Teaching and Learning with Microsoft® Office 2007 and Expression Web

A MULTILEVEL APPROACH TO COMPUTER INTEGRATION

SECOND EDITION

Timothy J. Newby
Purdue University

Judith Oates Lewandowski
Indiana University, South Bend

Allyn & Bacon
is an imprint of

PEARSON

Boston | New York | San Francisco
Mexico City | Montreal | Toronto | London | Madrid | Munich | Paris
Hong Kong | Singapore | Tokyo | Cape Town | Sydney

Vice President and Executive Publisher: Jeffery W. Johnston
Acquisitions Editor: Darcy Betts Prybella
Editorial Assistant: Nancy J. Holstein
Senior Managing Editor: Pamela D. Bennett
Project Manager: Sarah N. Kenoyer
Production Coordinator: Kelly Ricci/Aptara, Inc.
Design Coordinator: Diane C. Lorenzo
Cover Design: Jason Moore
Cover Image: Superstock
Operations Specialist: Susan W. Hannahs
Director of Marketing: Quinn Perkson
Marketing Coordinator: Brian Mounts

For related titles and support materials, visit our online catalog at
www.pearsonhighered.com.

Library of Congress Cataloging-in-Publication Data
Newby, Timothy J.
   Teaching and learning with Microsoft Office 2007 and Expression Web : a multilevel approach to
computer integration / Timothy J. Newby, Judith Oates Lewandowski.—2nd ed.
p . cm.
   Includes bibliographical references and index.
   ISBN-13: 978-0-13-171024-5
   ISBN-10: 0-13-171024-9
 1. Microsoft Office. 2. Microsoft Expression Web. 3. Application software. 4. Microsoft software—Study
and teaching. I. Lewandowsk, Judith Oates. II. Title.
QA76.76.A65N45 2009
005.3071—dc22
                          2008007088

Allyn & Bacon
is an imprint of

Printed in the United States of America

10 9 8 7 6 5 4 3 2 1   BRR 12 11 10 09 08

PREFACE

Vision of the text 	***Teaching and Learning with Microsoft® Office 2007 and Expression Web*** has been designed to give busy (and often overwhelmed) teachers and students a quick way to understand the basics of key software applications. Our vision is threefold: • to provide a foundation of the basics of common application software • to provide a vision and a path of how to integrate and utilize the software within classroom settings (*Note:* Our goal is for you to frequently say, "Yes, I can use this!") • to create a learning environment that is engaging, interesting, and effective
Why so basic?	Three points we want you to remember: 1. Teachers have more demands put on them now than ever before. 2. *Application software* (e.g., word processors) are more powerful (i.e., have more features) and can offer more help to the teacher than ever before. 3. More than 90 percent of the time that teachers spend working on the computer they are using *basic* features of the most common software programs. An understanding of the *basic* features will help you use the computer in the classroom. Once that foundation is prepared, you will know what information to request and how to find it as additional, more advanced features are needed. Without the basic foundation, you won't know when, why, or how to use those advanced features. That would only lead to frustration—and we really don't want you to experience more of that than necessary.
Why was this text written?	As for most projects of this nature, this text came about because of specific needs. In teaching our pre-service and in-service teacher courses, we needed a text that would a. quickly get students up and running with the basic Office software suite of programs b. provide examples and projects relevant to individuals who were or wanted to be teachers c. help learners develop the skill, as well as the desire, to integrate these powerful tools into their own classrooms in a manner that would significantly enhance the learning experiences of their present and future students
How does this text address those needs?	There were several basic philosophies used throughout the development of this text. • **Don't overkill.** Select and use basic key features of the software, but don't try to teach everything. Have learners understand the potential of the software, but let them be aware that they don't have to know it all in order to use the software effectively. As experience and confidence grow, more features can be added to their repertoires.

- **Help individuals quickly gain independence.** Although some step-by-step "hand-holding" procedures may be needed in the beginning, quickly show learners how to find features and resolve problems on their own. Help them recognize when and how to obtain answers to questions they will have as they use the software.
- **Support their efforts, but have students grow their own ideas and applications.** Students should quickly come to feel this information is relevant now and in their futures. Provide them with examples they can relate to, and support their use of the software to address their own projects and needs. Using the software on their own projects quickly develops the relevance needed to ensure the investment of effort that sustains the long-term use of these tools.
- **Envision the impact of integration.** The impact of such tools on personal productivity should be immediately apparent; however, an extended goal is to demonstrate the potential of integrating the software in the classroom in order to enhance the educational experiences they develop and experience with their future students.

What is the target content?

The text focuses on teaching Microsoft Windows Vista, Office 2007, and Expression Web. However, MS Office for Macintosh users will also be highlighted throughout.

Why use Microsoft's Office 2007 and Expression Web?

Basically, two reasons drove this decision. First, this software is prevalent in the majority of homes and schools. Second, because they are from the same "family" of software, they work in an integrated manner with many common toolbars, tool ribbons, menus, etc. For the novice, a feeling of familiarity when going from one program to the next is important in building confidence as well as in increasing the speed of acquisition.

Why use a three-level approach?

A three-level approach is utilized within this text to help students who enter the course at various levels of expertise.

- Level 1 is for the true beginner or novice. It is designed to give step-by-step "hand holding" help on accomplishing basic tasks with the software. It also offers a good review of key features for the more experienced user.
- Level 2 requires the use of additional and often more advanced features of the software—with guided assistance and help in finding the help that is needed. In this level, the student uses the software's *Help feature* to find solutions to questions and problems encountered. Key words and content locations are given as support to help the student grasp how to use Help effectively. In addition, guidance is given in the form of added procedures, images, and insights on how to implement the features. The goal is for students to gain independence and confidence by answering their own questions with the assistance of Help—but also not to become frustrated by the search process.
- Level 3 addresses integration of the software. Examples are given and students practice designing and developing technology-integrated learning experiences. Moreover, the relationship of the use of the software with the National Educational Technology Standards (NETS) is emphasized.

How are the chapters outlined?

All chapters are structured in a similar fashion. However, each is independent and thus the chapter sequence can be modified to fit the schedules and desires of the course instructor.

I.   **Introduction**

This section explains the goals of the chapters, the purpose of the software, reasons for learning, and some basic ideas of how it can be used by teachers and students.

II.   Orientation

This section allows one to view and work with the main workspace of the target software. Key ribbons and menus of tools are examined and key words, organizational concepts, and specific features are highlighted and explained.

III.   Level 1

One or more short scenarios or cases are given that incorporate projects previously completed using the targeted software. Key steps in the process of constructing each project are highlighted and students are guided through a step-by-step procedure to create a similar project.

IV.   Level 2

The scenario from Level 1 generally continues within this lesson and an additional, more complex project is outlined and completed. Users are then directed to alter the program and construct their own version. In this case, users are encouraged to use the program's Help to determine how to complete specific processes. Key words and phrases relevant to completing the task are listed for the individual to use with Help if it is needed. Insights and guidance are also given on how to utilize needed features. The focus is on using Help to acquire the desired results.

V.   Level 3

Integration is the focus of this level. Beginning with a presented lesson plan, users are shown how integration of the software can occur. Moreover, they are given opportunities to attempt to develop technology-enhanced lesson plans given specific situations. They are taught to use the Integration Assessment Questionnaire, and they explore and reflect on the relevant NETS Standards and how their work pertains to those standards.

What are the text's key features?

Lists: The text attempts to present most information in a concise fashion utilizing frequent bulleted and numbered lists.

Workouts: Workouts are regular exercises and projects that the student is directed to work through. These are designed to get the student actively involved early and often with the software. Many of these exercises are augmented by materials found on the texts' Web site **(www.prenhall.com/newby).**

Modeling: Example products and exercises are used to help students understand what is desired and how it can be achieved.

Reflective/guiding questions: These are used to encourage students to go beyond the immediate application of the software to envision how it could be integrated and transferred to other situations and settings.

Examples: Hundreds of examples of the utilization of the software are given across all age groups and content areas.

Help emphasis to gain independence: The use of the softwares' Help programs are highlighted, practiced, and implemented within this training in order to encourage independence and confidence in solving problems encountered when using the software.

Writing style: Concise—get to the point—and move on.

Mentoring videos: Short, concise videos can be accessed via the text's Web site **(www.prenhall.com/newby).** These videos show the exact steps needed to complete all outlined features within the text—for all chapters and all levels in each chapter.

How are the technology standards addressed?

Both teacher (NETS*T) and student (NETS*S) standards from the National Educational Technology Standards are listed in the Appendix. Within Level 3 of each chapter the utilization of the standards is discussed, and students demonstrate how they are used and assessed as the software is integrated within self-generated lesson plans.

What has been added to the second edition?

Several key items have been added to this second edition.

1. Chapter 1: Systems Navigation. This chapter is now based on **Windows Vista.** Although it is still relevant for other operating systems, the screen captures are based on Microsoft's newest system software.

2. Chapters 2–6: **Office 2007 software.** With the upgrade to Microsoft Office 2007, all chapters have been completely updated to include explanations and screen captures of all tool ribbons and other features of Microsoft Word, Excel, PowerPoint, and Publisher.

3. Chapter 6: **Publisher**. In this edition, we include a new chapter on Microsoft Publisher. This chapter follows the same format as all other chapters (three levels) and has desktop publishing projects that are integrated with other chapters within the text. This chapter also expands the printed publications and shows how to develop Web pages with Publisher.

4. Chapter 7: Web editing. With the demise of Microsoft FrontPage, we have focused the Web editing chapter around **Microsoft's Expression Web** software. New projects are incorporated to reflect the features of this new, more powerful, cleaner software.

5. Chapter on **Microsoft Access.** Although Access is not traditionally used by most classroom teachers, there is a need for a basic understanding of what it can do and how it can be used. Written in the same format as the other Office 2007 chapters, the Access chapter is available on the text's Web site **(www.prenhall.com/ newby).**

6. Within each chapter we have made a number of changes:

   a. Within Level 2 in each chapter, the emphasis in the first edition of the text was to show where to locate information within **Help** to complete certain tasks. That is also emphasized in the second edition; however, we have **greatly expanded each section to include additional information, insights, and guidance** on how to accomplish needed tasks. Level 2 still requires the student to work toward greater independence in working with software, but more resources and support are given to ensure students' success in accomplishing the tasks.

   b. In each chapter, **additional examples** have been provided to show more insights and ideas on how software can be used and why it should be used. In addition, many examples are expanded across the different softwares so the integration of the various types of software can be experienced by students. That is, a word processing task scenario may be expanded to show how a database application can be used within a related situation.

   c. Within Level 1 and Level 2 in each chapter, several **problem scenarios** are created. These scenarios are short problem situations addressed through use of target software. Such cases help the user more readily see how software may be used in real teaching and learning situations. It addition, the scenarios allow for increased levels of relevance.

   d. Within Level 3 in each chapter there is a section on the use of **National Educational Technology Standards (NETS)** for both teachers and students. Although this section was included in the first edition, a revised set of standards for students has been released. This new NETS for students has been incorporated throughout.

7. **Mentoring videos.** New to this edition is a set of short videos created for each of the chapters. Within each Level 1 and Level 2 feature explanation of the text, there is a matching video that visually and aurally shows exactly how the step is completed. Each of the videos is accessed via the text's Web site and readers can review how the text explains completion of specific steps and then go to the Web site to see and hear an explanation and demonstration of that exact step. The videos are designed to be short (approximately 60 seconds) and very easy and efficient to access.

8. **Instructor's manual.** Over the years we realized that we have generated much information and many experiences on how to teach these applications within our labs and within the online versions of our courses. We have compiled an instructor's guide and placed it on the text's Web site for access and use.

How can the authors be contacted?

The easiest and fastest way is generally through e-mail, but here is all of the needed information.

Tim Newby
Purdue University
Room 3138, BRNG
100 N. University St.
W. Lafayette, IN 47907-2098

Phone: 765-494-5672
Fax: 765-496-l622
Email: newby@purdue.edu

Judy Lewandowski
Indiana University—South Bend
Greenlawn Hall
1700 Mishawaka Ave.
South Bend, IN 46634

Email: jllewand@iusb.edu

How is the text currently being used?

We use this text for both undergraduate and graduate students. The undergrad course has over four hundred students each semester. We will be happy to share our ideas on how we structure the course with this text, to give you the benefits and the challenges, as well as to share our syllabi and Web site activities. We also enjoy visiting classes via phone or Internet video links and discussing issues with students and faculty. Just let us know what we can do to help.

Acknowledgements

No book can be completed without the help of numerous individuals. In particular we wish to acknowledge both our in-service and pre-service teachers who have presented hundreds of questions to ponder, consider, and respond to within this text. Through the years, their questions have heavily influenced the vision, design, and development of this work.

We would like to thank the following individuals for reviewing and offering their constructive suggestions on the first edition: Terri Buckner, University of North Carolina, Chapel Hill; Richard A. Smith, University of Houston, Clear Lake; and David VanEsselstyn, Long Island University.

BRIEF CONTENTS

CONTENTS

Chapter 2	**WORD PROCESSING—MS Word: The Basics of a Writing Assistant**	**29**

INTRODUCTION:
WHAT'S THIS ALL ABOUT?

> **Read Me First!**
>
> In many cases, as you open a new purchase that requires a little assembly (e.g., computer, bicycle, shelf unit for your office), there's a set of directions that indicates you should **READ ME FIRST**. You may not have to assemble this book, but it's wise to take a look at this introductory section. It sets the tone, provides insights, and helps you get set for the learning that's about to begin. It helps you to know what is expected and what you can expect from exploring and working on these pages. Things just go smoother when you begin here.

What are we trying to do?

We want you to be able to use computer software such as word processors, databases, spreadsheets, and software associated with the Internet. More importantly, we want you to use the software in ways that enhance your teaching, your curriculum, and your impact on your students (or future students). That is our goal, plain and simple.

Is this only "classroom software?"

We wrote this book as if we had on the eyeglasses of a teacher and/or a student. That means, our examples and projects are focused on how teachers and students can use this software to enhance learning. These basic applications, however, can be used by individuals in all walks of life and in all times of their lives.

Don't shy away just because you are going to cooking school, are in the military, or want to become a fireman, dancer, or magician. We have all been in the classroom before—these examples and projects should make sense from all different perspectives.

How does this relate?

This is the big question that we want you to ask over and over again as you go through this material. Think to yourself, "How does this relate to my teaching?" "How does this relate to the work that I have to do?" "How does this relate to a positive impact on my curriculum and ultimately on my students?" "How can the implementation of this software impact my learning?"

We provide you some examples and some ideas of how these concerns tie together and how they work. Always be mindful of ways to find relevance for your personal classroom or learning situation. Constantly look for ways to make these tools work for you. It is then that you will come to view them as something worthwhile and not just another thing to learn this week and never use again.

We want you to reflect back on these tools and think, "How did I ever get along without them?"

Why should I learn this?	• Saves time • Saves energy • Improves quality There isn't a job in this world that doesn't require these three objectives—and this is especially true for those of us in the teaching profession. It would be great if we could just hand you those benefits. However (here's the catch), for you to reap them, you have to invest a bit of time and energy. Our goal is to make your investment as efficient and painless as possible. We figure that if we can have fun along the way and help you get some of your work done as you learn this stuff, you'll stick with us.
Why use Microsoft Office and Expression Web?	Two reasons: 1. This software is very prevalent on home, business, and school computers. 2. Many of the same tools, menus, and so on are used from one application program to the next (this will help speed the learning process and the feelings of familiarity). **Note:** We realize there are *different versions of this software* and that there are other publishers of software that you may be more familiar with. We focus on important skills that can be learned with whatever software you have available—it may not be done in exactly the same way as the Microsoft products—but it will be close, and you'll soon learn how to figure out the small differences.
Where are we going?	The key tools we explore include the following: • Navigating the system (Windows Vista) • Word Processing (MS Word) • Spreadsheet (MS Excel) • Data management (MS Excel) • Presentation software (MS PowerPoint) • Desk top publishing (MS Publisher) • Web editor (MS Expression Web) Each of these topics receives attention. We suggest that you go through the section on Navigating the System first (just to lay the needed foundation); however, after that, go with what you need. If you are in a class, your freedom might be limited (professors like to do that), but if you're working on this independently, look over what you need to get done and where the emphasis in your life is—then go in that direction. **Note:** Start thinking now about current or future projects that you might be able to work into the projects for each of these applications. Remember, we want you to use your own. From the very beginning we want you to see the importance of this software for helping you and your students achieve.
How are we going to get there?	Basically, the format of each of the applications is similar. You will explore some basic background (short and sweet) about the software and complete some quick exercises. This will familiarize you with the software (what it looks like and how it works) and orient you about the basics of what, when, and why it is important. **Level 1 Application:** This is directed at the novice. We provide you examples of something produced with the software. We supply step-by-step guidance so you can produce something similar that can be altered for use in your own classroom.

Level 2 Application: To achieve increased independence, a second set of examples are given at this level. Key features of the products are highlighted and you will learn how to find critical "how-to" information as you create your own set of products using the software. That is, less step-by-step guidance but more general suggestions are provided. Remember, our goal here is *not* to "hold your hand," but to help you become more self-sufficient. We want to show you how to find the answers to your questions. Then when you're on your own, you should be better prepared to find your own solutions to the unique problems you confront.

Level 3 Application: With the basics learned, this level provides opportunities to explain, teach, and integrate the software within classroom settings. It's a time to solidify your own understanding of the basics, but most important, to consider the possibilities of its use and application for yourself as well as your learners. Here we want you to envision how this could be used and give you additional ideas on how to integrate and apply your new skills.

Mentoring Videos: All along the way there are references to the "mentoring videos." These are short (most are about 60 seconds in length) video demonstrations of each of the steps within the various levels. For example, in Level 1 of the chapter on word processing we may explain the steps needed to cut and paste information. If you feel you need to see how that works, you can simply go to the text's Web site (**www.prenhall.com/newby**) and select the video that will demonstrate it on your computer. You can watch these videos over and over until you understand exactly how the feature works and why it works the way that it does.

Do you really need to learn about these software programs?

Maybe . . . maybe not. There are several ways of finding out, but because most of you are associated with teaching and/or learning, we felt that a short assessment (nice words for *test*) would be in order. So take a crack at this, then ponder over your answers.

Circle the number on the scale about how closely the statement resembles something you could or should have said about yourself.

	That's Me				Not Me
1. I have been told that the computer will reduce my workload, but every time I try to use it, it costs more time, energy, and effort than it is worth.	5	4	3	2	1
2. I feel comfortable using the computer for some things, but I'm frustrated because I know I should be using it to do a lot more.	5	4	3	2	1
3. When asked to "cut and paste," my thoughts wander to grade school, blunt-nosed scissors, and Elmer's glue.	5	4	3	2	1
4. I think I have lost things in my computer and I have a feeling I'm not going to get them back.	5	4	3	2	1
5. When I hear the word *spreadsheet,* I think back to the last time I attempted to make my bed.	5	4	3	2	1
6. Everyone else seems to know a lot more about how to use the computer than I do.	5	4	3	2	1
7. In the past, I have usually found someone else to use the computer when I needed something done.	5	4	3	2	1
8. Computers and feelings of inadequacy, for me, seem closely related.	5	4	3	2	1

Now add up your total score and divide by 8 to calculate your average response. Check the scale below for our suggestions on using this book and learning the software.

3.0+	You've got the right book and there are lots of good things in store.
2.0–3.0	Buzz through the Level 1 exercises, and quickly get to the Level 2 assignments.
1.0–2.0	Review the Level 1 and Level 2 materials, see if there are some examples that you haven't experienced or thought about, then look closely at the integration and examples found in Level 3.

How much knowledge of Web or Internet use is required?

We are assuming that most people have at least a minimum level of knowledge of accessing and using the Web. Throughout this text, you are given resources to examine that are "on the Web." For those who have limited experience, we have developed a **mentoring video** (**www.prenhall.com/newby**) to help guide you through some basic elements of using the Web.

Is there a connection between information in this text and the NETS Standards?

Just as standards are being developed, examined, and used throughout all aspects of education, so too they are being generated and applied for computers and other technologies within the realm of education. The Appendix lists the National Educational Technology Standards (NETS) for both teachers and students. Within each chapter devoted to word processing, spreadsheets, databases, presentations, or Web page development, we highlight and emphasize those standards that are being addressed by the various learning activities and workouts. Look for these as a part of the Level 3 Workouts. Within those Workouts we highlight sections that apply to specific standards and insert reflective questions that should help you contemplate and visualize the relationship of a standard to the learning activity you are completing and/or designing.

What are some philosophies guiding this book?

1. **We aren't going to teach you everything.** There's no need for that. The programs we work with can be wonderful for the right job—they can also be overwhelming if you get involved in unnecessary applications. Our goal is to focus on what you need, and we show you how to find solutions to specific problems you come across.
2. **We believe in application.** If you use it, you won't as easily lose it. We quickly have you working with this book right alongside of your computer. Actual participation (you working the keyboard) is much better than watching someone else do it—we want and need you to be an "active participant."
3. **Kill two birds with one stone.** We want you to develop skills with the computer programs that will help you in *your* work. Make this information as relevant as possible. Look around and find some projects that need to get done at work, home, or school. As we show you different programs, think of ways that you could get an assignment done by finishing something that you have to do anyway.
4. **Let's keep it short and sweet.** You have limited time and we know that. We use all kinds of job aids, numbered and bulleted lists, and other means to help shorten the amount of reading that you need to do, to help you find what needs to be found.
5. **Having fun is NOT a crime.** We think that we can have some fun going through this assignment. We try to add some smiles along the way—which you can either enjoy or ignore. We have had a lot of classroom experience, and some of them are hilarious and can be used to illustrate different points in this text—so we have chosen to include them to some degree.

6. **We are not the final word.** You are going to find out (if you don't already know), that there are several ways to get the job done. That is the way that most things work, and it is definitely the way most well-designed software works. We show you how we do it, but in some cases you may know of other ways. If it works for you, use it.

7. **Keep frustration under control.** Listen, you're working with computers—computers are one facet of technology—and technology means that funny things will happen—and usually happens when you least expect it and least need it to happen. So be prepared and the problems will be only molehills, not huge mountains, to overcome.

How should you use this book?

A few points to note here:

- We don't think most of you should read this text like a novel. Use the margin headings to get to the information that you need in as efficient manner as possible.
- After reading this introduction, jump to the chapter that will service your current needs. That is, if you have a need for upgrading your skills with spreadsheets, go to that chapter and work there. You don't have to work through the other chapters first. A salient way to figure out what you should do next is to look at the "hot" projects that you need to get done as soon as possible. If there is a project that could be enhanced with the development of a Web site, then perhaps you should look to the chapter on that application, but if you have a pressing project on an upcoming presentation, then by all means go to the chapter on PowerPoint. You'll learn this much quicker and in greater detail IF you are working on a project that has relevance to you.
- We have included **mentoring videos** to help you reference and quickly recall some of the basics. The videos are on the text's Web site (**www.prenhall.com/newby**) and can be quickly accessed and viewed. There will be times when it helps to see a short demo of a specific feature within your selected program. These videos can also be used to help you remember some "forgotten" skill that you once had. Once you get through the chapters, use these features to help you retain and continue to use the key features of the software.

A special note to Macintosh users

As you can probably guess, a PC was used during the initial development of this text. However, on the desk next to the PC was a Mac. Once a chapter was completed, the Mac was then used to review all that was written and suggested. Although most of the figures are taken from the PC version, any major differences are noted and described for the Mac users. Generally, a bracket note within the text, such as [Mac Users . . .] is used to let you know about those differences.

Some "Rules to Live By"

1. **SAVE, SAVE, SAVE and then SAVE your work again.** Get in the habit of frequently saving your work. It isn't as hard as taking out the garbage and you can do it in a matter of 1–2 seconds. If you don't, you WILL get burned—it's only a matter of time. Don't depend on the software to do this for you—sometimes that may rescue you, but in many cases it won't.

2. **Think CONTENT first, PRETTY later.** In most cases it is better to enter and edit the content of your work first, and worry about the formatting (making it look good) later. If you get sidetracked on working on the "pretty" (which is frequently done in today's world), your message may never be developed.

3. **SIMPLE IS BETTER.** With so many bells and whistles found in these programs, it's very easy to get into the "throw in the kitchen sink" syndrome. Just because you have hundreds of type fonts, pictures, hyperlinks, audio or video clips available, it doesn't mean that you should try to include them all.

4. **KEEP YOUR EYES OPEN.** Look for examples of different ways to design and present your information. Sometimes other teachers, texts or magazines, Web-based documents, or even your students may offer some answers to problems and predicaments that you find yourself in. Pay attention and the solution may present itself.

5. **Store and use EXAMPLES and TEMPLATES.** Once you have either developed or located a good example, store it so that you can use it later. For instance, if you develop a spreadsheet grade book, a newsletter, a seating chart, a Web page, save copies so the next time you need to do something similar you can begin with that original as a template. The second time around you can speed up the process and actually make higher quality products. Templates launch you forward into your next project—use them.

Chapter 1

SYSTEM SOFTWARE
MS Windows Vista: The Basics of Navigating the System

Introduction

What should you know about system software?

If you don't know the rules of the game, it's very difficult to succeed. With the computer there are some general things you need to know and do (in most cases, these will turn into automatic skills) so that your interaction with the computer is simplified. If you don't understand how these work, you're going to be fighting an uphill battle—forever. When it comes to understanding the "ground rules" of the computer, you need to know some basics about the operating system software. Here are some of the things you should be familiar with:

- How to communicate and interact with the computer
- How things are reliably created, organized, stored, and then retrieved
- What tools are available and how they are accessed
- How to get **Help**

Terms to know

desktop	window	mouse	point, click, hold, drag
help	folder	file	menu
toolbar	taskbar	icon	

What is the system software and what does it do?

System software tells the computer how to perform its fundamental, basic operating functions (e.g., turn on, save things, run application programs). In other words, it is the master control program. When the system software is functioning properly, life is good—when it isn't, life can be miserable.

What are some commonly known system software?

Two types of system software (sometimes called "platforms") dominate the school and home market at the present:

Microsoft's Windows

Apple's Macintosh

What gets a little confusing is that new and improved versions of these systems are continually being introduced. For example, you might be working on Windows 98, 2000, XP, or Vista; however, you might also have experience working with the Mac OS 8, 9, or even X.

Although there are some basic differences between the main systems (and even within the different versions of a system), their purpose is very similar—to control how the computer functions.

Why bother learning how to use and navigate the system software?

From the time the computer is turned on until it is shut down, the system software is involved and actively participating. Its role is similar to that of the director of a play. The audience may not see the director, but the director directly controls what transpires on the stage.

Understanding the system software will allow you to control the following:

- Starting up and shutting down the computer
- Storing, moving, and retrieving your work
- Installing and uninstalling other software on your computer
- Finding **folders, files,** and so forth in your computer storage areas
- Controlling how peripherals (e.g., keyboard, **mouse,** monitors, scanners) interact with the computer
- Using application software (e.g., word processors, spreadsheets)

Orientation

What's the workspace look like?

When you walk into a new school building for the first time, it's often easy to get lost. We have found it helps if you can find out where you are (perhaps by visiting the main office) and then see a picture of the building and how it is laid out. Key landmarks (e.g., the main hallway, the faculty lounge, the numbering system of the rooms) then can be noted and the logic of the building begins to be clarified.

Similarly, this is how we need to handle the computer and its various applications. We will begin each explanation section with an overview "map" of what the workspace looks like so that you can get a feel for how it's laid out and what the major landmarks, or tools are.

Review Figure 1.1. This is a view of a Windows-type computer "**desktop**." After starting the computer and allowing it to go through its "getting ready" stage, the desktop appears. This is a key landmark and a place where you will frequently find yourself visiting and working.

MAC USERS

Don't worry. You also have a desktop with similar items on it—e.g., an easy-to-access main menu, a trash can, a hard drive **icon** to access items on the hard drive, and so forth.

What's the "desktop"?

In a normal working office, the top of the desk is where most of the work is completed. There are tools (e.g., pencils, paper clips, writing paper) that are sitting on the desktop so that when needed they are readily available. This is very similar to the computer's desktop. It is here that one has ready access to the needed tools and files so that real work can be accomplished.

Figure 1.1 View of a Windows Vista desktop

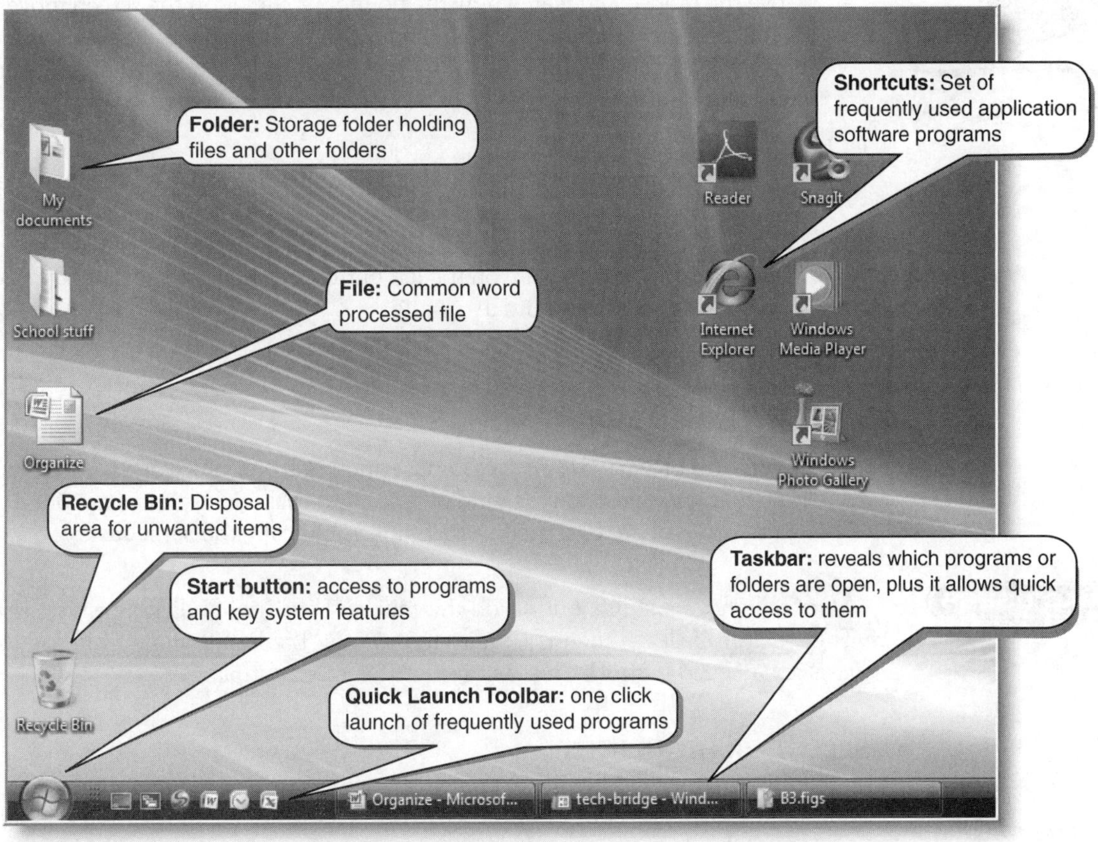
Shortcuts: Set of frequently used application software programs
Folder: Storage folder holding files and other folders
My documents
Reader
SnagIt
School stuff
File: Common word processed file
Internet Explorer
Windows Media Player
Organize
Windows Photo Gallery
Recycle Bin: Disposal area for unwanted items
Start button: access to programs and key system features
Taskbar: reveals which programs or folders are open, plus it allows quick access to them
Recycle Bin
Quick Launch Toolbar: one click launch of frequently used programs
Organize - Microsof...
tech-bridge - Wind...
B3.figs

> **Note:** Don't be concerned if your desktop looks a bit different than the ones in this Figure 1.1. The top of the desk in your home or office probably looks different from that of any other person's desk. We can customize the desktop to fit your needs—just like you have done on your personal desk. Generally, there are some basics that you will find (e.g., Recycle Bin, taskbar and toolbars, some folders) in and around the desktop. Look for those key landmarks.

Getting it to do what you want

The centerpiece of a good relationship is the ability to communicate. Teachers have to be good at this—you have to handle a variety of students, parents, administrators, and so forth—all of whom may require different communication skills.

Guess what? When working with the computer, communication is also essential. Yes, it can be even more frustrating than telling little Billy not to bring his pet lizard to school for the eighth time. Early on, your biggest problem will be finding the way to effectively communicate to the computer what you want done. Sounds a lot like the give-and-take within any relationship, doesn't it?

For most computer systems today, **the mouse and keyboard are the critical means of communication**. So look them over, tap on them, play with the keys, and note what the different buttons do. You'll be using them before long.

The "power of the mouse": *pointing, clicking, selecting, and dragging*

The power of the mouse (or any mouse substitute—such as the trackball, touchpad, pencil eraser) is that it allows you to tell the computer what to pay attention to and, in many cases, exactly what to do.

Here are the key skills:

POINT:

Move the mouse and watch how the pointer or cursor on the screen moves with it. You need to be able to tell the computer which things to work with—the power of the mouse is that it allows you to **point** to exactly what you want the computer to attend to.

CLICK:

Note that the mouse has a button or two (maybe more) on it. When you depress a button once quickly, it is called a "**click.**" A click gives the computer important information about what to do with the item you are pointing at. Generally, for a PC the majority of clicks are on the left button. At times you will need to expand your clicking repertoire into a

- Double (or even a triple) click
- Right click
- Click and hold

If you do not have access to a mouse (perhaps you are working on a laptop), note that there is still some kind of point and click mechanisms provided. Don't worry. They all are designed to accomplish basically the same task.

Macs only have a single button on the mouse. Thus "right" clicking isn't possible. There are drop-down menus (similar to those on the PC) that are available to access any needed item. The rest of the clicking is very similar.

SELECT OR HIGHLIGHT:

Often you need to identify a specific item (e.g., a picture, word, number) that you want the computer to work on. To do this, you typically put the mouse pointer on top of the item and click. In some cases, you'll need to click and **hold** in front of the item, then **drag** over the item until it is fully selected. When it is "selected," it will change colors (typically becoming darker). If you want it to be "deselected," you just click anywhere else on the screen. Here is an example of a selected word:

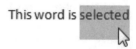

Here are examples of selected and nonselected folders:

non-selected   selected

DRAG:

This is where you point at some object, click and hold (don't release the button), and then move the mouse. The item you have clicked on will then move (drag) or be highlighted in some way. For example, this is one way that you can move a file from one place on the screen to another. Point at the file, click and hold, and drag it to the new location.

For more information about the use of the mouse (e.g., clicking, dragging), view the mentoring video on this text's Web site: **www.prenhall.com/newby.**

The "power of the keys"

For the computer to be really helpful, there are times when you need to spell out what needs to be done. That's when the keyboard comes in handy. Yes, there will be times ahead in which the keyboard may become obsolete—however, for the near future you will continue to type in the words and commands that are needed via the keyboard.

Start Menu

The Start **menu** (see Figure 1.2) is important for you to become familiar with. This is where you go to gain access to most of the key functions of the computer. Review Figure 1.2. The inserted callouts highlight a few of the important activities that can be accomplished through the use of the Start menu. This is the place where you go to launch specific programs, complete a search for specific documents and/or folders, gain access to your flash drive, and change settings on the computer (i.e., through the control panel).

Help and Support

With our use of the computer, right after getting a good orientation of the computer layout, it is important for you to know where you can get some help if it is needed.

The main operating systems today have **Help** sections built into their programs. We will constantly be suggesting that you turn to **Help** to get answers to your questions. In most cases, **Help** will give you the answer you are looking for.

To find the **Help** section, look in the **Start** menu (see Figure 1.2) and note the **Help and Support** button that has been highlighted.

MAC USERS

On the desktop's main menu, look for the Help menu (**Help>>>Help Center**).

Figure 1.2 Start menu from Windows Vista

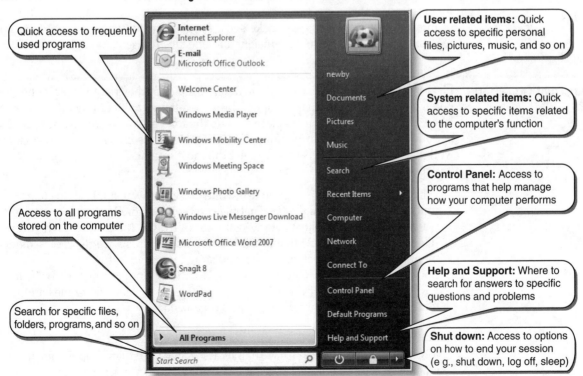

Quick access to frequently used programs

User related items: Quick access to specific personal files, pictures, music, and so on

System related items: Quick access to specific items related to the computer's function

Control Panel: Access to programs that help manage how your computer performs

Access to all programs stored on the computer

Help and Support: Where to search for answers to specific questions and problems

Search for specific files, folders, programs, and so on

Shut down: Access to options on how to end your session (e.g., shut down, log off, sleep)

The three BIG metaphors

The following three metaphors will help you learn the basics about the computer:

1. **Office filing systems metaphor.** Any well-run office (whether at home or at a business) has a means of storing important information. Today, most offices still have file cabinets with drawers full of folders. Each folder contains valuable documents containing all kinds of information. Similarly, for the computer to be used efficiently, a filing system devoted to storing key documents and files within folders is used.

2. **Restaurant metaphor.** Each time you go to a restaurant to eat, you have a selection of food and drink from which to choose. This is most readily accomplished by looking over the menu. Likewise, the computer has menus from which to make a selection of what you want to achieve.

3. **Construction worker metaphor.** Just as a builder has a toolbox and a number of tools he accesses and uses when building a new home or business, the computer user has access to many tools available within the computer software. Some tools are used more frequently by the builder, but knowledge of many of the others allows him to accomplish great things. The same philosophy applies with using the computer.

    Often, throughout this text, we refer to these metaphors to help you quickly grasp the new information. Get used to them—you'll be using them yourself before long.

Why do I need to organize and clean my room?

With the large storage capacity of a computer (one of its greatest assets), you need to have an organizational plan. This will allow you to store and retrieve your stuff easily.

Organization plays a key role. If you don't attend to how your files and folders are organized, you'll quickly find that working on the computer can be more frustrating than it needs to be.

In the next few sections, we make some suggestions on what you can do to help organize your computer so it is efficient and effective to use.

Important Organizers

Files and Folders: To organize what's on the desktop and what's stored within the computer, we are a simple visual metaphor. Just like a filing cabinet in the office contains labeled folders and documents placed inside the folders, so too are objects organized in your computer's system platform. The filing system is critical to organizing your workplace (the computer) so you can get the most from it.

An example of files and folders:

1. Whenever you create something using one of the software applications (e.g., word processing), we will call it a *file*. That file can then be stored by putting it on top of your desktop OR by filing it away within a folder. On the picture of the desktop (Figure 1.1) look for a file that is called "Organize." This is a word-processed document that has been created, named, and stored on the desktop.

2. Look at the desktop in Figure 1.1 again. Note that there is a picture, or "icon," of a folder that is called "School Stuff." This folder is a place where files and other folders related to school can be put and organized.

> **Note 1:** Both files and folders have names associated with them. This is a great convenience! You can name these so that you can remember what they contain.

> **Note 2:** You have an endless supply of folders and the size of each can be expanded to hold a huge amount of files, other folders, programs, and so on. You never have to go to the store and buy another package of folders.

> **Note 3:** If you want to name them a specific way, you can easily do so. Likewise, if tomorrow you figure out a new way to name your folders and files, you can rename them with relative ease.

Recycle Bin.   An important part of organizing is *getting rid of the stuff you no longer need*. This is easily done by dragging the item to the Recycle Bin (trash) that's located on the desktop. Once there, it's possible to take out the recycles or trash and "empty" it from your system. *Note:* Discarding trash or recycles on the computer is generally a lot easier (and less smelly) than taking out the kitchen garbage. A comforting thought is that the Recycle Bin or Trash is a temporary holding spot. If you delete something you later decide you need, you can open the Recycle Bin and retrieve your disposed material. However, once you decide to empty the Recycle Bin, the contents are gone for good.

MAC USERS   The Trash serves this purpose.

Menus and toolbars

Why menus?   Why not? Restaurants have found them effective. Menus allow you to see lots of choices of food to eat or (as in the case of the computer) activities to perform.

Menus on the computer are often pulled down (or up) and are there until you have made your selection. Once used, they (similar to the restaurant variety) disappear until called on for other selections.

In all programs we discuss, there will be menus and toolbars that you can access and select from. It's really a very efficient way to access different tools and other important things (The Start Menu, Figure 1.2) is a good example of a menu of items from which to choose computer activities). Generally, by selecting a menu button, file name, and so on, the menu of alternatives is revealed in some way (e.g., a drop-down menu appears, a new window is revealed, a pop-up window comes into view). Once a selection is made, the menu then disappears until it is called back into service.

Toolbars and taskbars.   The computer is capable of many tasks. Subsequently, there are numerous tools and commands that can be used to accomplish these various tasks. To help with this process, many of these tools have been placed on convenient toolbars that can be shown (or hidden) as you determine their need. Figure 1.1 highlights the "Quick Launch Toolbar" that allows you to launch a specific program with one click right from the desktop. The same figure also highlights the taskbar, which reveals which programs, files, and folders are currently open and can be immediately accessed with a single click.

Within all programs, tools must be accessed in some way. As shown in Figure 1.3, tools with a common purpose are generally grouped together in some way within a command set, within a group, or on a toolbar of some kind.

Windows, windows, everywhere

Take a look at Figure 1.4. This is an example of several **windows** being open on one computer screen. Windows allow you to peer into different programs and different parts of the program.

Figure 1.3 Common font commands found within a word processing program

Note how the windows can be made of different sizes and can be made to overlap each other. As you begin to work with the computer, you'll find that navigating through these windows, and being able to have multiple windows exposed at a single time, can be very helpful. The window you are currently working on (the one on "top") is known as the *active window*. When you have a number of windows on the screen at one time, you can make a specific one active by pointing your mouse directly within the space of that window and clicking once. It will highlight and come to the top (i.e., it will overlay or be on top of the other open windows).

Look more closely at Figure 1.4. Note the highlighted section in the corner of the active window (see the upper right corner). These buttons allow you to control the active

Figure 1.4 View of multiple open windows

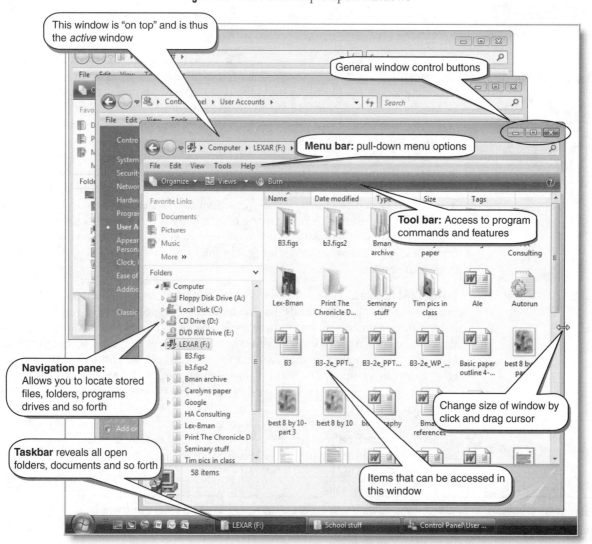

window (i.e., hide the window temporarily so you can see what else is on the screen, change the size, or close it altogether). If you want to change the size of the active window, put your cursor directly over a side, bottom, or corner of the window and the cursor changes into a two-headed arrow. Click and drag the window to your preferred size and release the mouse button. To see a demonstration of how to work with active windows, review the mentoring video on the text's Web site: **www.prenhall.com/newby.**

Although the controls look a bit different, they work basically the same way. The idea is that you can open multiple windows and you can readily alter their size.

Think about the application advantage of these multiple windows. For example, you could be grading an assignment that one of your students has submitted and at the same time have the grading rubric in another window that is showing on the screen at the same time. Or you might find it fun to have a word processed document up in one window and you can copy a section of it and paste it into another program (like a graphics program) without having to do much at all other than select, copy, and then go to the other window and paste.

Orientation Workout: Explore the territory

Turn on your computer and attempt the following on the desktop:

1. Click the **Start** button and see how it reveals its main menu. Get used to selecting certain parts of the menu and using it to launch various windows or programs.

Open items on the Main Menu bar and explore the Apple menu, as well as the File, Edit, Special menus, and so on.

2. Open several items (e.g., WordPad, Help and Support). Practice opening, changing size, minimizing, moving, and closing various windows. Check out the menus available within the various windows you open. Also use the Quick Launch Toolbar to launch some of the given programs. In addition, use the taskbar to open windows that have been minimized.
3. Try manually changing the size of a window by clicking and holding the side, top, bottom, or corner edge of a window and dragging it slowly (note how the mouse pointer turns into a two-headed arrow as you move it over the edge of the window).
4. Get used to moving the windows from one location on the desktop to another. Point, click, and hold the mouse pointer on the bar along the top of the active window (the title bar). Now drag the mouse and see if the window moves in your desired direction.

Note: Each of these key features is demonstrated in a set of mentoring videos on the text's accompanying Web site. Go to the **www.prenhall.com/newby** >>> **Chapter 1** >>> **Mentor Videos.**

Level 1: Designing, Building, and Using a Good Filing System

What should you be able to do?

At this level, your focus is on knowing how to navigate and access the various tools and features provided within the system software. Moreover, it is important to understand how things are organized and how you can name, rename, and organize files and folders. The emphasis here is on organization—putting things in places where you can find and retrieve them later. If you don't have some grasp of this, it won't be long before you will be frustrated trying to find stuff you seem to have misplaced.

What resources are provided?

Basically, Level 1 is divided into a few common scenarios, selected solutions, and practice exercises (i.e. Workouts). The scenarios have been constructed to allow you to examine common problems and how they can be addressed through the use of the system software. To do this we have provided the following:

a. Quick reference figures that identify (via visual callouts) all of the key features that have been incorporated within the solution presentation. These allow you to rapidly identify the key features and reference exactly how to include such features within your own work.
b. Step-by-step instructions on how to incorporate all highlighted features within your work.
c. Video mentoring support that guides you through the integration of each of the highlighted features (see the text's Web site **www.prenhall.com/newby**).
d. Workout exercises that allow you to practice identifying and selecting which software features to use, when to use those features, how they should be incorporated, and to what degree they are effective.

How should you proceed?

If you have <u>little or no experience</u> with Windows Vista or some other similar system software, then we suggest you do the following:

1. Read and review Scenario 1.
2. Examine the quick reference figure (Figure 1.4) and its highlighted features.
3. Using the step-by-step directions given for each highlighted feature, use the software and practice using each of the features.
4. If you have any confusion or difficulty with these features, access the videos and monitor the features as they are demonstrated and discussed within the short video clips.
5. Once you feel comfortable with these features, go to Scenario 2 and repeat these same steps with the new features introduced for that scenario. Monitor the quick reference figure (Figure 1.6) closely.
6. After both scenarios have been reviewed, go to the Workout and work through the problems and exercises as it outlines.

If you have <u>experience</u> with your operating system, you may want to review the scenarios and the quick reference figures first. If any of the features are unfamiliar, then access and use the step-by-step procedures, as well as the mentoring support videos, as needed. Once the review has been completed, then move directly to the Workout exercise.

Scenario 1: Organizing your electronic file cabinet

To set the stage, let's imagine that your school has just received a new grant where all of the teachers at your grade level have been given laptop computers to use (for some of you this may require *a lot* of imagination). Two weeks before the start of fall classes you receive your computer, but other than how to turn it on, no training will be available until after the first day the students return. You know how hectic the start of school can be and you would really like to be comfortable using the computer before the doors open and the kids show up.

When the computer coordinator drops in to see how things are going with the new computer, you ask for her advice. She suggests that you might try a few things. Here are several of her suggestions:

Figure 1.5 Example folder structure

1. Explore on your own.
2. Plan how you think the computer will be used.
3. Walk through (with her guidance) some basic implementation activities.

Your technology coordinator suggests that you plan how you will set up the storage system. That is, how will you know where you will put things you create, where to look for them when you need them at a later date, and so on. This will require the use of folders. Here are some simple steps to follow:

a. With a paper and pencil, outline the structure of an efficient filing cabinet. For example, if you have an organized filing system at work, look through it and see what works and what could be improved. You may want to replicate this on your computer.
b. Determine how to label the folders in your filing system and which folders can be "nested" or put within other folders. For example, look at the filing system showing in Figure 1.5.

> **Note:** Don't get too complex or fancy. There's nothing worse than trying to locate a file that's stored in a folder, in a folder, in a folder, that is in a folder (you get the idea). Keep it simple. Also, you can always change folders, rename them, put new things in, and take other things out. Over time, you'll find that you need to change and alter your structure.

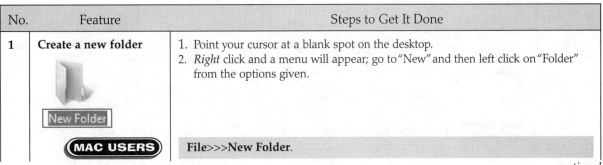

No.	Feature	Steps to Get It Done
1	**Create a new folder**	1. Point your cursor at a blank spot on the desktop.
		2. *Right* click and a menu will appear; go to "New" and then left click on "Folder" from the options given.
	MAC USERS	**File>>>New Folder.**

continued

No.	Feature	Steps to Get It Done
2	**Name a new folder** Essays	1. Once a new folder has been created (and before you do anything else), type in the name that you have selected for your folder. It will appear below the folder icon. 2. Once you have it typed in, press Enter.
3	**Rename a folder** Essays	1. Point the mouse pointer on the current name of the folder and click twice (slowly). The name should become selected (highlighted). ***Note:*** If it's easier, you can also point the mouse on the current folder and right click once. A menu will appear and you can select to "Rename" the folder from the alternatives given. 2. Once the old name is selected (highlighted), type in the new name and it will replace the old one. 3. When you are finished entering the new name, press Enter.
4	**Open a folder to see what is inside**	Put the pointer on top of the folder and double click. A window will open and you will now be able to see the contents of the folder.
5	**Create (or place) one folder inside another folder** Essays School stuff	1. Open the existing folder (double click on the folder). 2. With that open, follow the instructions for creating a new folder (see Feature 1). The new folder will be created automatically within the open folder. **Note:** You can also create a new folder on the desktop and then click on the new folder, hold and drag it over the top of the folder you want it to go inside of. When the destination folder becomes selected (changes color or shade) then you can release the mouse button. The folder you were dragging will now be dropped into the target folder. To see if it worked, open the target folder and see if the new folder is there.
6	**Delete a folder** Essays Recycle Bin	1. Put the mouse pointer on the folder to be deleted. 2. Click, hold, and drag the folder to the Recycle Bin. 3. Once the Recycle Bin is highlighted, let go of the mouse button. The folder should now be within the bin. **Note:** Additionally, you can delete a folder by putting the cursor on the folder, *right* click, and select the *delete* option from the pop-up menu. The folder will automatically be placed in the Recycle Bin. Mac Users: Drag the folder to the Trash. **Note:** Double click on the Recycle Bin and a window will open. You can look to see if your folder really is in there.
7	**Take out the recycles** Open Explore Empty Recycle Bin Create Shortcut Delete Rename Properties Recycle Bin **MAC USERS**	When you are sure you want to delete something that has been put in the Recycle Bin, you may want to get rid of it for good. 1. Point the mouse pointer at the Recycle Bin and right click. 2. Choose the option for emptying the bin. **Special >>> Empty Trash** . . .

Level 1a Workout: Getting organized with folders

Once you have reviewed these different steps and written down your idea of a filing system with various folders, do the following:

1. Create a set of folders as outlined in your plan.
2. Name each of the folders (use names that are relevant to you and your work.
3. Practice nesting some of the folders inside of others.
4. Rename some of the folders.
5. Select and remove some of the folders by putting them in the Recycle Bin or Trash.

As additional practice, go to the text's Web site, **www.prenhall.com/newby,** and review its contents. Do the following:

- Navigate to the Chapter 1 Navigation folder (**www.prenhall.com/newby** >>> **Chapter 1** >>> **Workout 1a** >>> **Navigation** folder). Copy the folder and paste it on the desktop of your machine. A mentoring video has been created to demonstrate and guide you through this task (see text's Web site: **www.prenhall.com/ newby**).
- Once it has been placed on your desktop, open the **Navigation** folder. You'll see a number of different folders (all of which are empty) nested within that folder. Play with these. Practice naming, renaming, deleting, putting one inside of another, and so forth. The idea is to become accustomed to doing it.
- Develop some type of logical structure for the folders. Create additional folders as needed.

Review what you have just done. It may not look like much, but it is actually quite important. Don't think that folders were the only things you have explored. You have also worked on pointing, left and right clicks, click and holds, dragging, and so on. You have also explored the Start menu and seen the locations of various programs that will be used later.

> **Note:** If you understand how to create, label, and move these types of folders, this little skill will transfer very easily when you name files, place them within folders, recall them from folders, and so on. This is a major function of the computer and now you know something about how to store and retrieve. Good job.
>
> More information about folders, desktops, and creating, storing, and deleting can be found in Windows **Help**.

> **Another note:** Pay attention to the necessity of organization. It will amaze you at how fast the number of folders, documents, images, and what-not will pile up in your computer, specifically on your desktop. Soon it will be overwhelming to find what you need. Begin early to organize your data into a set of folders that help identify where your stuff is and how to find it efficiently.

Scenario 2: Make it personal

Recently, I was talking with a group of high school students when suddenly a cell phone began to ring. They all stopped talking immediately and listened to the ring, and then one reached into a nearby backpack, pulled out his cell, and began a conversation. Based on the ring, not only did this student know his cell was the one ringing, but he also knew who was making the call. To accomplish this, he had personalized his ring tones. In further examination of his phone, it was also easy to note how he had personalized, for instance, the exterior (e.g., cover with added color), the screen background, list of frequently called numbers, etc.

That student's personalization of his cell may have been done for a number of reasons (e.g., to make it more efficient, aesthetically appealing, or just to be different). This type of personalization can also be done with your computer through implementing features of the system software. For example, the background on your desktop can be readily altered to include a picture of your favorite place or person, the size and shape of the cursor can be changed, or even the look of the windows, taskbars, and Start menu can be altered to fit your personal needs, preference, and desires. In some cases, these changes may be made only to get a new and different appearance; in other cases (e.g., accessibility issues), the changes may be required.

Figure 1.6 is the Personalization window found within Windows Vista (**Start button** >>> **Control Panel** >>>**Appearance and Personalization** >>> **Personalization**). Many of the ways in which you can change the appearance of your computer can be accomplished through this window. In the step-by-step procedures that follow, you can explore the various types of changes that can easily be made to personalize your machine.

> **Note:** In some cases (e.g., school lab computers), customization or personalization of the computer may not be allowed or may require special permission to complete. If multiple users access the computer, specific systematic appearances may be most efficient for that type of environment. Make sure you check with the system administrator before making any changes.

Figure 1.6 Personalization window

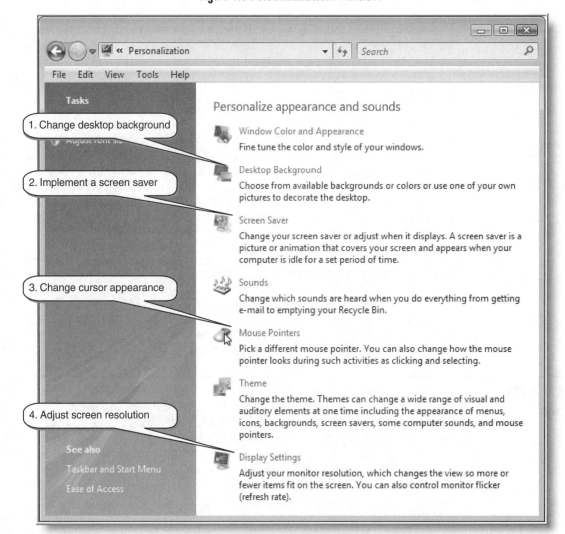

No.	Feature	Steps to Get It Done
1	**Change the desktop background**	1. Open the Personalization window (**Start button** >>> **Control Panel** >>> **Appearance and Personalization** >>> **Personalization**). 2. Select **Desktop Background**. 3. Under the drop-down menu for "Picture Location," select the type of background you prefer (e.g., solid color, a sample picture, a picture from your personal file). 4. Also select how the picture should be positioned as a background.
2	**Implement a screen saver**	1. Open the Personalization Window (**Start button** >>> **Control Panel** >>> **Appearance and Personalization** >>> **Personalization**). 2. Select **Screen Saver**. 3. In the **Screen Saver** group, click on the drop-down menu and select one of the options. 4. Preview your selection in the preview window. 5. Continue to select various options and preview each. 6. In the **Wait:** selection area of the window, select the desired wait time that the computer should be inactive before the screen saver comes up on the screen (e.g., 5 minutes).
3	**Change the appearance of the cursor**	1. Open the Personalization Window (**Start button** >>> **Control Panel** >>> **Appearance and Personalization** >>> **Personalization**). 2. Click on **Mouse Pointers** to open the **Mouse Properties** window. 3. Within the **Mouse Properties** window, click on the **Pointers** tab. 4. From the **Scheme** group, use the drop-down menu to select a different scheme for your pointer. 5. Preview the selected scheme in the **Customize:** section of the window. 6. Select and review various cursor schemes. Once your final preference is selected, click on the **OK** button and that scheme will be applied.
4	**Adjust screen resolution**	1. Open the Personalization Window (**Start button** >>> **Control Panel** >>> **Appearance and Personalization** >>> **Personalization**). 2. Select **Display Settings**. 3. Select the level of resolution that you desire. 4. Click the **Apply** button and note the changes. Make further changes as desired. **Note:** If you have your computer hooked up to two monitors at the same time (or you wish to do so), this is the window where you can select to have them work as a single, large screen (select "Extend the desktop onto this monitor").
5	**Alter the screen for individuals with low vision (or other accessibility needs)**	1. Review Figure 1.7 (**Appearance and Personalization** window). 2. Open the **Appearance and Personalization** window (**Start button** >>> **Control Panel** >>> **Appearance and Personalization**). 3. Click on the **Ease of Access Center**. 4. Click on **Start Magnifier**. 5. When the **Magnifier** window appears, select a desired magnification level (**Presentation** group >>> **Scale factor**). Also select the dock position (e.g., top) where the magnified section of the screen should be positioned. 6. Preview the magnified section of the screen. **Note:** To turn off the magnifier, right click the **Magnifier** button in the taskbar and select "Close." **Note:** Review and attempt (e.g., Narrator) the other options to adapt your computer for other accessibility needs.

continued

No.	Feature	Steps to Get It Done
		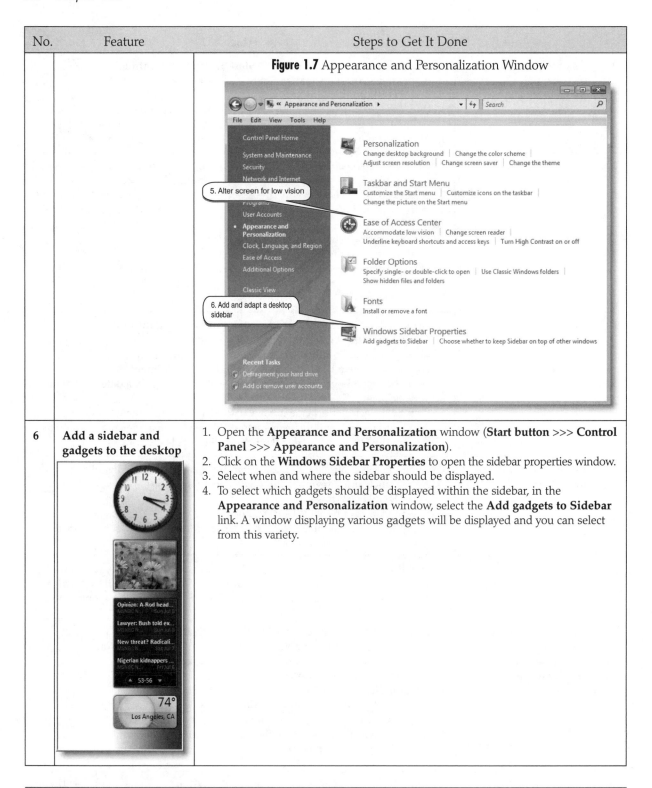
6	**Add a sidebar and gadgets to the desktop**	1. Open the **Appearance and Personalization** window (**Start button** >>> **Control Panel** >>> **Appearance and Personalization**). 2. Click on the **Windows Sidebar Properties** to open the sidebar properties window. 3. Select when and where the sidebar should be displayed. 4. To select which gadgets should be displayed within the sidebar, in the **Appearance and Personalization** window, select the **Add gadgets to Sidebar** link. A window displaying various gadgets will be displayed and you can select from this variety.

Level 1b Workout: Your personal touch

After reviewing the various ways that you can do to change the appearance of your computer system, you should try a few of these things. If you're working on your own personal computer, these changes should be easy to make; however, if you're working in a school computer lab, such changes may not be allowed. Restrictions are frequently imposed within computer labs to keep the computers uniform for the efficient use of the maximum amount of individuals.

If you do have the option of changing the various computer settings, here are a few things that you should attempt to do to personalize your computer's settings (each

can be accomplished through the Personalization and Appearance window that can be found through clicking the **Start button** >>> **Control Panel** >>> **Appearance and Personalization**):

1. Imagine that you want to add a new background to your computer's desktop. Create one that includes your picture or a picture that you have selected beyond the standard pictures offered by the software.
2. Suppose you are currently taking a personal management course that requires the monitoring of the New York Stock Exchange. In fact, you have "invested" $100,000 in various stocks and you now want to easily monitor their daily performance. Can you add a gadget to your sidebar that will allow for this monitoring to easily occur?
3. Imagine sitting in a computer lab when you notice that the person next to you is having difficulty seeing the screen and following the mouse cursor movement. You offer to help. You need to show that individual how to change some setting to magnify the screen and to enlarge the mouse cursor to a maximum size. Practice doing this on your computer.
4. You've found that you really aren't very good at opening folders by double clicking them. It is difficult to keep your hand steady and it seems to take forever to get the dumb things open. Find a way to change the double click to a single click to open folders on your computer.
5. You've found a new piece of software that you are using quite frequently. To launch it, however, you have to go into the All Programs section of the Start menu and then through several other folders before it's finally located. Isn't there a way to just add that program to your Start menu? Also, there are a number of programs on the Start menu that you never use. Can you get rid of them, or at least just remove them from this convenient location? Resolve these tasks through the same Appearance and Personalization window.

Level 2 Help, I Need Some Info

What should you be able to do?

Here, the focus is on getting efficient, effective, and reliable help when it is needed. This is a skill that will be needed and used over and over again as you work with the computer.

> **Note:** There's too much information within each of these programs for any sensible person to totally learn and retain. Knowing where and how to access that information is a skill well worth the effort to learn.

Introduction

At this level of performance, we want you to become more independent. That is, we want you to begin to answer questions that you have a need to answer—not something we have conjured up for you. This will allow you to search for and find needed information, to get tasks done, to solve problems, to overcome difficulties, and so on—even when it is just you and the machine.

Don't worry—there will always be questions. You will encounter endless novel situations that will require the use of extra resources. Specifically, the use of the computer's built-in **Help** should become a natural place for you to turn to.

> **Note: Help** doesn't have all the answers, but it does answer many of the common problems individuals run into. You are much further ahead by using **Help** as your knowledgeable personal computer assistant.

Another note: Guess what? There are **Helps** within almost all of the major software application programs available today. That is, if you're working in a word processing program, there will be a word processing **Help** that you can refer to. Likewise, if you're working with a spreadsheet, there's a specific **Help** for spreadsheets also. Isn't it nice to know that these people were thinking about you when they were developing their products?

Getting some Help

Have you ever bought a new car and then proceeded to ***memorize*** the owner's manual? Why not? Don't you want to know everything about your new purchase?

For most of us, that type of memorization task would be too time-consuming, would take too much energy, and would be too boring with little return. You and I know that when specific information is needed about the car (e.g., Where is the jack located? What is the procedure to change a tire?), we can turn to the owner's manual and find the needed information.

Guess what? This is also true for the computer. The nice thing about the computer, however, is that it has a section where you can electronically look up answers to your questions and solutions for your problems. This is known as the **Help** program. In Microsoft's Windows Vista operating system, you can access Help and Support by clicking **Start** button >>> **Help and Support**.

Why do you *really* need to know how to use Help?

This question is similar to "Why do I need to know how to use an encyclopedia?" that some of your students may have asked. Those of us who have worked on this book—and any book out there that has to do with the computer—can't foresee all the situations that you'll find yourself in need. In one way or another, you'll find questions that we haven't thought of and definitely haven't attempted to answer.

The goal, then, is to help you find the way to get your own answer. For the long haul, this will be a much better approach than writing a huge text with "all of the answers" that we would want you to memorize. That is a little unrealistic and unwanted.

Help is very efficient and, in most cases, for the novice user it will have more than enough information to get you what you need.

Scenario 3: Creating the self-sufficient parent

Lexy was having difficulties with her mother. It wasn't a disagreement about Lexy's homework getting done, her friends, or even how many minutes she used on last month's cell phone bill. Lexy's problem had to do with her mother's nonstop questions about the computer. It seemed that each evening Lexy's mom would wait until Lexy was just settling down to a favorite TV show and then the inquisition would begin. In most cases, it began with a simple, "Hey Lexy, can you show me how I can get my computer to . . . ?"

Lexy quickly figured out that the best way to solve her problem was to help her mom learn to help herself. Today, for example, Mom was having difficulty figuring out how to install a new program that she needed to preview for her boss.

"You know Mom, you can answer many of your own questions, by just accessing the computer's Help." Lexy then proceeded to show her mom that she could quickly access Help by clicking on the **Start** button and then clicking on **Help and Support** (see Figure 1.8). When she showed her how that was accomplished, she then gave her mom a little assignment: to type in her specific question about installing a program into the search section of **Help** (see Figure 1.8) and see what topics come up. She was then to select one of the topics that was most relevant and examine if the given procedure was helpful. Mom indicated she would try. Lexy monitored and gave suggestions. Then the computer questioning seemed to abate—which gave Mom more time to ask Lexy about lots of other things—cause moms like to do that.

Figure 1.8 Windows Help and Support

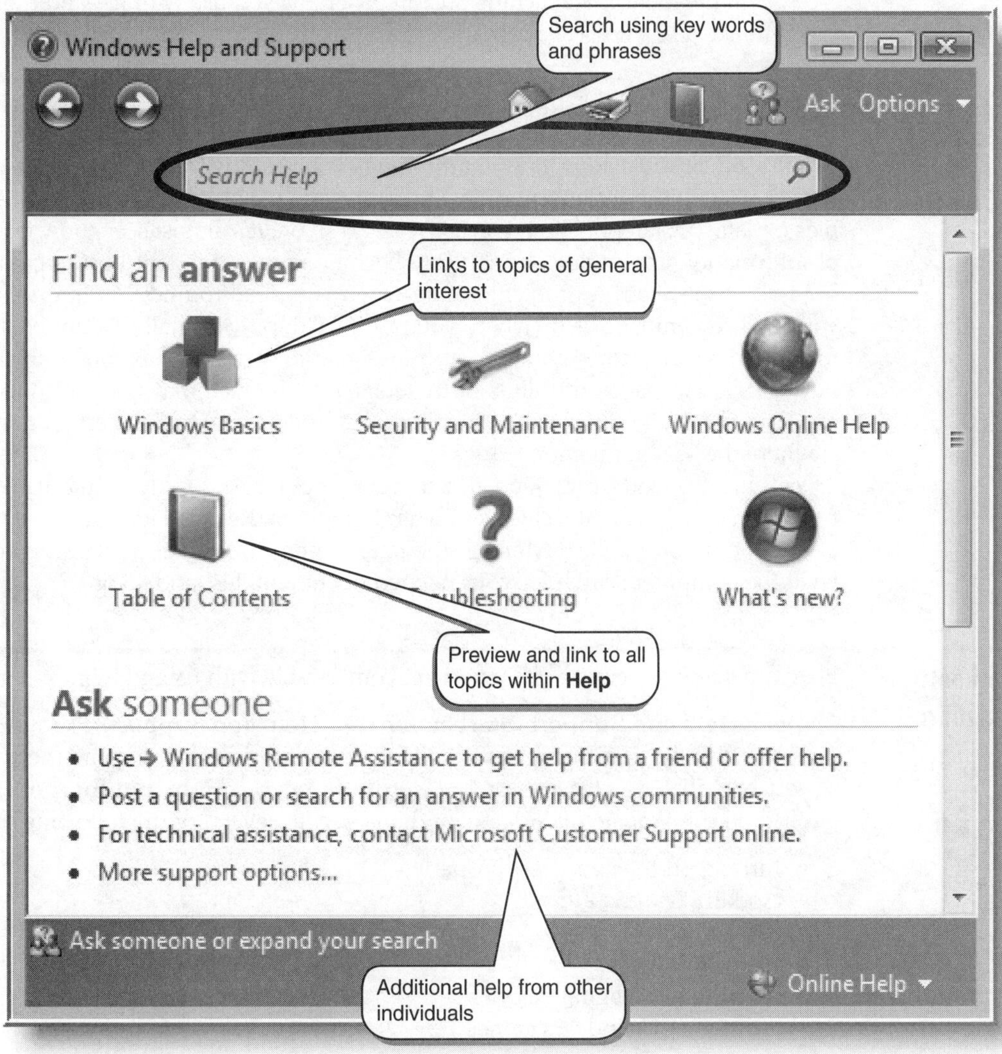

Using Help

Basically, **Help** works like an electronic encyclopedia. It is arranged by topics. If you need something, you tell **Help** the key word or phrase and it will look it up for you and report back the related topics found. You can then select the specific items you feel may have the answer that you seek and the computer will highlight all of the information that it has on the topic.

Sounds simple, doesn't it? There are a couple of things to remember:

- You need to know what the key word or phrase is. If you don't have something at least close to your topic, the computer won't know what to look for. We've given you a bunch of key jargon words for this section of the text as examples of key words that can be looked up in **Help.**
- Sometimes your selected key word gets you close, but not exactly in the right place (this happens sometimes when you're looking for a book in the library). Don't be afraid to look around and see if some of the topics are related and how they relate to your topic. These may help you find exactly what you are looking for.
- There are times when **Help** may cause you frustration. Perhaps there isn't the needed information, the information provided is confusing in some way, or you know the information is in there but you can't seem to find it. Skills at using **Help** are like anything else, they get better as you use them. Throughout this text we emphasize using **Help** because it's a skill you should develop to gain greater

independence with your use of the computer. Your other choice is to memorize everything about this machine and all programs you use with it—and that doesn't seem like a very logical alternative.

Using the Search function

Once you become accustomed to using the computer for many of your daily tasks, you'll soon be amazed at how many things you store within it. Soon you will have thousands of pieces of information. Those bits and pieces may include photos, letters, files of data, book reports, math exercises, and so on. It's almost scary how fast the bits of information accumulate. We quickly become very dependent on the computer to hold all of this stuff. A problem occurs when you need to find that information and you can't remember exactly where you put it. With only a small amount of stored information, looking through using your own pair of eyes may be more than sufficient; however, if you have thousands of folders, each of which may contain multiple files and documents, it may take a tremendous amount of time to find certain things. That is where the search function comes in.

Within Microsoft Vista, you can use the computer to quickly search its own contents by merely giving it a clue as to what to look for. Review Figure 1.2 and note that at the bottom of the **Start Menu** is the place where you can enter the key words and have the computer search for your needed document, file, and so on.

Level 2 Workout: Stretching with a little Help

Here are a few exercises to help you get comfortable with using **Help**.

1. Open **Help and Support** (**Start** button >>> **Help and Support**). Examine (review Figure 1.8) the various topics in the **Help and Support** window and the area to insert potential search terms or key words. Within the **Help and Support** window, click on the *Windows basics* link and investigate several of the following topics:

   - Turning off the computer properly
   - Working with windows
   - Using Paint
   - Using Wordpad
   - Working with digital pictures
   - Learn about Windows games

2. Within **Help and Support,** select the **Table of Contents.** Examine the various categories of information and how they are organized. If you have a question within a general category (e.g., files and folders), you can click on that category and see the various links to all kinds of information. Follow these examples and see what types of information can be obtained from the Help and Support Table of Contents:

   - How do you burn a CD or DVD? (Start at the **Files and folders** category within the **Help and Support** table of contents.)
   - How do you play music and videos? (Start at the **Music and sounds** category of the **Help and Support** table of contents.)
   - How do you open a calculator for use on the computer? (Start at the **Programs tools and games** and then look under **Windows programs and tools.**)
   - What is a firewall and how is it used? (Start at **Security and privacy** within the **Help and Support** table of contents.)

   Don't spend a huge amount of time playing with this, but do get a feel for what this has to offer. There are some really great bits of information readily available to you within **Help and Support.** Get a feel for what's there and what can be accessed when it's needed.

 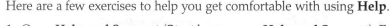

Help>>>Help Center>>>Mac Help.

3. Insert key words and terms in the *Search Help* area (see Figure 1.8) and practice looking up bits of information that may be useful. For example find out how to

- "Change languages"
- "Define HTML"
- "Use speech narration"
- "Create shortcuts"
- "Find a file or folder"
- "Install a program"

Try out several of your own terms and see what types of results are produced. Stump your friends by exploring several of the topics in **Help**. Create some questions about the new things you have found and check with friends, neighbors, colleagues, etc. to see if anyone else knows what you now know.

4. Go to the text's Web site, **www.prenhall.com/newby,** and review the mentoring video that has been created to demonstrate Help and its various functions.

Level 3: Integration and Application

What should you be able to do?

The focus at this point is for you to begin to think of ways that this information can be applied. Using these examples, generate ideas on how to use the features of the system software to facilitate your students' learning and the work that you do.

Introduction

Now it's time to stretch. You need to now understand how to use this information on your own and teach it effectively to your students or future students.

Ideas on using the system software as a learning tool

There are a number of ways that the system software can be used to increase the learning of others. Here are some examples to get you thinking about possible ways to use various features of the operating software:

1. Develop a mind-set of finding the answers for oneself by focusing on how to find answers to problems or questions that haven't yet been encountered. An example of this would be setting up a computer scavenger hunt that involves the use of the system software's **Help** feature. Have students find information that deals with things such as *optimizing performance*, *print queues*, or even *updating drivers*.
2. Develop skills at planning and creating effective organizational filing systems. Have students design a filing system that they can defend as being effective for the storage of their key documents and files. After they have designed it, have them review what others have planned, make revisions, and then create and use the actual folders and nested folders on their computers.
3. Use the system software **Find** feature to locate specific documents, folders, and so forth, on the computer. Have students find specific files on the hard drive and explain the path to the file's location.
4. Learn to adapt the computer settings to best fit the user's preferred style. For example, using the Control Panel, change the settings on the monitor to enhance (or diminish) the size of the screen display, adapt the speed with which the cursor blinks, change the size and shape of the mouse pointer, or even alter the size and looks of the icons displayed on the desktop. Also have the students learn how to change these back to its original setting.
5. Develop the ability to open several folders in separate windows at a single time and transfer documents or subfolders between the different folders. In addition, develop the ability to copy folders and documents and put them on different disks for storage purposes.

Ideas on using the system software as an assistant

1. Use the computer's system software features to help maintain the computer. Features of the system software such as *Disk Defragmenter* and *Scan Disk* can be used to improve the performance of the computer by keeping it in an efficient working order.
2. Use *Windows Explorer* as a means to view where saved items are located and how they can be rearranged or manipulated.
3. Determine the size of a specific file and/or the size of disk space.
4. Use the control panels to alter how the computer functions and looks.
5. Create and use shortcuts to facilitate the effectiveness of accessing key programs and files.
6. Add and/or remove programs from the Start menu for easy access.
7. Use the system to enhance the access of physically challenged students.

Chapter 2
WORD PROCESSING
MS Word: The Basics of a Writing Assistant

Introduction

What should you know about word processors?

Word processing is *a* (if not *the*) major software tool used by teachers and students. You need to know a few basics to use it effectively. In this opening section, we want you to know the following:

- What a word processor is, what it can do, and how it can help in teaching and learning
- How to justify the use of the word processor as an effective tool—by knowing when and why it should or shouldn't be used

Terms to know

font	graphic	style
table	format	margins
ruler	columns	headers
footers	alignment	page setup

What is a word processor and what does it do?

A word processor is a computer application that allows you to enter, edit, revise, **format,** store, retrieve, and print text. When you work with text the way that teachers and students do, word processors quickly become a valuable tool. For just a second, review that list of verbs once again, in relation to the teaching profession. You need this tool!

What are some commonly used word processors?

- Microsoft's Word
- Corel's WordPerfect
- Sun Microsystems' StarOffice/OpenOffice Writer
- The word processor within Microsoft's Works
- The word processor inside of AppleWorks

> **Note:** We focus on Microsoft's Word in this text. However, **what we present can be done in any of the other word processors listed.** So if you don't have access to Word, don't be alarmed—you can still complete the projects and learn the basic skills.

Why bother learning how to use a word processor?

- We haven't found anything yet to replace reading and writing. As long as those two skills are needed, there will be a need for the processing of words.
- Most of us don't have perfect memories. Word processors are a good way to record ideas, thoughts, research, and instructions, and then be able to recall them later.
- We live in a world of repetition. From the written standpoint, word processors help so you don't needlessly start from scratch when confronted with a project that may be the same or similar to one encountered previously. Thus the second time around, you spend your time on improvements instead of reinventing the same thing.
- It just looks better. If this text were handwritten (by me), you would gag. Word processing allows others to be able to quickly decipher what is written. As much as we would like to say that we judge things based on their content, how something looks also matters. Good word processing can help with how information is perceived and processed by the reader.
- It isn't just words anymore. Today's word processors not only handle words, they also incorporate the use of all kinds of graphics and pictures. These can lead to more proficient and better communication (and possible learning).
- No longer is word processing a lone wolf. That is, what is produced with a good word processor can be coupled with other programs and made even more powerful. Hooking up your words with powerful graphics programs, databases, spreadsheets, and even the Internet can open all kinds of possibilities for classroom projects, fun explorations, and increased efficiency.

How can word processors be used at school? A brief list of ideas

By the teacher:

- Newsletters
- Classroom handouts
- Student assignments and tests
- Calendars
- Lesson plans

By the student:

- Essays (expository, narrative, persuasive)
- Book reports
- Answers to comprehension questions
- Creative writing
- Written science reports

Orientation

What's the workspace look like?

Figure 2.1 is an example of the workspace of a common word processor (MS Word). Note where you can enter in your information and some of the common commands, command groups, and specific tools that can be accessed and used.

What commands can be used?

As in all MS Office applications (e.g., MS PowerPoint, MS Excel), there is a ribbon of tools that runs across the top of the work screen. Within each ribbon the actual tools that can be used to input, format, and edit the words to be processed are grouped under the various **command tabs** (e.g., Home, Insert, Page Layout, References).

Figure 2.1 View of a Microsoft Word word processing work area

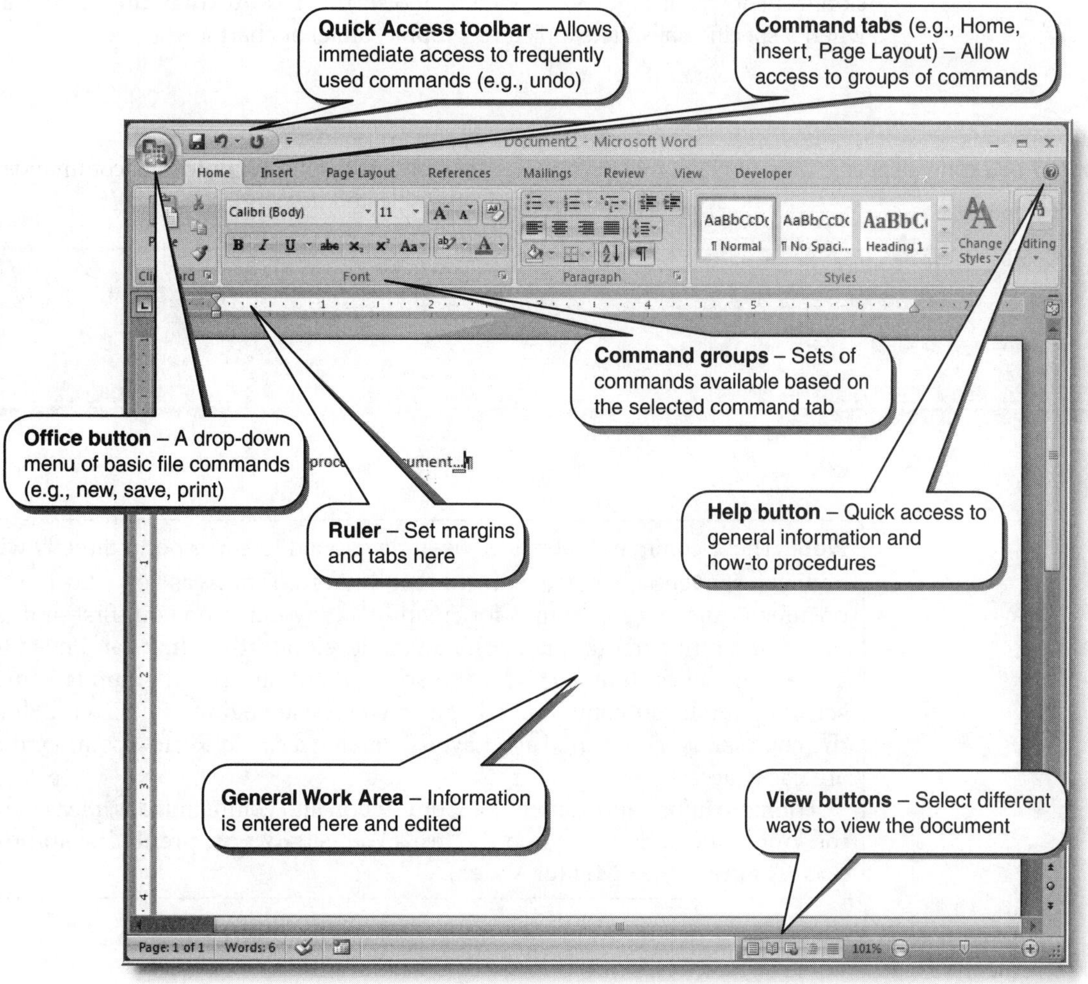

Quick Access toolbar – Allows immediate access to frequently used commands (e.g., undo)

Command tabs (e.g., Home, Insert, Page Layout) – Allow access to groups of commands

Command groups – Sets of commands available based on the selected command tab

Office button – A drop-down menu of basic file commands (e.g., new, save, print)

Ruler – Set margins and tabs here

Help button – Quick access to general information and how-to procedures

General Work Area – Information is entered here and edited

View buttons – Select different ways to view the document

Selecting a specific tab reveals an associated command set or group. Once a command tab has been selected, this specific group remains visible and ready for use. Items within the set may appear as individual items or as a **gallery** of related items. For example, selecting the Insert tab (see Figure 2.2) in Word reveals a group of commands that deals specifically with the insertion of such things as tables, illustrations, links, headers and footers, and of course the text itself.

The tabs have been developed to make your life easier. No longer do you have to go through hundreds of potential drop-down menu items to find the needed tool; the tabs allow you quick access to related groups of commands.

Figure 2.2 The Ribbon holds the command tabs, command groups or sets, and individual commands

It should be noted that there are additional commands that are needed on occasion. As shown in Figure 2.3 (Picture Tools), these **contextual commands** appear when a specific object like a picture, graphic, table, or chart is selected.

Figure 2.3 Selecting a specific item (e.g. graphic, picture) in the workspace reveals contextual commands that can be accessed and used with the selected item

> **Note:** These command tabs have been developed to correspond directly with how you sequentially create a document in Word. That is, as you start the document, the key commands for creating and working on your first draft are found under the first tab (Home). As you develop further drafts and need to add additional content, pictures, and so on, then the needed group is found by selecting the Insert command tab. Next, when you begin to finalize the draft, the commands within the Page Layout, References, and Review command tabs are easily accessed.
>
> For more information about the Word ribbon and command tabs, please review the Word Orientation video on the text's Web site (**www. prenhall.com/newby >>> Chapter 2 >>> Mentor Video**).

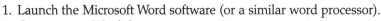

Orientation Workout: Explore the territory

Turn on your computer and attempt the following:

1. Launch the Microsoft Word software (or a similar word processor).
2. Create a new Word document.
3. Explore the various tabs on the ribbon and examine the different command groups.
4. On the new document attempt the following:

   - Enter a few lines of text.
   - Select some of text and alter its format (e.g., size, **style**).
   - Use the different view buttons and select different ways to view your document.
   - Alter the paragraph structure by changing the manner your text is aligned and if it is double or single spaced.
   - Practice cutting and pasting portions of your text.

Level 1: Designing, Creating, and Producing Written Documents

What should you be able to do?

At Level 1, the emphasis is on using various tools and techniques of an electronic word processor to format a document given specific guidelines and step-by-step procedures.

What resources are provided?

Basically, Level 1 is divided into common teaching scenarios, selected solutions, and practice exercises (i.e., Workouts). The scenarios have been constructed to allow you to examine common problems and how they can be addressed through the use of this software. To do this, we have provided the following.

a. Completed word processed documents (see the text's accompanying Web site: **www.prenhall.com/newby** >>> **Chapter 2** >>> **Workout Level 1**) that you can review and compare and see how the features are used to address the problems presented within each scenario.
b. Quick reference figures that identify (via visual callouts) all of the key features that have been incorporated within the solution presentation. These allow you to rapidly identify the key features and reference exactly how to include such features within your own work.
c. Step-by-step instructions on how to incorporate all highlighted features within your work.
d. Video mentoring support that guides you through the integration of each of the highlighted features (see the text's accompanying Web site: **www.prenhall. com/newby** >>> **Chapter 2** >>> **Mentor Videos**)
e. Workout exercises that allow you to practice identifying and selecting which software features to use, when to use those features, how they should be incorporated, and to what degree they are effective.

How should you proceed?

If you have <u>little or no experience</u> with MS Office 2007 and particularly Word, then we suggest you do the following:

1. Read and review Scenario I.
2. Examine the quick reference figure (Figure 2.5) and all of the highlighted features.
3. Using the step-by-step directions given for each highlighted feature, use the software and practice using each of the features.
4. If you have any confusion or difficulty with these features, access the videos and monitor the features as they are demonstrated and discussed within the short video clips (**www.prenhall.com/newby** >>> **Chapter 2** >>> **Mentor Videos**). Select the short clip that demonstrates the use of the needed feature.
5. Once you feel comfortable with these features, go to Scenario 2 and repeat these same steps with the new features introduced for that scenario. Monitor the quick reference figure (Figure 2.8) closely.
6. After both scenarios have been reviewed, go to the Workout and work through the problems and exercises as it outlines.

If you have <u>experience</u> with Word 2007, you may want to review the scenarios and the quick reference figures first. If any of the features are unfamiliar, then use the step-by-step procedures as well as the mentoring support videos. Once the review has been completed, then move directly to the Workout and create your own Word document by incorporating many of the highlighted features.

Scenario 1: A little story

Sally sat staring at a stubby, chewed pencil on her desk. Her second graders had just wiggled on home for the day, and she was too tired to move. She smiled as she thought about the 2.5 million silly second-grade questions she had answered that day, how much chalk was on her dress, and how many times she had to tell Jenni Hatcher to quit acting like a bird—although the bird was actually easier to control than the spotted dinosaur that Jenni had been the day before.

From the hallway behind her, Sally heard Brinna Washington's voice. Brinna was laughing as she looked in at Sally and said, "Don't worry girl, it does get better." During these first two weeks of the school year, Brinna had already shown herself to be a needed friend and mentor. She had great timing for giving support and adding tidbits of advice.

Brinna continued, "During my prep time this afternoon I was thinking about how overwhelmed you must be feeling right now. Two years ago, I was in your exact position, and it wasn't that much fun. So I made you a little helper gift. I put it on the flash drive that I borrowed from you this morning." She then handed Sally an envelope that obviously contained the flash drive and a short note. "It's nothing special," continued Brinna, "but it's something I wish I had when I first started teaching."

"Thanks . . . but you know that I don't do much on the computer," replied Sally.

"Oh, I know that—but you will," Brinna responded as she disappeared into the hallway.

Sally unfolded the note and looked over what was written:

Sally—

This flash contains a folder that holds three files. They should be easy to open on your machine in your classroom or on the one you have at home. The first file contains a short newsletter that I sent to my kids last week. You'll see that it's real simple, but it might give you an idea of what could be sent home and what you can build on. The second file is a simple science lesson plan that I was working on for next week. See if you want to use it, or adapt it in some way. We might even want to join our classes together to work on it. And the last file is just something that helps me keep things in perspective. I keep a copy inside my day planner and try to read it every once in awhile.

Hope this helps—

Brinna

P.S. Did you do a bird unit today? I kept hearing bird sounds coming from your room — aren't second graders great!!

A few minutes later, Sally was packed up and heading out to her car for the trip home. In her new "My School Bag" tote bag she carried the flash drive. She'd take a look at the files over the weekend and see what treasures her friend had given her.

Let's take a look at the first item that Brinna offered Sally—"*The Happenings...*" newsletter. It is a simple word processed document that can be used as a template for other letters that may use a similar format. Several key word processing formatting features are used within the letter. Figure 2.4 and 2.5, respectively, serve as "before" and "after" pictures of the newsletter. Within Figure 2.5 callout bubbles have been inserted to identify the key features that were incorporated to enhance the formatting of the document.

- Using Figure 2.5 as the guide, follow the numbered features in the step-by-step procedure to learn how each of the features is employed.
- If additional guidance is needed, go to the mentoring videos in the text's accompanying Web site (**www.prenhall.com/newby** >>> **Chapter 2** >>> **Mentor Videos**) and select the short clip that demonstrates the use of the needed feature.

Figure 2.4 Letter from Mrs. Washington *before* formatting

The Happenings...
Mrs. Washington's Second Grade, Room 8

Week of August 26–30

Hello everyone,

This is the second in our weekly series of newsletters. Things have started to settle down into a regular weekly routine. Hopefully you have all had the chance to look over some of the work that is being done in our class.

Highlights of this week:
We've started our group science project on "Whales." The kids were fascinated by the stories we read from our library books. I think some of them were surprised at the size of a blue whale when we attempted to draw one the right size with chalk in the school parking lot! We are now monitoring the "Whale Search" Web site. If you have access to the Internet at home, try it out and let the kids show you what they have discovered.

In math, we are working with manipulables. We are trying to count about everything possible in our room. If your child counts things at home, that is why.

We have spent a lot of time in the "reading lounge" this week. After a long summer vacation, it is time to get into the habit of regular reading. Encourage this at home. Pick something fun and have your child read to you out loud.

Things to look forward to:
More whale work is coming. We will soon be creating a world globe that highlights many of the key areas that whales can be found in today's world. We will also create one that represents where the whales were 100 years ago. It should make for an interesting comparison.

We will be doing some classroom reading and math assessments next week. These are to help identify any areas that need special attention and encouragement. I will send home individual reports to each of you about your child's performance and my thoughts.

A little help from parents:
Extra boxes of tissues are needed. Could you send an extra box in the next week or two? Thanks.
The school fund raiser is upon us. We will need help in the organization and distribution departments. I will be sending home a sign-up sheet next week. Be looking for it.
Weekly spelling tests will be starting next week on Fridays.

Thanks for all of your support and help. This should be the best year ever!!!!
Mrs. Washington

Figure 2.5 Letter from Mrs. Washington *after* formatting

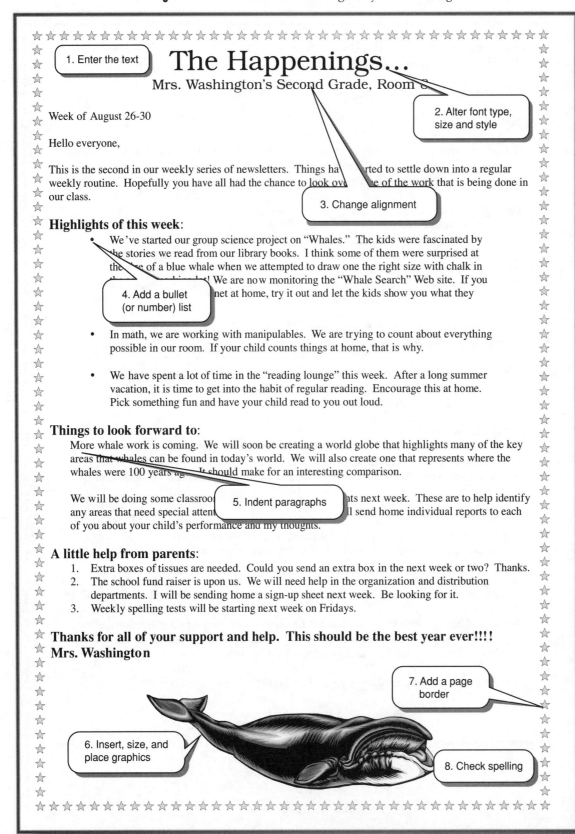

No.	To Do	How to Get It Done
1	**Enter the text**	1. Start Word and create a new document (**Office Button** >>> **New**). 2. Remember one of the key rules —"think content first, then make it pretty." That applies here. You first enter the information for the document into the computer. **Note:** If you want to use the content from "The Happenings…" newsletter (see Figure 2.5), it's available on the text's accompanying Web site (**www.prenhall.com/newby** >>> **Chapter 2** >>> **Workouts**>>>**HappeningsNewsletter**). 3. Generally, don't worry about how the document looks at this point. You just need the content to be accurate. Making it look fancy will be part of the formatting to follow. **Note:** Check out the **Mentor Video**, "Copying, Cutting, and Pasting," on the text's Web site for guidance and demonstrations on different ways to enter information. The video can be accessed as (**www.prenhall.com/newby** >>> **Chapter 2** >>> **Mentor Video**).
2	**Alter font type, size, and style**	1. Select (highlight) the title of the newsletter "The Happenings…" 2. Review the **Font** set of commands (**Home tab** >>> **Font** group) as shown in Figure 2.6 3. Click on the down arrow to reveal the gallery of different font types (e.g., Times New Roman) and preview the different alternatives by moving your cursor over the different names of types. Click on your preferred type. 4. Use the down arrow on the font size (e.g., 12) to reveal selected font sizes that can also be previewed in a similar fashion. Follow the same procedure to preview and select the size of the font you desire. 5. Using this same font group of tools, you can change the font style (e.g., **bold,** *italic*, <u>underline</u>), font color, and background highlighting within the document. 6. For additional alternatives, select the expansion arrow and a font dialog box will open. **Note:** You can also use the Quick Styles feature (**Home tab** >>> **Styles** group) as shown in Figure 2.6. Similar to the previous steps, highlight the text you want to alter, then preview how it will look by moving the cursor over the formatted styles that are on the ribbon. Click on your selection to make the change. **Figure 2.6** Home tab with various formatting commands highlighted
3	**Change alignment**	1. Select the first two lines of the newsletter. 2. As shown in Figure 2.6, click on the center **alignment** tool (**Home tab** >>> **Paragraph** group). **Remember:** *Alignment* allows you to quickly line up text on the left, the right, equally between right and left, or in the center of your page.
4	**Add a bullet or number list**	1. Highlight all items in the list to be bulleted or numbered. For your newsletter, select all three paragraphs under the "Highlights of this week" heading. 2. Click on the bullet list icon (Figure 2.6) within the **Paragraph** group of commands within the **Home tab**. 3. Review what has been done to your document. Bullets should now appear in front of the items or paragraphs that were selected. The items are indented, and there's an extra bit of white space between each bulleted item.

continued

No.	To Do	How to Get It Done
		4. Next, on the newsletter highlight the three paragraphs under the subheading "A little help from parents . . ."
		5. Click on the number list icon (Figure 2.6).
		Note: If the default bullets or numbers are not appealing, you can change them. After selecting your list of items, click on the down arrow icon next to the bullet or number icon. A gallery of alternative versions of the bullets and numbers will appear. Preview the items by moving your cursor over the alternatives and then click on your selection.
5	**Indent paragraphs**	1. Locate the **ruler** at the top of the document (if it's not showing, go to **View tab** >>> **Show/Hide** group >>> **Ruler**). Note the sliders or paragraph markers sit on both sides of the ruler. The left one pertains to the left text margin and the right one to the right text margin.
		Ruler with paragraph indention markers
		2. Select the text where you want to alter the paragraph indents (e.g., select the text under the heading "Things to look forward to:").
		3. On the bottom square (left marker) icon, left mouse click, hold, and drag the mouse slowly to the right. A vertical dashed line will appear and it will move the margin of the selected text to the right. Adjust it in and out to get a sense for how this works. This adjusted margin only pertains to the highlighted paragraphs of text. If nothing is highlighted, it pertains to the paragraph where the cursor is currently located.
		4. See what happens if you point only at the top triangle marker and move it to the right or left. The first line will change on your selected text. If you wish to indent the first line of the selected paragraphs, then you would use this tool. Note what happens when you only move the bottom triangle. This is known as the "hanging indent." This leaves the first line where it is and moves the rest of the paragraph. Try each of these to see how they can be used to set and reset any text that is selected.
		5. Use the right margin marker set (triangle on the right of the document on the ruler) to set the right **margin** of the selected text.
		Note: If you begin your document by setting the first line marker, the left marker, and the right marker, all the paragraphs that follow will use this same margin setting. Later you can come back and change any and all of the settings as is needed. If you have already entered the text, then highlight those sections that need to have similar margins and set it one time.
6	**Add, size, and place a graphic** Clip Art task pane	1. **Get the graphic** (e.g., picture, clip art). a. On the main ribbon, click **Insert tab** >>> **Illustrations group** >>> **Clip Art** . . . The Clip Art task pane will appear. b. In the Clip Art task pane, enter a key word that describes the type of clip art you are searching for (e.g., "sports") and then click on the **Go** button. Various small versions of the clip art should appear in the task pane. c. Scroll through the different alternatives presented in the task pane. Use the "Other Search Options" to refine your search if needed (e.g., where to search, types of media to search for). d. Click on your selected clip art and the picture will automatically be inserted within your document.

No.	To Do	How to Get It Done

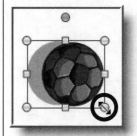

The Clip Gallery window will appear. Make a selection from this gallery or choose to go online and select from additional choices.

2. **Size the graphic**. If your inserted clip art is the perfect size for your document—great, leave it as it is. However, in many cases, the size will not be perfect. So point your mouse at the picture and left click once. You'll note that a box is drawn around the picture and "handles" are placed at each of the corners and in the middle of each of the sides. The handles are small circles and squres. You can grab a handle by putting your mouse pointer on the handle (note that your pointer will change into a double-headed arrow), left click, and hold it. Dragging a handle causes the picture to be altered. Try different handles and see what happens to the shape and size of the picture.
3. **Place the graphic**. Once your picture is inserted and sized appropriately, you can move it to a different location on the slide by putting the mouse on top of the **graphic**, clicking, holding, then dragging it to the new location.
4. **Adapt or adjust the quality of the graphic**. You should also note that once you have selected your picture (the picture has the box around it with the handles), a special set of **Picture Tools** becomes available (look for the **Picture Tools** tab immediately above the **Format** tab on the main ribbon). You can use these tools for the following:
   - Adjust the picture (brightness, contrast, color)
   - Change the picture style (border, shape, special effects)
   - Arrange the picture in relation to other items (bring to the front, send to the back)
   - Size (crop, alter height and width)

Note: Working with clip art and other graphic files may take a bit of practice. Some won't look as nice when their size is changed to a drastic degree — others work great. You'll also find that access to the Internet gives you an endless supply of various clip art photos, pictures, and so on that you may want to insert within your documents.

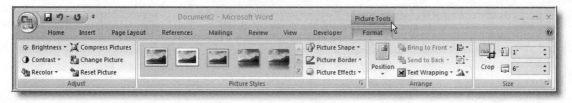

Picture Tools

7	**Page border**	1. Click **Page Layout** >>> **Page Background** group >>> **Page Border.**

2. The "Borders and Shading" dialog box will appear (see Figure 2.7). Click the Page Border tab if it isn't already selected.
3. Under the section titled Settings click on the Box option. Notice what happens in the Preview section on the right-hand side of this window.
4. Under the section titled Art, click on the down arrow and scroll through all of the different borders that could be selected. Select one that you think would look cool. Look at the Preview box to see what has occurred.
5. Explore this window and try several different settings. See what appeals to you by watching how the changes impact the Preview box. When you have made your final set of selections, click OK.

Note: This "Borders and Shading" dialog box will become very handy. Make sure you take time to try the different options under the "Borders" tab and also the "Shading" tab within this dialog box. You can learn to draw boxes around specific bits of text, color the boxes, or even shade the backgrounds within the boxes.

continued

No.	To Do	How to Get It Done

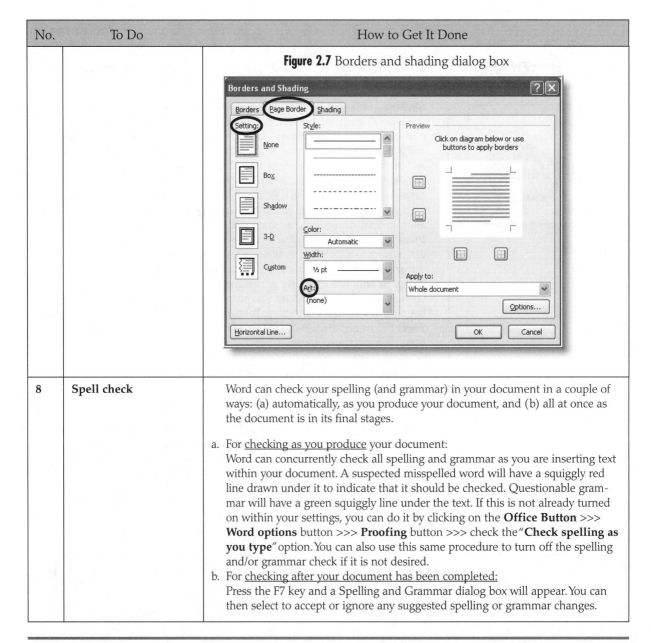

Figure 2.7 Borders and shading dialog box

| 8 | **Spell check** | Word can check your spelling (and grammar) in your document in a couple of ways: (a) automatically, as you produce your document, and (b) all at once as the document is in its final stages.

a. For <u>checking as you produce</u> your document:
Word can concurrently check all spelling and grammar as you are inserting text within your document. A suspected misspelled word will have a squiggly red line drawn under it to indicate that it should be checked. Questionable grammar will have a green squiggly line under the text. If this is not already turned on within your settings, you can do it by clicking on the **Office Button** >>> **Word options** button >>> **Proofing** button >>> check the "**Check spelling as you type**" option. You can also use this same procedure to turn off the spelling and/or grammar check if it is not desired.
b. For <u>checking after your document has been completed:</u>
Press the F7 key and a Spelling and Grammar dialog box will appear. You can then select to accept or ignore any suggested spelling or grammar changes. |

Scenario 2: The story continues

Remember, Brinna from the opening scenario had actually given Sally three different documents to take home. The second document is shown as Figure 2.8. This figure also has various formatting features highlighted for easy identification.

One thing that an experienced teacher like Brinna knows is that the use of examples can be critical. In this case, the document is a lesson plan about blubber. Sally may not need this specific content, but the example of how to use the word processor to help in the creation of similar documents may be invaluable. Look closely at Figure 2.8 and note the key features we have included: **tables,** footnotes, **headers** and **footers,** page numbers, borders, hyperlinks, and shading. Are these features critical for you to become a good teacher? Probably not. But they'll help you organize your documents and make them more readable for those who may be reviewing them. That's important for your students.

> **Note:** For the full blubber lesson plan, go to the text's Web site (**www.prenhall. com/newby** >>> **Chapter 2** >>> **Workouts** >>> **Blubber**) and open the "blubber" file. If you find this a useful template, select and cut the content and add your own content to the structure already designed for you. .

Figure 2.8 Lesson plan with highlighted formatting features

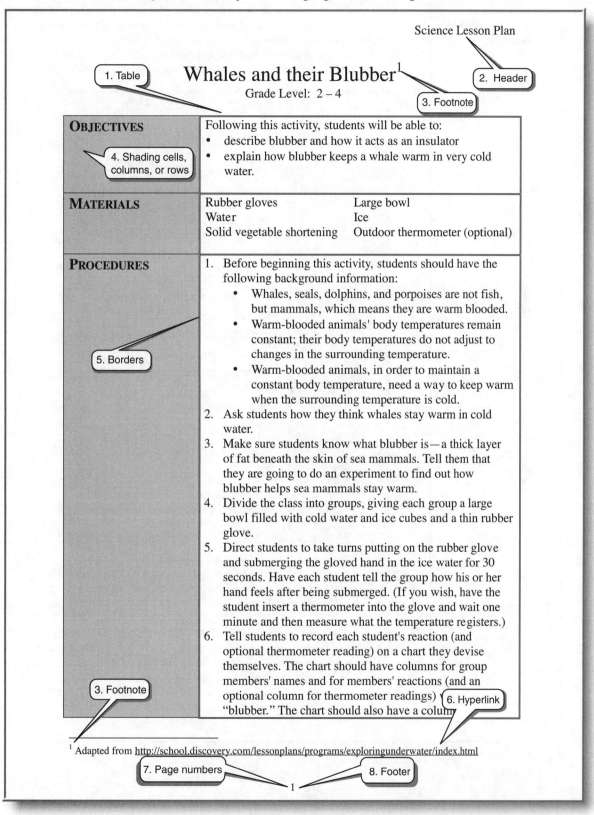

Science Lesson Plan

1. Table

Whales and their Blubber[1]
Grade Level: 2 – 4

2. Header

3. Footnote

OBJECTIVES	Following this activity, students will be able to: • describe blubber and how it acts as an insulator • explain how blubber keeps a whale warm in very cold water.
MATERIALS	Rubber gloves Large bowl Water Ice Solid vegetable shortening Outdoor thermometer (optional)

PROCEDURES	1. Before beginning this activity, students should have the following background information:
	  • Whales, seals, dolphins, and porpoises are not fish, but mammals, which means they are warm blooded.
	  • Warm-blooded animals' body temperatures remain constant; their body temperatures do not adjust to changes in the surrounding temperature.
	  • Warm-blooded animals, in order to maintain a constant body temperature, need a way to keep warm when the surrounding temperature is cold.
	2. Ask students how they think whales stay warm in cold water.
	3. Make sure students know what blubber is—a thick layer of fat beneath the skin of sea mammals. Tell them that they are going to do an experiment to find out how blubber helps sea mammals stay warm.
	4. Divide the class into groups, giving each group a large bowl filled with cold water and ice cubes and a thin rubber glove.
	5. Direct students to take turns putting on the rubber glove and submerging the gloved hand in the ice water for 30 seconds. Have each student tell the group how his or her hand feels after being submerged. (If you wish, have the student insert a thermometer into the glove and wait one minute and then measure what the temperature registers.)
	6. Tell students to record each student's reaction (and optional thermometer reading) on a chart they devise themselves. The chart should have columns for group members' names and for members' reactions (and an optional column for thermometer readings) ... "blubber." The chart should also have a colum

4. Shading cells, columns, or rows

5. Borders

3. Footnote

6. Hyperlink

[1] Adapted from http://school.discovery.com/lessonplans/programs/exploringunderwater/index.html

7. Page numbers

8. Footer

No.	Feature	Steps to Get It Done
1	**Tables:** creating and formatting	1. Place your cursor in the document where you want the table to be inserted. 2. Click **Insert tab** >>> **Tables** group >>> **Table.** 3. Pull the mouse over the revealed grid to preview the creation of your table and click on the desired size (e.g., number of rows and **columns**). **Note:** You can also click on the **Insert Table** button. "An insert table" dialog box will appear. In this box you can select the exact number of rows and columns you want your table to contain. 4. Once the table has been created, the **Table Tools** for both the **Design** and the **Layout** of the table appear (see the tab directly above the **Design tab** and the **Layout tab**). These tools allow you to format various styles of tables, add shading, borders, add and remove columns and rows, add gridlines, size cells, merge or split cells, and so on. Each time you select a table, the **Table Tools tab** appears and can be accessed.

Table tools for the *design* of the table

No.	Feature	Steps to Get It Done

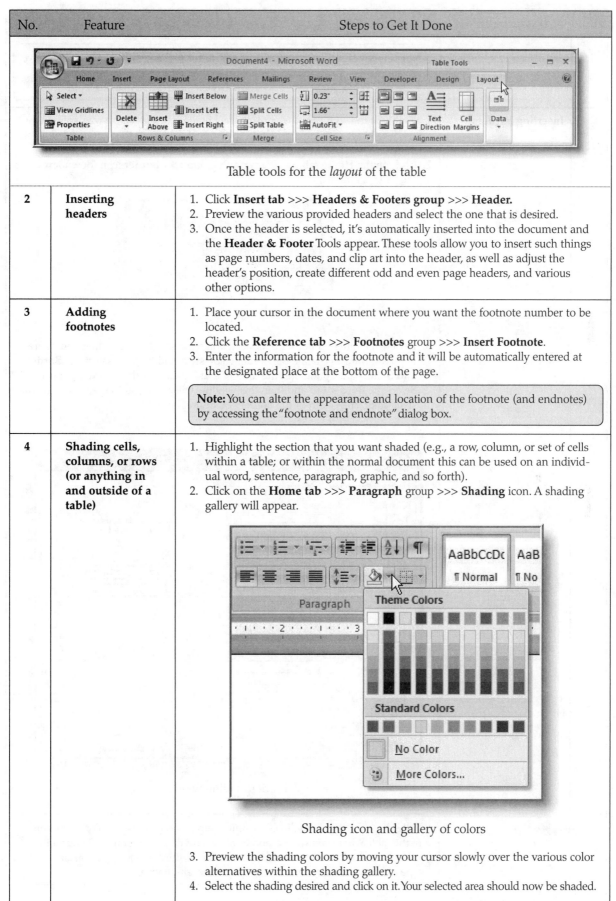

Table tools for the *layout* of the table

No.	Feature	Steps to Get It Done
2	**Inserting headers**	1. Click **Insert tab** >>> **Headers & Footers group** >>> **Header.** 2. Preview the various provided headers and select the one that is desired. 3. Once the header is selected, it's automatically inserted into the document and the **Header & Footer** Tools appear. These tools allow you to insert such things as page numbers, dates, and clip art into the header, as well as adjust the header's position, create different odd and even page headers, and various other options.
3	**Adding footnotes**	1. Place your cursor in the document where you want the footnote number to be located. 2. Click the **Reference tab** >>> **Footnotes** group >>> **Insert Footnote.** 3. Enter the information for the footnote and it will be automatically entered at the designated place at the bottom of the page. **Note:** You can alter the appearance and location of the footnote (and endnotes) by accessing the "footnote and endnote" dialog box.
4	**Shading cells, columns, or rows (or anything in and outside of a table)**	1. Highlight the section that you want shaded (e.g., a row, column, or set of cells within a table; or within the normal document this can be used on an individual word, sentence, paragraph, graphic, and so forth). 2. Click on the **Home tab** >>> **Paragraph** group >>> **Shading** icon. A shading gallery will appear. Shading icon and gallery of colors 3. Preview the shading colors by moving your cursor slowly over the various color alternatives within the shading gallery. 4. Select the shading desired and click on it. Your selected area should now be shaded.

continued

No.	Feature	Steps to Get It Done
		Note: Specifically within that table, you can follow the previous procedures above or you can also find a similar shading gallery by clicking Design tab (directly under the **Table Tools tab**) >>> **Table Styles** group >>> **Shading** button.
5	**Inserting borders**	1. Highlight the section you want to have a border around (e.g., a row, column, or set of cells within a table or within the normal document this can be used on an individual word, sentence, paragraph, graphic, and so forth). 2. Click on the **Home tab** >>> **Paragraph** group >>> **Border** icon (down arrow for the various options).

Bordericon

3. Review the different border options. If you don't see the option that you desire (e.g., you want to change the border color, style, width), then select the **Border and Shading...** option and the "Border and Shading" dialog box will appear. Select the **Border tab** and then this window will allow you to specify exactly the style, color, and width of the border you desire.

BorderShading window

Note: If you are working directly within a table, you can also select the portion of the table where you want a border to be, and then click on the **Design tab** (directly under the **Table Tools tab**) >>> **Draw Borders** group. Color, size, and type of border can also be selected from these alternatives.

No.	Feature	Steps to Get It Done
6	**Adding hyperlinks**	1. Type the text you would like to serve as the link. If you choose to use the Web address as the text that appears, simply type in the address and press the space bar. The link is automatically created and the font and style changes to indicate its link to the Web. 2. If you would prefer to use customized text for the link, insert the text, select it, click the **Insert tab** >>> **Links** group >>> **Hyperlink** button. The **Insert Hyperlink** window will appear. Insert Hyperlink window 3. In the "Text to display:" section of this same window, you may also modify the text you have chosen to display in your document. 4. In the "Address:" section of the window, type in the Web address of the Web site you want linked. **Note:** This is one case where spelling counts! In either method of including a hyperlink, be sure to type in the Web address accurately and completely (don't forget the http://)! **Another Note:** With the use of this window, you can also link to more than just Web sites (e.g., specific documents, an e-mail address).
7	**Adding page numbers**	1. Click on the **Insert tab** >>> **Header & Footer** group >>> **Page Number** icon. A gallery of options for the placement of the page number will appear. Click on the position that you desire. 2. Page numbers can also be placed within the header or footer of a document. For example, to include it within the footer (the header page number also works in this same fashion): • Click the **Insert tab** >>> **Header & Footer** group >>> **Footer** icon and select the type of footer that you desire for your document. (**Note:** If you already have a footer within the document simply open your current footer.) • Once the footer has been inserted or opened, click on the **Header & Footer Tools tab** (above the **Design tab**) >>> **Header & Footer** group >>> **Page Number**. • As you select the page number placement, you will also notice an alternative to "Format page number . . .". Selecting this alternative will display a **Page Number Format** window that will allow you to select the various ways to present your page numbers (e.g., 1, 2, 3; i, ii, iii; a, b, c, and soon.). This window will also allow you to select alternative page number starting points (e.g., if you desire to start on page 32—(or whatever)—instead of page 1).

continued

No.	Feature	Steps to Get It Done
8	**Inserting footers**	1. Click **Insert tab** >>> **Headers & Footers** group >>> **Footer.** 2. Preview the various provided footers and select the one that is desired. 3. Once the footer is selected, it is automatically inserted into the document and the **Header & Footer Tools** appear. These tools allow you to insert such things as page numbers, dates, clip art, and so forth into the footer, as well as adjust the footer's position, create different odd and even page footers, and various other options.

Level 1a Workout: Practice using the basic Word features

To actually acquire the needed skills with word processing, you need to practice using Word. It generally isn't good enough to just read and watch how these features are developed. One way for you to accomplish this is by creating and formatting your own documents. As these documents are created, select and integrate the different features within your own work.

Here's a basic outline of what you need to do:

1. Review Figures 2.5 and 2.8 and all the various highlighted features that have been within those figures.
2. Go to the text's accompanying Web site and open the unformatted versions of these two figures (**www.prenhall.com/newby** >>> **Chapter 2** >>> **Workouts** >>> **Happenings** or **Blubber**).
3. Using the given unformatted versions of the newsletter ("The Happenings…") and the lesson plan ("Blubber"), go through the list of features and practice adding those to your documents. Don't worry about matching the example figures exactly—that isn't the point. You can adapt and change the features as you add them. Remember this is a practice workout—*practice integrating as many features as possible.*

> **Note:** Refer to specific feature numbers and the given step-by-step procedures as needed. Additionally, use the mentoring videos to help guide you through any specific procedure that needs additional clarification.

Level 1b Workout: Creating your own document

The benefits of word processing become very apparent as you begin to create and format your own documents. Think about all the documents. that you will need to create for your work, home, or school. Select one or two of those that are currently in need of being completed and do the following:

1. Generate a simple draft copy of the content of the document. If you have difficulty thinking of a topic, go to the Level 3 section of this chapter (subsection on further ideas on using word processing as a learning tool) and review all the various example topics given (e.g., write your teaching and/or technology integration philosophy; write answers to questions posed for a scholarship application; create documents for work – such as work schedules, safety procedures, or letters to new customers; compose a written itinerary of your next vacation and all that you plan to do and see). If you can find something that needs to be done anyway, then the effort invested has greater value and what is learned will be retained longer.
2. Review the features demonstrated within Figures 2.5 and 2.8 from Scenarios 1 and 2.
3. Format your new document with as many of the features demonstrated in those figures as possible. Use Table 2.1 as a checklist to guide your efforts.

> **Note:** Remember and implement the first rule to live by: Save, Save, Save, and then Save your work again. Make sure you do that—or it will return back to haunt you sometime down the road.
>
> Also think about Rules 3, 4, and 5. Keep things simple, watch for how others accomplish what we have described above, and make sure you think about saving the lesson plan as a template that can be adapted and used later as needed.

Table 2.1 Level 1 Workout and Practice Checklist
Creating and Formatting a Document

Document Content	___ Content is accurate and current.
	___ Content is relevant and cohesive throughout the document.
	___ Content achieves the proper "level" for the intended audience.
	___ Content is free from spelling and grammatical errors.
Document Format	___ A new document was created.
	___ Font size, style, and type were varied within the document to add emphasis to headings, and so on.
	___ Paragraph margin settings were adapted using the margin markers on the ruler.
	___ Appropriate graphics (e.g., clip art, pictures, images) were properly selected, sized, and placed within the document.
	___ A table was incorporated within the document.
	___ Borders were employed to add highlights to specific parts (page, paragraph, words, and so forth) of the document.
	___ Shading was used to add highlights and variety to specific parts (words, paragraphs, parts of a table, and so on).
	___ Automatic page numbers were employed within multipage documents.
	___ Live hyperlinks to specific Internet sites or other documents were incorporated.
	___ Headers and/or footers have been incorporated.
	___ Footnotes or endnotes were used to add reference material or additional clarity to the material.

Level 2: Tables, Templates, and Other Good Stuff

What should you be able to do?

You should learn to recognize additional word processing features and gain confidence using Help to create, edit, and format several original documents.

The key here is not to memorize all that the word processor is capable of—it is better to know some of the basics and when, where, and how to find assistance for everything else.

Getting some Help

Similar to **Help** in Windows, there is also **Help** in MS Word and most other sophisticated word processing software. To use **Help**, click the **Help** button on the tab bar of the main ribbon.

Clicking the **Help** button opens the **Help** window. From here you can browse general help topics, bring up a general table of contents of all help topics, complete a search for a specific question that you might have, and so on.

Home	Insert	Page Layout	References	Mailings	Review	View	Developer	⊘

Word Help button

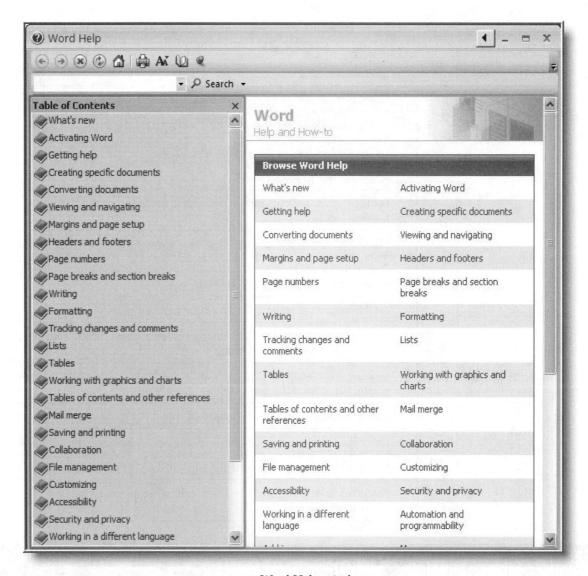

Word Help window

When you type in key words or even a full question, Help will respond with a variety of potential answers for you to investigate. Help generally does not have all of the answers – but it will have a lot of them. Make sure you get a good sense for how it works and how often it can be of assistance. Don't forget to go to the text's Web site **www.prenhall.com/newby,** >>> **Chapter 2** >>> **Mentor Video** and review the mentoring video that has been created to demonstrate Help and its various functions.

Scenario 3: "The Station"

The final document that Brinna gave Sally was The Station by Robert J. Hastings. For us, this word processed document shows other formatting features that will be beneficial. Figure 2.9 shows the printed document and highlights the key formatting things that have been done to it. It is given here as an example of some of the possibilities available to you or your students with word processing software.

As you explore this example, note how the title and author's name are centered at the top of the page, but directly underneath all lines of the quote are placed within two columns. This requires the document to be divided into sections so that in one section something can occur that you may or may not want to occur in other sections. Also note

Figure 2.9 "The Station" with highlighted formatting features.

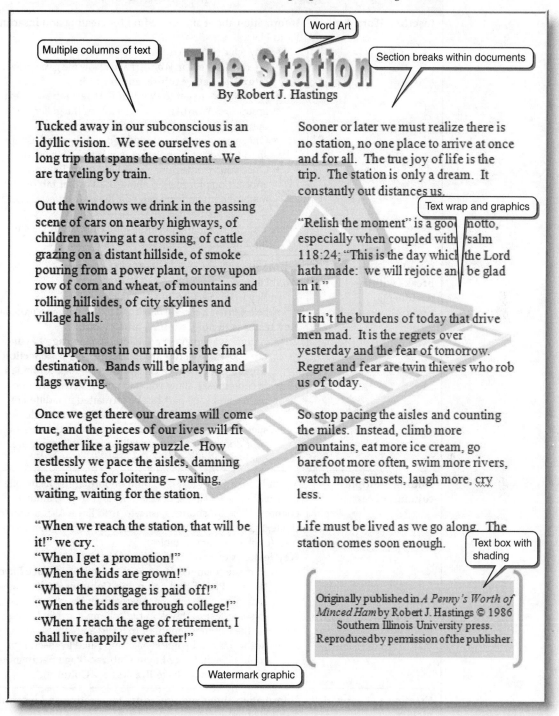

Originally published in *A Penny's Worth of Minced Ham* by Robert J. Hastings © 1986 Southern Illinois University Press. Reproduced by permission of the publisher.

that we have inserted a picture of a railroad station, but in this case we have created it as a watermark, enlarged it, and used it as a background to the words in the quote.

Once you have examined this figure, review how to find the key information about implementing these features within your documents. In addition, mentoring videos have been created, and can be accessed on the text's Web site, that will guide you through the use of each of these features (see **www.prenhall.com/newby** >>> **Chapter 2** >>> **Mentor Video**).

Feature	Steps to Get It Done
Inserting Word Art	**Information about and procedure for creating and inserting:** Word Help 🔵 • Key word: **WordArt.** • Select *Add or delete WordArt* and follow the given procedure **Key features to note, explore, and try out:** • A quick way to get to WordArt is **Insert tab** >>> **Text group** >>> **WordArt** >>> select from the gallery of options/types. • Once your option is selected, a dialog box will ask for specific size, type, and exact words to be included. • Once your WordArt is selected, WordArt Tools will appear (look for the tab above the **Format tab** on the main ribbon) and you can edit the style, effects, size, and how it is arranged. • You can move and position your WordArt by clicking, holding, and dragging it to the new location.
Creating section breaks within documents	**Information about and procedure for inserting:** Word Help 🔵 • Key word: **Section break.** • Select *Insert a section break* and follow the given procedure. **Key features to note, explore, and try out:** • A quick way to insert a section break is **Page Layout tab** >>> **Page Setup** group >>> **Breaks** >>> **Section Breaks** (pick the type that you need—e.g., continuous). • Section breaks allow you to cut your document into parts—and each part can be formatted in a different manner. For example, you want a different header for a specific part of your document, you want the pages of your document to be vertically oriented in some areas but horizontally oriented in other sections.
Adding multiple columns of text	Multiple columns of text is a common formatting technique used within newspapers, newsletters, and so on. Multiple columns allow for shorter, easier-to-read lines. As it is entered, the text generally wraps continuously from one column to the next (unlike columns in tables). **Key features to note, explore, and try out:** • To create columns of text, go to the following: **Page Layout tab** >>> **Page Setup** group >>> **Columns**. Make your selection from the different alternative types of columns. • In some cases, a break in the column is needed to equalize the columns' length or to insert a graphic, and so forth. This can be quickly accomplished by inserting a column break (**Page Layout** tab >>> **Page Setup** group >>> **Breaks** >>> **Page Breaks** >>> **Column**).
Creating a watermark picture	**Information about and procedure for creating and inserting:** Word Help 🔵 • Key word: Watermark – • Select *Brand a document with a watermark or background* and then select *Turn a picture into a watermark or background* and follow the given procedure. **Key features to note, explore, and try out:** • The standard way of producing a watermark is **Page Layout tab** >>> **Page Background** group >>> **Watermark**. At this point, you can select from the gallery of watermarks or you can select a "Custom Watermark" and select a picture or other text to include.

Feature	Steps to Get It Done
	Note: Using some text (e.g., Urgent) as a watermark, would be the easiest and most efficient route; however, if you want to use a picture as a watermark, it may be easier—and allow better control—to insert a picture, adapt that picture (e.g., alter the contrast, color, and brightness, as well as the size), and then arrange it by sending it behind the text. Refer to Feature 6 from Scenario 1 (add, size, and place a graphic) to review how to adapt pictures and graphics.

Text wrapping with graphics	Text wrapping allows you to insert a picture or object within your document and then control how the text is formatted in relationship to that object (e.g., above, below, around, on top of, or behind the object).
	Information about and procedure for creating and inserting:
	Word Help
	   • Key word: **Wrap text.**
	   • Select **Wrap text around a picture or drawing object** and follow the given procedure.
	Key features to note, explore, and try out:
	   • After inserting your graphic, make sure the graphic is selected and then click on the **Format** tab >>> **Arrange** group >>> **Text Wrapping** and make your selection of the type of wrapping you desire
	
	Note: It may take a few attempts to get the text to wrap in the manner that is most desirable. Try different alternatives.
	
	Another Note: You may also need to change the placement of the graphic (refer to Scenario 1, Feature 6). A little change of its location on the page often significantly changes how the text is wrapped.

Adding a text box	A text box is a specialized container of text within a document. It can add interest and break up the normal flow of the text. This container can be sized, colored, and positioned on a page. It is frequently used to highlight a special quote, place information in a side bar, or add some point of interest. Text boxes are both predesigned and custom created. **Key features to note, explore, and try out:** • A quick way to get to the action buttons is **Insert tab** >>> **Text** group >>> **Text Box**. **Note:** You can position the text box by selecting it, placing your cursor over one of the outline box lines, clicking, holding, and dragging it to its new location. **Another Note:** After selecting the text box, **Text Box Tools** are accessible (above the **Format tab**). These tools allow you change text direction, add box styles, effects, size, and arrange the position and the text wrapping.

Note: Each of these key features is demonstrated on the mentoring videos within the text's accompanying Web site. Go to the **www.prenhall.com/newby** >>> **Chapter 2** >>> **Mentor Videos.**

Level 2 Workout: Practice using additional Word features

Now you try it.

1. Find a favorite quote, poem, newspaper article, or short essay that you have wanted to give to someone, hang up in your room, or whatever.
2. Enter the document into the word processor.
3. Divide it into appropriate sections.
4. Put some of the document into multiple columns.
5. Align and format the title and all key headings.
6. Insert an appropriate picture, clip art, or graphic and place it within the document so that the words are wrapped correctly.
7. Pull out salient quotes of interest and include within a text box.
8. Use Table Table 2.2 as a checklist to make sure you have included a number of key features that have been highlighted within Scenarios 1, 2, and 3 of this chapter (see Figures 2.5 and 2.8).

> **Note:** Invoke Rule 1: Save your work.

Table 2.2 Level 2 Workout and Practice Checklist
Using Additional Formatting Features within a Word Document

Document Content	___ Content was accurate.
	___ Content was free from spelling and grammatical errors.
Document Format	___ A new document was created.
	___ Font size, style, and type were varied within the document to add emphasis to headings, etc.
	___ WordArt has been incorporated.
	___ Paragraph margin settings were adapted using the margin markers on the ruler.
	___ Appropriate graphics (e.g., clip art, pictures, images) were properly selected, sized, and placed within the document.
	___ A watermark graphic was included and properly positioned and arranged.
	___ A text was incorporated and highlighted with appropriate shading.
	___ Text boxes were appropriately positioned and arranged with proper text wrapping.
	___ The document was divided into multiple sections.
	___ Multiple columns were incorporated within specific sections of the document.

Level 3: Integration and Application

What should you be able to do?

Here you need to think of how to use word processing both in terms of yourself and your students. You should be able to apply the examples given to generate ideas on how to integrate and apply the word processor to improve personal productivity as well as student learning.

Introduction

Within Levels 1 and 2 of this chapter, we focus on word processing from the perspective of learning to use it. However, to extend its use, you need to think about word processing as a means to enhance the learning experience of students. There are times when integrating word processing within a learning situation may improve the learning opportunities and possibilities of the learners. However, there are other times when such integration would be more of a hassle than potential benefits may warrant. Learning to tell the difference can help you be successful in what you develop and use in your classroom.

Word processing integration

Creating the enhanced learning experience: A partial lesson plan

Topic: A study of the people, places, and culture of an African country

Overview: Mr. Carpenter is an eighth-grade social studies teacher at Lowell Middle School. He constantly searches for ways to increase his students' interest in the topics they explore and learn in his classes. Recently he had the opportunity to speak with one of his past students, Jonathon Rogers, who had attended Lowell a number of years ago. Jonathon is now a graduate student at a nearby university.

During their discussions, Jonathon explained to Mr. Carpenter that during the coming school year he was going to work on an internship for an international health organization. He would be traveling to the country of Zimbabwe in southern Africa to help with the organization's distribution of health supplies and educational materials. He would live and work with the Zimbabwean people throughout the next school year.

Through a little brainstorming, Mr. Carpenter and Jonathon determined that with mail and possibly e-mail they could establish a connection between Mr. Carpenter's social studies classes with some of the culture, politics, education, and geography that Jonathon would be experiencing. The students at Lowell could perhaps come to vicariously learn through the eyes and ears of Jonathon as he explored another country halfway around the world.

Specific learning task: To begin the course of study on Zimbabwe, the students in Mr. Carpenter's classes were to make simple comparisons between Zimbabwe and the United States. Members of the classes were divided into smaller cooperative research groups. Each group selected a major topic of interest (e.g., education, geography, politics, health, culture) that they would investigate to make their comparisons.

Sample learning objectives: Students will be able to do the following:

1. Compare and contrast the key similarities and differences between the countries of Zimbabwe and the United States.
2. Identify and explain several common issues impacting the people of both countries, as well as issues isolated within one country or the other.

Procedure:

1. Break into the groups and brainstorm the key questions of inquiry to investigate about the selected topic.
2. Research answers for the questions from the view of both Zimbabweans and U.S. citizens.
3. Create a comparison table that lists the questions and potential answers determined through research. Reference the answers to the questions that were found within the research.
4. Write a reflection paper about the key findings reported within the comparison table. Explain the major similarities and differences noted between the two countries.
5. Send the comparison tables to Jonathon and have him select several of the questions to ask people he encounters in Zimbabwe. Have him respond and enter those responses within a new column on the comparison table.
6. Based on the full findings of the group and the responses by Jonathon, the group will develop a final written executive summary of their findings to be distributed to all members of their class. The final version should include additional questions that the group now wishes to investigate if given the opportunity to do so.

Questions about word processing integration

Obviously, this lesson could be completed with or without the use of word processing software. Use these reflective questions to explore the value of potentially integrating word processing within such a lesson as outlined by Mr. Carpenter.

- Within this lesson, in what way could word processing be used by Mr. Carpenter, by Jonathon, and by the members of the social studies classes?
- How could word processing help with the development of the initial group brainstorming of the key questions?
- How could word processing be used to complete research on the selected topics? Could word processing increase the potential creativity and/or the breadth of the students' research?
- In what way could the use of word processing be helpful in the design and development of the comparison table? Would its value increase as information was input and periodically updated?
- How could word processing facilitate the development and production of the assigned reflective paper? Could word processing allow for additional insights and levels of creative thought and/or comparison?
- Could word processing facilitate increased levels of communication between Jonathon and the classes of social studies students?
- Could word processing impact the creation, production, and dissemination of the final executive summary report?
- Are there potential problems and pitfalls if word processing is integrated within this lesson and its respective assignments?

Level 3a Workout: Integrating word processing

Now it's your turn. Complete the following steps to this Workout as you think about the future use of word processing within an applied setting.

1. Read each of the following situations. Imagine being directly involved in the planning for each of these projects. Select one (or more if you wish) for further consideration.

Roller Park Proposal:

The mayor of Billingsburg has asked the city parks engineer to create a proposal for a park that would focus on roller blade activities for the city youth. The park could be located on city land adjacent to the new city swimming pool. To accomplish this task, the city engineers have contacted the local middle schools and high schools and asked the students to make recommendations for the proposal. They want students to suggest layouts of the parks, types of jumps, obstacles, and activities that should be integrated, proposed fees for the use of the park, and so on. They have even asked the students to propose the types of safety features that should be included.

The Greatest Decade:

During the twentieth century many wonderful, sad, horrifying, and satisfying events occurred. But was there one decade that shines above the rest as making the greatest impact? How and why should one decade be selected over the others as being the "most significant" decade of the twentieth century? How can the strengths and weaknesses of each decade be effectively exposed, compared, and debated?

Senior Citizens and Young Mentors:

The activities chairperson at Heritage Retirement Center is constantly being asked for lessons on basic computer skills. Many residents of the Center desire to use the available computers to type letters, send e-mail, and surf the Internet. The activities chairperson contacts a neighborhood elementary class of fourth and fifth graders to come to Heritage and mentor the residents. Her thoughts are to have the children and the residents work together to produce a newsletter that could be published and distributed. The contents of the publication could be stories from the lives of the residents.

Making a Copy:

The high school media specialist is worried that many of her students may not fully understand the ramifications of copyright infringement. She notes that they seem to freely copy and distribute music CDs, pictures from the Internet, and even papers for various school class reports. She decides that perhaps a discussion is in order where small groups of students will debate the pros and cons of copyright law in today's digital world.

2. Based on your selected project, consider the following questions found within the Integration Assessment Questionnaire. Mark your response to each question.

Integration assessment questionnaire (IAQ)

Will using **WORD PROCESSING** software as a part of the project:			
Broaden the learners' perspective on potential solution paths and/or answers?	__ Yes	__ No	__ Maybe
Increase the level of involvement and investment of personal effort by the learners?	__ Yes	__ No	__ Maybe
Increase the level of learner motivation (e.g., increase the relevance of the to-be-learned task, the confidence of dealing with the task, and/or the overall appeal of the task)?	__ Yes	__ No	__ Maybe
Decrease the time needed to generate potential solutions?	__ Yes	__ No	__ Maybe
Increase the quality and/or quantity of learner practice working on this and similar projects?	__ Yes	__ No	__ Maybe
Increase the quality and/or quantity of feedback given to the learner?	__ Yes	__ No	__ Maybe
Enhance the ability of the student to solve novel, but similar, projects, tasks, and problems in the future?	__ Yes	__ No	__ Maybe

3. If you have responded "Yes" to one or more of the IAQ questions, you should consider the use of word processing to enhance the student's potential learning experience.
4. Using the example lesson plan, develop a lesson plan based on your selected project. Within the plan, indicate how and when the learner will use word processing. Additionally, list potential benefits and challenges that may occur when involving this software within the lesson.

Level 3b Workout: Exploring the NETS Standard connection

Developing a lesson plan, as suggested in the previous Workout, which integrates the use of word processing, directly addresses several of the National Educational Technology Standards (NETS) for both teachers (NETS·T) and students (NETS·S). For a full listing of the standards, refer to the Appendix.

Part A:

In a straightforward manner, NETS·T Standard V.C. for teachers and NETS·S Standard 6.b. for students indicate that one should be able to apply technology to increase productivity. With the use of word processing, it is relatively simple to demonstrate the increased productivity you can achieve (e.g., rapidly editing and reproducing a saved lesson plan). However, reflect on the following questions and consider how the integration of word processing may also impact other areas addressed by different technology standards:

- How can the use of word processing help develop students' higher order skills and creativity? Is there something about the use of the word processor that may enhance the exploration of alternative ideas, thinking patterns, solutions, or that may positively impact overall student creativity? (NETS˙T III.C.; NETS˙S 4)
- In what ways could word processing be used to facilitate the communication and collaboration between teachers, students, parents, and subject matter experts on specific projects that ultimately impact student learning? (NETS˙T V.D.; NET˙S 2, 5. b.)
- How can word processing improve how the collection, analysis, and assessment of student work or data are completed? Could this increased information be used to improve the learning environment and experience? (NETS˙T IV.B.; V.B.; NET˙S 4)

Part B:

Go to the International Society for Technology in Education (ISTE) Web site http://cnets.iste.org. Within that site, select to review either the student or the teacher NETS Standards. Once you have selected the standards to review, select either the student or teacher profiles and look for the corresponding scenarios. Review the scenarios and determine how the word processor could be used within several of those situations.

While visiting the ISTE Web site and exploring the scenarios, go to the lesson plan search area and select a number of different lesson plans of interest. Review those and determine the role (if any) of word processing within the development, implementation, and assessment of the lesson. Note this from both the perspective of the teacher developing the lesson and from the perspective of the student participating in the implemented lesson.

Further ideas on using word processing as a learning tool

When students are involved in using the word processor, the task frequently revolves around generating a written report of some kind. The word processor is a great tool to facilitate reflection, generation, and editing of materials.

> **Note:** These ideas are to help you generate your own ideas of what can be done. Don't let it bother you if they're not the right content or grade level, use the idea and adapt it to be helpful within your own situation. These are meant to be stimuli for additional ideas.

Here are a few ideas that may help you see how the word processor might be beneficial:

1. Create a table and have the students fill in the blanks, or have them create the frame for themselves. For example, on the axis on the left side include different types of Native Americans and where they lived. Along the top table row or axis, put categories of clothing, shelter, tools, or food sources. Have the students fill in the cells of the table and make predictions about the relationships between climate and their tools, shelter, and so forth.
2. Compose and format different types of letters (e.g., business, personal, memo, cover letter, persuasive communication, and letter to the editor) and then compare the different styles of writing.
3. Have students conduct research by generating data gathering instruments (e.g., questionnaires), describing procedures, and then summarizing the results.

4. Have learners create an assessment rubric that outlines all criteria for a group project presentation.
5. Have students write a group report using comments and tracking in the word processor to monitor who makes which comments and suggestions within the document.
6. Have students develop a brochure about a specific historical topic (e.g., colonial America), their personal work history and skills (e.g., jobs they have worked and what they have done), or places they may someday travel (e.g., Australian Outback).
7. Have learners use the word processor's outlining function and brainstorm and design a required group presentation.
8. Given specific paragraphs from the writings of famous authors, have students identify and highlight nouns, verbs, adjectives, and so on, in various electronic highlighter colors.
9. Have students review a paragraph or document that contains highlighted target words. Have them use the thesaurus and change the words to add clarity to the document.
10. Have students work in groups to develop divergent viewpoints about historical controversies (e.g., American Japanese internment camps; Iraq War; Antitrust settlements of AT&T and/or Microsoft). Their written points and counterpoints can then be summarized, shared, and discussed within a single document.
11. Have students evaluate a set of instructional materials (e.g., a biology CD) and give their opinions on its value, what they felt was worthwhile and what they felt could have been improved to make it more effective.
12. Have students develop (or complete) a matching game that consists of a table of anatomy terms in one column and a picture of various anatomical structures in the other column.
13. Have learners create original poetry and combine it with an inspirational photo as a background to their written work.
14. Have students use voice recognition software and compose a short story about living in a world without the use of one's eyes and/or hands.
15. Have students identify three college scholarship applications that require short essays as part of the application process. Have them create word processed responses to those essay questions.

Additional ideas on using the word processor as an assistant	

1. **School conduct report.** Create a table that highlights all of the rules of class conduct and cells to report when the rule is not followed.
2. **Communication report.** Create a template that allows you to monitor how often notes are sent to parents or supervisors about a student.
3. **Certificates.** Create of certificates for extra effort and merit.
4. **Progress reports.** Develop reports to keep students (and parents) informed of what has been accomplished and what is still needed.
5. **Work sheets.** Construct various types of work sheets and/or directions for projects.
6. **Individual education plans (IEPs).** Develop IEP templates that can be altered and adjusted for each individual student.
7. **Calendars.** Develop and use daily, weekly, and/or monthly assignment or work calendars.
8. **Weekly lesson planning.** Develop a table template of all weekly planning for lessons and subjects.
9. **Badges and labels.** Production of name badges for students, class helpers, and parents. and/or labels for files, folders, and so forth.
10. **Programs.** Develop programs and handouts for school productions.
11. **Newsletters.** Write weekly or monthly classroom newsletters containing relevant information for students and parents.

12. **Permission slips.** Develop permission slips for events such as field trips, bus rides, and authorized school activities.
13. **Makeup work assignments.** Develop a template for helping students who have missed school so they know what was missed and when it is to be completed.
14. **Volunteer schedules and job responsibilities.** Create a document that explains job responsibilities and schedules for individuals who volunteer at the school.
15. **Reminders.** Write memos to remind students about their assignments or to sign up to complete tasks (e.g., bring snacks or give a report).
16. **Class activities.** For example, develop a short script for a play that includes text columns for sets, narration, different pictures and scenes. Use graphics to draw basic areas of the stage and where actors and scenery will be placed.

Chapter 3
SPREADSHEETS
MS Excel: The Basics of a "Number Cruncher"

Introduction

What should you know about spreadsheets? 	Spreadsheets are designed to help you work with numbers—not just the normal adding, subtracting, and so forth, but also for comparing, making predictions, and evaluating. Beyond numbers, this software deals with text in a way that teachers can find very helpful. Within this introduction to spreadsheets, we want you to discover the following: • What a spreadsheet is, what it can do, and how it can help in teaching and learning • How to justify the use of the spreadsheet as an effective tool—knowing when and why it should or shouldn't be used
Terms to know	cell row column formula function chart worksheet
What is a spreadsheet and what does it do?	Spreadsheets are remarkable tools that allow you to organize, calculate, and present data (generally, this data has something to do with numbers—but not always). These tools organize the world into a grid of rows and columns. A grade book is a familiar example for most teachers. Within an electronic spreadsheet grade book, you not only can quickly find and organize data for each student, but the spreadsheet can be set up to do the needed calculations automatically for you. Just as quickly, you can rearrange how the grade book looks and how grades are calculated. Figure 3.1 shows a very simple form of such a grade book.

Figure 3.1 Simple grade book spreadsheet

Student's Name	Project 1	Project 2	Project 3	Total
Anderson, Timbre	13	14	13	40
Butler, Landon	14	15	15	44
Jersey, Alexis	12	11	13	36
Johnson, Brayden	15	14	15	44
Nesbit, Max	11	10	9	30
Rendolf, B. Jane	15	15	15	45

What are some commonly used spreadsheets?

- Microsoft's Excel
- Lotus 1-2-3
- Corel's Quattro Pro
- Sun Microsystems' StarOffice/OpenOffice Calc
- The spreadsheet program within Microsoft's Works
- The spreadsheet program within Appleworks

> **Note:** We focus on Microsoft's Excel in this book. However, **what we present can be done in any of the other spreadsheets listed**. So if you don't have access to MS Excel at home, don't be alarmed—you can still complete the projects and learn the basic skills.

What bother learning how to use a spreadsheet?

- **To cut your time.** Just think about it—if you have six class periods in a day with 20–25 students in each period, and over the course of the grading period you record a dozen assignments, three quizzes, and two tests, you have over 2000 scores to record! Think of the time it takes to calculate totals, subtotals, averages, and so on, during the course of a semester. The spreadsheet can calculate automatically for you.
- **To cut your mistakes.** If you are continually entering and reentering the same data over and over, you'll eventually punch in the wrong number. Having the computer do the calculations for you can be a way of overcoming many of the little problems that creep in because of fat fingers, tired eyes, and low power cells (yours and the calculator's).
- **To use the work of experts.** Maybe you don't know much about certain statistical, accounting, or other formulas and functions. Many of these are built into an electronic spreadsheet. Instead of creating the **formula,** you just make a selection and the computer completes the calculation.
- **To allow predictions.** This software allows you to imagine what the possibilities are if the current course of action continues or if some changes are made ("What if. . .").
- **To allow for quick repurposing.** Instead of constantly rebuilding from scratch (e.g., creating a new grade book for next semester's class), you can use a spreadsheet that is similar and just needs some quick adaptations. This is often faster than starting over.
- **To help you see things differently.** Through the use of charts that can be quickly and easily generated from the spreadsheet, what was once a bunch of rows and columns of numbers may now be seen as simple, understandable trends and answers to problems that were unnoticed before.

How can spreadsheets be used at school? A brief list of ideas

By the teacher:

- Grade books
- School class expense budget
- Track fund-raiser sales
- Highlight relationships and trends graphically
- Create class seating charts
- Track and monitor assessments

By the student:

- Math assignments
- Assignment planners
- Personal budgets
- Science reports for calculating and reporting results
- Chart personal goals and progress

Orientation

What's the workspace look like?

Figure 3.2 depicts the workspace of a common spreadsheet (MS Excel). Note that the workspace consists of designated *rows* and *columns* (where a row and a column intersect is known as a *cell*). Similar to other programs, there are toolbars and menus placed around the workspace.

What commands can be used?

As in all MS Office applications (e.g., MS Powerpoint, MS Word), there's a ribbon of tools that runs across the top of the work screen. Within each ribbon the actual tools that can be used to input, format, and edit the numbers to be analyzed are grouped together under the various command tabs (e.g., Home, Insert, Page Layout, References). Selecting a specific tab reveals an associated command set or group. Once a command tab has been selected, this specific group remains visible and ready for use. Items within the set may appear as individual items or as a gallery of related items. For example, selecting the Insert tab (see Figure 3.3) in Excel reveals a group of commands that deal specifically with the insertion of, for example, tables, illustrations, charts, links, Word art, and text boxes.

Figure 3.2 View of Microsoft Excel spreadsheet work area with simple grade book

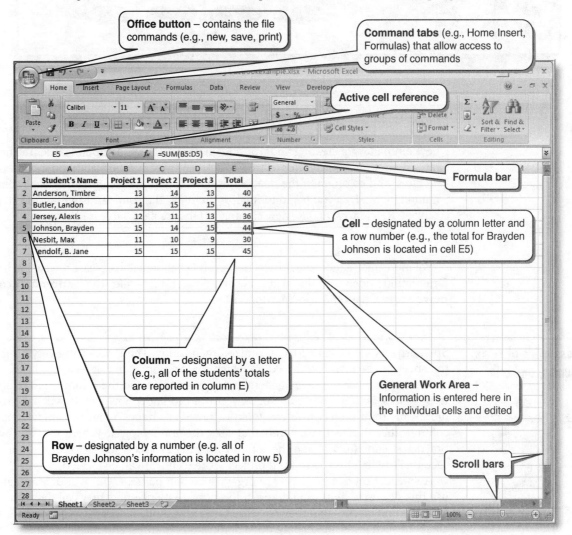

Figure 3.3 The Ribbon holds the command tabs, command groups or sets, and individual commands

The tabs have been developed to make your life easier. No longer do you have to go through hundreds of potential drop-down menu items to find the needed tool—the tabs allow you quick access to related groups of commands.

Note that there are additional commands that will occasionally be needed. As shown in Figure 3.4 (Chart Tools), these contextual commands appear when a specific object like a **chart,** picture, graphic, or table is selected.

Figure 3.4 Selecting a specific item (e.g., graphic, picture) in the workspace reveals contextual commands that can be accessed and used with the selected item

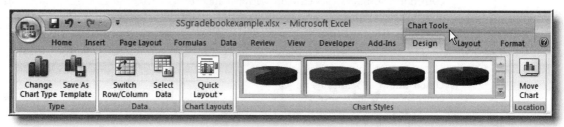

> **Note:** These command tabs have been developed to correspond directly with how you sequentially create a document in Word. That is, as you start the document, the key commands for creating and working on your first draft are found under the first tab (Home). As you develop further drafts and need to add additional content, pictures, and so on, then the needed group is found by selecting the Insert command tab. Next, as you begin to finalize the draft, the commands within the Page Layout, References, and Review command tabs are easily accessed.

For more information about Excel ribbon and command tabs, please review the Excel Orientation video on the text's accompanying Web site (**www.prenhall.com/ newby** >>> **Chapter 3** >>> **Mentor Video**).

Those grids of rows, columns, and cells

Spreadsheets are designed to maximize organization. Think about it. Everything on the sheet can be identified based on which row and/or column it resides within.

For convenience, numbers generally designate rows and the columns are referred to by letters. So if in your grade book you want to know how well Brayden Johnson did on his third project, you can look for Brayden's name under the student name column, then locate the column that lists the third project. Where the row with Brayden's name (row 5) and the column with the Project 3 scores (column D) intersect, that's where Brayden's third project score (cell D5) will be located.

A spreadsheet is a great way to organize certain parts of your world. Mapmakers use this system to help you find exact locations—city planners may call them streets, avenues, and blocks—but they have the same idea. And, of course, accountants know all about such grids for keeping track of income, expenses, and totals.

What can go in the cells?

In an electronic spreadsheet, something interesting happens. Within any one cell you can insert words (*Project 1*, *Student's Name*, and so forth), numbers (actual scores on projects), variables (=*B5*, which tells the spreadsheet to find cell B5, copy what it finds there, and insert whatever it finds into the current cell), or even mathematical formulas or **functions** (*B5 + D5*, which instructs the spreadsheet to add the number found in cell B5 to that found in cell D5).

This opens up all kinds of possibilities. Pretty soon you can envision a grade book that has your students' names in one column, as well as a set of cells that includes scores for all of their assignments, projects, and so forth. Additionally, you should begin to see that there may be cells containing formulas that add up all of the scores for individual students, provide averages, show high and low scores, and so on. All of these can be accomplished simply by controlling what happens in the cells.

The "power of manipulation": Using functions and formulas

The power of the spreadsheet is in how it manipulates numbers. Within those cells it is possible to write formulas or equations that complete calculations on the data recorded in the spreadsheet. So not only does the spreadsheet organize, it can also manipulate data through addition, subtraction, and so forth.

Look at the simple grade book example in Figure 3.2. In cell E5 we have inserted a simple addition formula to add up all of Brayden Johnson's scores. When the cell is highlighted, a formula (=B5+C5+D5 or stated another way = Sum (B5:D5)) can be inserted on the formula bar line, however, once activated, cell E5 automatically (and very quickly) reveals the total of those scores. Once that formula is inserted, if a change to any of Brayden's scores occurs, the total found in cell E5 *automatically updates*.

The power of "What if. . ."

Sometimes it helps if you can imagine what would happen if _____ (you fill in the blank). What if . . . I had married my high school boyfriend? What if . . . I decreased my calorie intake of food by 20% for the next two months? What if . . . I made 10% more than I do now? What if . . . Brayden Johnson had scored a 15 on Project 2?

We doubt that the first "What if . . ." will be helped by a spreadsheet; however, for the last three it can play an important part. Because it can calculate so quickly with such relative ease, you can plug in formulas and then readjust those formulas to immediately see different types of results based on certain variable factors. That is, you can make projections or estimations of how things would be "if . . . ."

Imagine what you can do with your students, then, when you discuss world populations and the impact of a population growth that increases by 6 % instead of 3% over the next 10 years. Perhaps you could get them to understand the mind-set of those in a third-world nation who attempt to leave their country when inflation hits an all-time high and the value of their country's money drops by 30% over a short period of time.

It's very powerful to be able to "see into the future." Most individuals can't do this with consistent accuracy (although some profess to have this ability—call 1-900-ICANSEE). However, with a spreadsheet some different scenarios can be played out so that predictions can be accurately made if specific situations occur.

Seeing the possibilities

Spreadsheets are the darlings of number manipulators. However, some of us can't see everything we need when given a big grid of numbers. Another wonderment of spreadsheets is that they can take the numbers and convert them to various graphs and charts with relative ease. In this way, instead of seeing a column of numbers you can see a bar, line, pie, or column chart. Magically, the numbers turn into revealing pictures.

Sometimes looking at data differently allows important correlations to stand out. For example, for a small middle school student listing all of the average weekly temperatures for Indianapolis, Indiana; Bahrain, Saudi Arabia; and Santiago, Chile, may not mean much other than a big bunch of numbers. Showing those same numbers but as overlapping different colored line graphs, however, may suddenly turn on light bulbs about how temperature vary across these widely dispersed cities. You could easily do the same for personal budgets, speeds on the 100-dash, cars crossing various bridges over the same river in downtown Chicago, and the growth of a classroom of students over the course of a semester.

> **Note:** It doesn't take a brain surgeon to figure out that by combining the "What if . . ." function with the graphing function, you can start to readily "see" possible relationships and how you can possibly prepare for those possibilities.

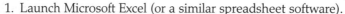

Orientation Workout: Explore the territory

Turn on your computer and attempt the following:

1. Launch Microsoft Excel (or a similar spreadsheet software).
2. Create a new Excel spreadsheet.
3. Explore the various tabs on the ribbon and examine the different command groups.
4. On the new spreadsheet, attempt the following:

   - Click on a cell and enter a word or a number.
   - Highlight the words or numbers you have entered in the cell and change its formatting in some way (e.g., with the Home tab selected, try clicking on various font commands).
   - With the same cell selected, note its location identified in the active cell reference (see Figure 3.2) and also note what's listed in the formula bar.
   - Practice cutting and pasting from one cell to another.
   - In column A of your spreadsheet, insert the number 10 in cell A2, put the number 12 in cell A3, the number 9 in cell A4, and the number 11 in cell A5. Once that is completed, do the following:

     i. Select cells A2, A3, A4, and A5.
     ii. Click on the Insert tab and select one of the charts from the chart commands (e.g., Pie).
     iii. Examine what you have created.
     iv. Try some of the other potential charts.
     v. Change some of the numbers in A2 through A5 and watch your chart as you input the new number. This is just a preview of things to come.

Level 1: Designing, Creating, and Producing a Useful Data-based Class Project

What should you be able to do?

At this level, the emphasis is on using various tools and techniques of the spreadsheet software to create a document given specific guidelines and step-by-step procedures.

What resources are provided?

Basically, Level 1 is divided into common teaching scenarios, selected solutions, and practice exercises (i.e., Workouts). The scenarios have been constructed to allow you to examine common problems and how they can be addressed through the use of this software. To do this we have provided the following:

a. Draft spreadsheet documents (see the text's accompanying Web site (**www.prenhall.com/newby** >>> **Chapter 3** >>> **Workout Level 1**) that you can use to practice and review how the features are used to address the problems presented within each scenario.

b. Quick reference figures (see Figure 3.6 and 3.10) that identify (via visual callouts) all of the key features that have been incorporated within the solution presentations. These allow you to rapidly identify the key features and reference exactly how to include such features within your own work.

c. Step-by-step instructions on how to incorporate all highlighted features within your work.

d. Video mentoring support that guides you through the integration of each of the highlighted features (see the text's accompanying Web site (**www.prenhall. com/newby**).

e. Workout exercises that allow you to practice identifying and selecting which software features to use, when to use those features, how they should be incorporated, and to what degree they are effective.

How should you proceed?

If you have <u>little or no experience</u> with MS Office 2007, particularly Excel, then we suggest you do the following:

1. Read and review Scenario 1.
2. Examine the quick reference figure (Figure 3.6) and all of the highlighted features.
3. Using the step-by-step directions given for each highlighted feature, use the software and practice using each of the features.
4. If you have any confusion or difficulty with these features, access the videos and monitor the features as they are demonstrated and discussed within the short video clips.
5. Once you feel comfortable with these features, go to Scenario 2 and repeat these same steps with the new features introduced for that scenario. Monitor the quick reference figure (Figure 3.10) closely.
6. After both scenarios have been reviewed, go to the Workout and work through the problems and exercises as it outlines.

If you have <u>experience</u> with Excel 2007, you may want to review the scenarios and the quick reference figures first. If any of the features are unfamiliar, then you may wish to access and use the step-by-step procedures, as well as the mentoring support videos. Once the review has been completed, then move directly to the Workout exercise and create your own worksheet by incorporating many of the highlighted features.

Scenario 1: Trying to make a difference

John Rena is trying to get his middle school science students to be more environmentally conscience. Even though many of them complain that their efforts really don't add up to too much, John wants to help them understand that they each can make a significant impact. To accomplish this, he has initiated an aluminum can recycling project. He begins by challenging each of his five classes to bring to school the empty aluminum beverage cans that they get from their own homes. Each class then counts, crushes, and stores the cans for pickup by the local recycling company. John has each class create a simple spreadsheet to keep track of how many cans are collected each month and he keeps a master spreadsheet of the totals for all classes. At the end of each month, the totals for all classes are tabulated and posted for all classes to see. In addition, money earned from the sale of the cans is then used for some needed school science equipment.

Take a close look at Figure 3.5. This is a very simple, incomplete spreadsheet of the results of Mr. Rena's science class's five-month recycling project. Figure 3.6 is the same thing; however, it highlights all of the unique features that have been done to the spreadsheet to get it to look and work as a finished product. Within Figure 3.6, call-out bubbles have been inserted to identify the key features that were incorporated to enhance the formatting of the document.

- Using Figure 3.6 as the guide, follow the numbered features in the step-by-step procedure to learn how each is employed.
- If additional guidance is needed, go to the Mentoring Videos (**www.prenhall.com/ newby** >>> **Chapter 3** >>> **Mentor Videos**) and select the short clip that demonstrates the use of the needed feature.

Figure 3.5 A draft spreadsheet (incomplete and unformatted) showing the number of empty aluminium beverage cans donated by Mr. Rena's science classes during the spring semester

	A	B	C	D	E	F	G
1	Class	Jan	Feb	Mar	April	May	Total per class
2	1st hour	923	1243	1198	1463	1507	
3	2nd hour	540	832	927	1103	1097	
4	3rd hour	752	647	527	1054	1209	
5	4th hour	621	845	829	995	1056	
6	5th hour	1105	1267	1015	1513	1483	
7	Total by month						
8	Class average						

Figure 3.6 A complete spreadsheet with finishing and formatting steps highlighted

1. Create a new workbook
2. Insert, align, and format column headings
3. Insert classes and all of their monthly data
4. Change column width
5. Add gridlines
6. Format cells and data
7. Insert formulas to calculate totals
8. Use fill handles
9. More formulas and fills

	A	B	C	D	E	F	G
1	Class	Jan	Feb	Mar	April	May	Total per class
2	1st hour	923	1243	1198	1463	1507	6334
3		540	832	927			4499
4		752	647	527	1054	1205	4189
5	4th hour	621	845	829	995	1056	46
6	5th hour	1105	1267	1015	1513	1483	
7	Total by month	3941	48		6128	6352	25751
8	Class average	788	967	899	1226	1270	5150

No.	Feature	Steps to Get It Done
1	**Create a new worksheet**	 1. Launch Excel. If a new worksheet doesn't appear, click on the Office button and select "New" from the drop-down menu. 2. Select the Blank Workbook and click on the Create button. A new, blank **worksheet** should appear and you can begin entering data. **Note:** When you have the New Workbook dialog box open, you can also select from various Excel spreadsheet templates (e.g., **Installed Templates** >>> **Personal Monthly Budget**). Such templates may help to speed up your work by providing much of the design work.
2	**Insert, align, and format column headings**	1. To insert a column heading, click on the cell where you want the heading to be inserted. For our example, click on cell A1 and then type the word *Class*. Hit the tab key and cell B1 will be highlighted. Type in *Jan.* Hit the tab key and continue until all of the headings have been entered. **Note:** It is not necessary to leave blank rows at the top of the spreadsheet workspace. If you want to add or delete rows (or columns) at a later time, that can be easily completed. 2. To align the contents of a cell (column or row), highlight the cell you wish to align and then click on the **Home Tab** and select your preferred alignment from the **Alignment** group (e.g., left, center, right) as shown in Figure 3.7. 3. To format items in a cell (row or column), select what you wish to format and then click the type of formatting (e.g., font type, size, boldface, italic) that you desire (**Home tab** >>> **Font** group). See Figure 3.7 for examples of the highlighted formatting features. **Note:** If you make a mistake, don't panic. Click on the cell that you want to change, then go to the Formula bar at the top of your spreadsheet (just under the command ribbon) and make your changes there. **Another note:** Copy, cut, and paste work fine in this application. If you find that you need to enter similar headings (e.g., Assignment 1, 2, 3, 4, . . .) and you don't want to type the same words over and over, you can copy the heading and then continually paste it into the cells as needed. **Figure 3.7** Home tab with various formatting commands highlighted
3	**Enter classes and main data of the spreadsheet**	1. Click on a cell (e.g., A2) and enter in the name of the first class of Mr. Rena. Click on the Tab key and enter that class's total cans donated during the month of January, click the Tab key and enter the total for the second month of the project, and continue until all classes and their respective data have been entered. Leave the "Total per class" column empty of all data. Additionally, don't put any data in for the "total by month" row. We'll do that in just a minute.

continued

No.	Feature	Steps to Get It Done
		2. If any entry errors are made, click on the cell and go to the Formula bar and make the needed editorial changes. Once finished with the editorial change, click the Enter key and the change will have occurred within the proper cell.
4	**Adjust column width (or row height)**	1. Directly beneath the Formula bar, each column is labeled with a letter. Click on the letter of the column that you wish to adjust (e.g., A). The whole column will be highlighted. Then move your mouse pointer to the line that divides the target column and the next adjoining column. The pointer will change into a two-headed arrow. 2. With the two-headed arrow showing, click and hold the mouse, and drag it to the right or left. You'll notice that as long as you have the mouse button held down, the width of your target column will change based on your mouse movement. 3. When you have determined the correct size, release the mouse and the column size has been altered. If you don't like it, you can immediately repeat the process and produce a different size. **Note:** This same procedure works for adjusting the height of rows. Click on the targeted row number and then move the cursor to the line between the adjoining row and your target and the two-headed arrow will appear. **Another note:** If you need to be precise, you can actually set a column width or a row height to an exact measurement. To do so, place your cursor in the proper row or column and then go to **Home tab** >>> **Cells** group >>> **Format** >>> select the option for column width or row height. A dialog box will appear that allows you to input the exact size you desire.
5	**Add gridlines**	1. Select all of the cells, rows, or columns where you want the gridlines or borders to be displayed. 2. Go to the **Font** group of tools (**Home tab** >>> **Font** group) and click on the border button. 3. From the drop-down gallery, select the type of gridline you desire (check out the different line styles, colors, thicknesses, and placements available). **Note:** You can also return to the Format Cell dialog box (**Home tab** >>> **Font group** >>> **Font dialog box expander**) and select the Border tab (see Figure 3.7) for additional options.
6	**Formatting cells (and the things in them)**	1. To change the alignment of column headings, cell data, and so on, select the cells you want to format. For example, select all of the headings from cell A1 to G1. Refer to Figure 3.6 and Feature 2 (Steps 2 and 3—formatting column headings). 2. Go to the **Home tab** >>> **Font** group and click on the **Font group dialog box expander** (see Figure 3.7). The Format Cells window opens. Examine all of the possibilities within this window (note the tabs along the top of this dialog box—click on a tab and it will show you additional functions that can be used). See Figure 3.8 for a peek at what you can play with. 3. To change font style: (a) click the Font tab, and (b) select the type, style, size, color, and any other effects that you desire. Click the OK button and what you selected will be applied to all selected cells. 4. To change the alignment (center, left, right, and so on) or to change the direction of the words within your selected cell(s), click on the Alignment tab within the Format Cells window. **Note:** At times you may wish to have certain cells (e.g., column headings) type the words vertically or at a slant. This Format Cells window is where you make such changes occur. 5. Other cell formatting functions include choosing borders for the cells, adding patterns to the cells, and protecting the cells in certain ways. All of these functions are completed through this Cell Format window.

No.	Feature	Steps to Get It Done
		Figure 3.8 Format Cells dialog box (Font tab selected) 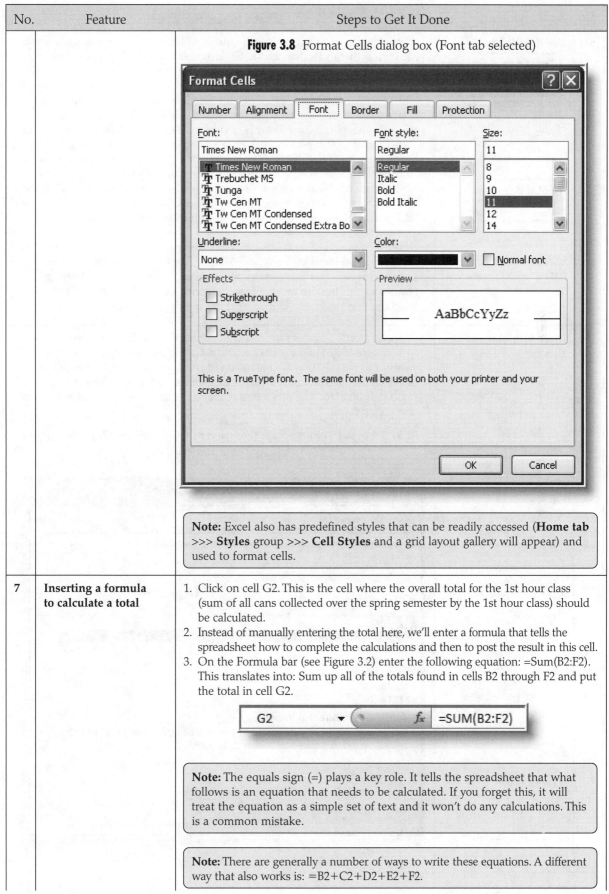 **Note:** Excel also has predefined styles that can be readily accessed (**Home tab >>> Styles** group **>>> Cell Styles** and a grid layout gallery will appear) and used to format cells.
7	**Inserting a formula to calculate a total**	1. Click on cell G2. This is the cell where the overall total for the 1st hour class (sum of all cans collected over the spring semester by the 1st hour class) should be calculated. 2. Instead of manually entering the total here, we'll enter a formula that tells the spreadsheet how to complete the calculations and then to post the result in this cell. 3. On the Formula bar (see Figure 3.2) enter the following equation: =Sum(B2:F2). This translates into: Sum up all of the totals found in cells B2 through F2 and put the total in cell G2. G2 ▼ f_x =SUM(B2:F2) **Note:** The equals sign (=) plays a key role. It tells the spreadsheet that what follows is an equation that needs to be calculated. If you forget this, it will treat the equation as a simple set of text and it won't do any calculations. This is a common mistake. **Note:** There are generally a number of ways to write these equations. A different way that also works is: =B2+C2+D2+E2+F2.

continued

No.	Feature	Steps to Get It Done
8	**Use the fill handle** 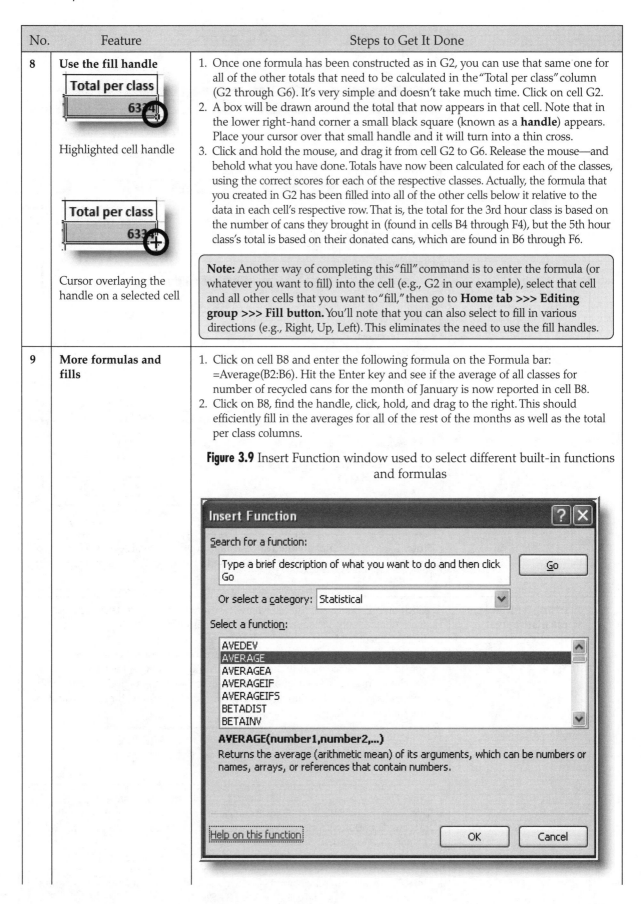 Highlighted cell handle Cursor overlaying the handle on a selected cell	1. Once one formula has been constructed as in G2, you can use that same one for all of the other totals that need to be calculated in the "Total per class" column (G2 through G6). It's very simple and doesn't take much time. Click on cell G2. 2. A box will be drawn around the total that now appears in that cell. Note that in the lower right-hand corner a small black square (known as a **handle**) appears. Place your cursor over that small handle and it will turn into a thin cross. 3. Click and hold the mouse, and drag it from cell G2 to G6. Release the mouse—and behold what you have done. Totals have now been calculated for each of the classes, using the correct scores for each of the respective classes. Actually, the formula that you created in G2 has been filled into all of the other cells below it relative to the data in each cell's respective row. That is, the total for the 3rd hour class is based on the number of cans they brought in (found in cells B4 through F4), but the 5th hour class's total is based on their donated cans, which are found in B6 through F6. **Note:** Another way of completing this "fill" command is to enter the formula (or whatever you want to fill) into the cell (e.g., G2 in our example), select that cell and all other cells that you want to "fill," then go to **Home tab >>> Editing group >>> Fill button.** You'll note that you can also select to fill in various directions (e.g., Right, Up, Left). This eliminates the need to use the fill handles.
9	**More formulas and fills**	1. Click on cell B8 and enter the following formula on the Formula bar: =Average(B2:B6). Hit the Enter key and see if the average of all classes for number of recycled cans for the month of January is now reported in cell B8. 2. Click on B8, find the handle, click, hold, and drag to the right. This should efficiently fill in the averages for all of the rest of the months as well as the total per class columns. **Figure 3.9** Insert Function window used to select different built-in functions and formulas

No.	Feature	Steps to Get It Done
		Note: The spreadsheet has lots of built in formulas. To view these go to the **Formula tab >>> Functions Library** group. An embedded gallery of formula types will be displayed. In addition, you can click on the **Insert Function** button within that same **Functions Library** group and an Insert Function dialog box will be launched. As shown in Figure 3.9, this box allows you to search for a specific function. Once you select the function, you can also view the structure of the formula and if you desire you can access help that gives examples and procedures to walk you through the setup and use of the formula.

Scenario 2: The story continues

Through the efforts of Mr. Rena's science classes, a total of over 25,700 cans were collected and recycled. Receiving approximately 1 cent per can, the school received a payment of $257.51 for their science equipment. Because of the success of the program, Mr. Rena asked several of his students to use the data and make a presentation to the school principal, petitioning for a new schoolwide can recycling project to be started in the following school year. Figure 3.10 represents a part of the visual presentation developed by the students. Notice that this data, when compared with that presented in Figure 3.6 has been changed for the presentation. For example, a title row and columns for number of students, student average, and money earned have all been added; at the same time, one row of data (class average) has been deleted.

Figure 3.10 Mr. Rena's Science class expanded spreadsheet of data of recycled cans with added data charts

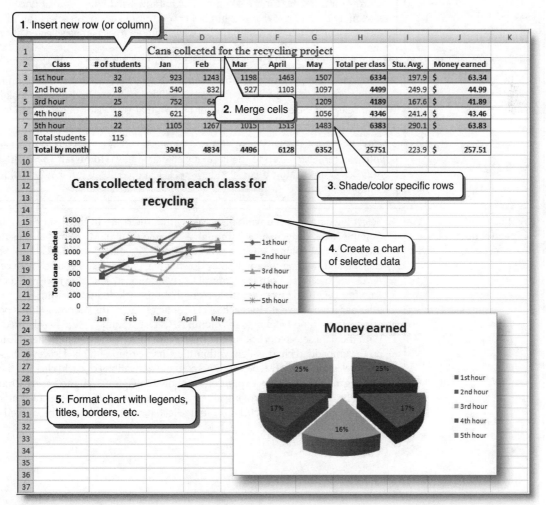

No.	Feature	Steps to Get It Done
1	**Insert a new row (or column)**	1. To insert a new row, place your cursor in the row (or column) immediately *after* where you want your new row (or column) to appear. 2. Go to **Home tab** >>> **Cells** group >>> **Insert** >>> select the option for **Insert Sheet Rows** (or **Insert Sheet Columns**). The new row is inserted into the sheet directly above (or to the left of) where your cursor was placed.
2	**Merge cells**	At times it is appropriate to have several cells merge to display data that would normally go beyond the single cell size. In Figure 3.10 this is done to format a title to the data table. 1. Begin by selecting all of the cells that you want to merge. **Note:** The cells must be next to each other in the adjoining row(s) or column(s). 2. Go to **Home tab** >>> **Alignment group** >>>**Merge & Center** gallery button. The cells will be automatically merged. The **Merge & Center** drop-down gallery also allows you the option to merge without centering or to unmerge cells when needed. 3. To format the data in the cell, select the cell(s) and specific data you want to format, then go to **Home tab** >> **Font** group and make your selection from the given alternatives (see Figure 3.7).
3	**Shade or color specific rows (or cells, columns)** *[toolbar image: Calibri · 11 · A A; B I U · ▦ · ◇ · A · ; Font]*	1. Select the row(s), column(s), or cell(s) you wish to shade. **Note:** To select a whole row (or column), click on the number associated with that row (or the letter for the column). The full row will highlight all at once. To select more than one row, press and hold the Control key as you select the various rows you wish to highlight. In this way, multiple rows can be selected at any time. 2. Return to the **Font** group of tools (**Home tab** >>> **Font** group) and click on the fill button. A grid layout of a color gallery will be displayed and you can make your selection. Select the color and/or pattern that you wish your selection to contain and then click OK. **Note:** You can also return to the Format Cell dialog box (**Home tab** >>> **Font** group >>> **Font dialog box** expander) and select the Fill tab (see Figure 3.8) for additional options.
4	**Create a chart of specific data**	1. Select the data that you want displayed within the chart. In the first chart of our example, we selected cells A2 through A7 (name of all of Mr. Rena's classes AND the title of that column ("Class"). We did this by holding down the Control key, clicking and holding the mouse key down while dragging the pointer from cell A2 down to cell A7. With the Control key continuously held down, recycled can data from C2 to G7 were selected. Note that this included the column month titles as well as the data for each of classes across all of the months. At this point, selected data (and headings) in column A, C, D, E, F, and G were highlighted. 2. With the data selected, click on the **Insert tab**. Review the possible charts listed on the embedded chart gallery within the **Chart** group of tools. However, to see a full selection of chart types and the possible derivations of each, click on the **Chart group dialog box expander**. As shown in Figure 3.11, the **Insert Chart** dialog box will appear. Scrolling allows you to review all of the types of charts available. Select one and click OK. Your selected chart should now be created and inserted within your spreadsheet document.

No.	Feature	Steps to Get It Done
		Figure 3.11 Insert Chart dialog box used to select different built-in charts 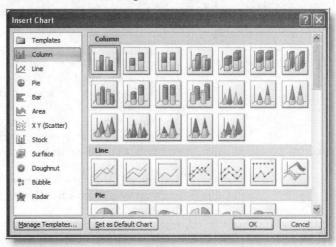

Note: If you decide you don't like your selected chart type—no problem. Simply click on the new chart and the **Chart tools contextual tab** will appear. Go to the **Chart Tools/Design tab** >>> **Type** group >>> **Change Chart Type** button. Clicking that button will return you to the **Insert Chart** dialog box, where you can select a different chart type and start the process over.

Another note: Two frequent mistakes that occur: (a) The title of the columns (e.g., Class, Jan, Feb, Mar) is not included as the rest of the data is being selected. The spreadsheet may still create the chart, but without the headings the chart will input its own set of titles that may or may not make sense to you. (b) If there is a title above the column headings, make sure you don't accidentally select it so that the chart wizard attempts to include it within the chart. Select only those relevant columns of headings and data.

No.	Feature	Steps to Get It Done
5	**Format changes on the chart**	Although charts can be quickly created, often changes to the overall design, layout, or format are needed for the charts to be optimally effective. Several of these possible adaptations have been highlighted in Figure 3.11. To alter charts after they have been created, consider the following steps: 1. For simple editing changes to elements (e.g., titles, legends) that already appear on the chart, simply click directly on the element that you want to change. A box and handles will appear around the element. Words within the box can then be selected and edited, or the element's location can be changed by clicking and dragging it to the new location. 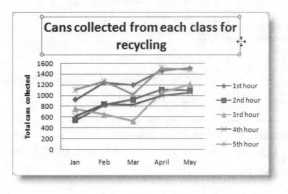

continued

No.	Feature	Steps to Get It Done
		2. For more major changes to the chart (see those highlighted in Figure 3.12), click on the chart to select it. This will cause the **Chart Tools** contextual tab for **Design, Layout,** and **Format** to appear. Use these tabs to access the needed tools for the following changes: a. <u>Change from lines to pies</u> . . . If you need to change the overall type of chart (e.g., see Figure 3.11 to view the pie type), go to **Chart Tools/Design tab** >>> **Type** group >>> **Change Chart Type**. The Insert Chart dialog box will appear (see Figure 3.11) and you can select a different type for your data. This is one of the easiest, quickest, and valuable major change you will ever attempt. *Do it a number of times to make sure your data is presented in the best possible way.* b. <u>Alter axis titles.</u> If the titles on your chart axis doesn't appear or is not in the correct position, you can change it by clicking **Chart Tools/Layout tab** >>> **Labels** group, or the **Axes** group of tools. c. <u>Add gridlines.</u> Play with the types and number of gridlines that can be added to a chart by going to **Chart Tools/Layout tab** >>> **Axes** group >>> **Gridlines** drop-down gallery. d. <u>Include a chart title.</u> Similar to changing an axis title, chart titles can be altered by going to **Chart Tools/Layout tab** >>> **Labels** group >>> **Chart Title**. e. <u>Include and adapt a legend.</u> To include a legend within the chart, go to **Chart Tools/Design tab** >>> **Chart Layouts** group >>> review the gallery of layouts and select one with a legend. To alter the position of the legend that has been included within the chart, go to **Chart Tools/Layout tab** >>> **Labels** group >>> **Legend** and select from the drop-down gallery options. f. <u>Add or alter chart border shading.</u> To add highlights and dimension to the chart on the spreadsheet page, border shading can be added. To do this, go to **Chart Tools/Format tab** >>> **Shape styles** group >>> **Shape Effects** and try various shadow and three-dimensional(3D) alternatives for your chart. **Note:** These are only a few of the design, layout, and format changes that can be included within your chart. Create a chart and explore the various options available for use.

Figure 3.12 Example chart with highlighted elements that can be altered

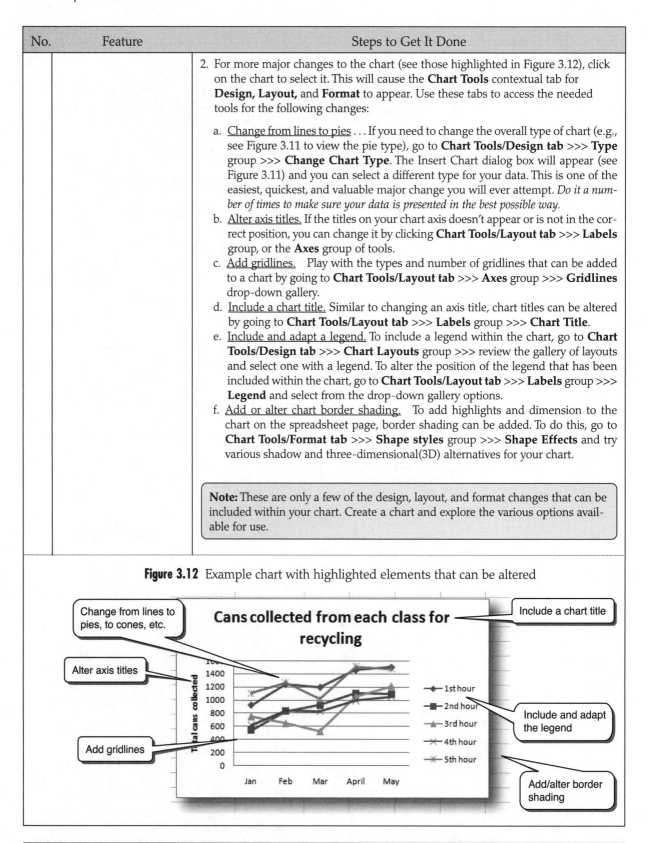

Level 1a Workout: Practice using the basic Excel features

Now it's time for you to practice using this spreadsheet software. With this first workout, we want you to review all that was presented within the step-by-step procedures. However, there are many other things that were not touched upon within this chapter,

so as you go about working on this exercise, please explore and experiment with some of the new things you encounter. Later, when you are working on a new project, you may find that those features you "discovered" are some of the features you find most helpful.

Here is a basic outline of what you need to do:

1. Review Figures 3.6 and 3.10 and all of the various highlighted features that have been within those figures.
2. Go to the text's accompanying Web site and open the unformatted version of these two figures (**www.prenhall.com/newby** >>> **Chapter 3** >>> **Level 1 Workout** >>> **Recycle**).
3. Using the given unformatted version, go through the list of features and practice adding them to your spreadsheet. It really isn't that important for you to match the text's example with your product, but try the feature to see how it works and how it can be adapted for your use. Explore and have fun with this. Remember this is a practice workout—*practice integrating as many features as possible.*

> **Note:** Refer to specific feature numbers and the given step-by-step procedures as needed. Additionally, use the mentoring videos to help guide you through any specific procedure that needs further clarification.

Level 1b Workout: Creating your own spreadsheet

To help you transfer the information from the text to something you'll actually use, it is time for you to use this software with some of your own data. You can use a spreadsheet to input and store important data, as well as organize, analyze, and present it in new and important ways. For the Workout, create a spreadsheet that includes your own data. You may get the numbers from your own data collection or you may get them from other sources such as the Internet, textbooks, magazines, and so on. What is important is for you to acquire some numbers that can be input into the spreadsheet, organized, formatted, analyzed, and output in some manner.

Some examples of data that you might use would include the following:

- Statistics from some of your favorite sports teams (e.g., softball hitting, pitching statistics)
- Comparisons of birth and death rates for several countries
- Number of illegal downloaded songs on college campuses over the last decade
- Boxes of Girl Scout cookies sold and profits made
- Gas prices from various areas of the country or the world at different times during the last few years
- Prices of several different common food or drug items from various stores
- Personal budget of income and expenses for the past 6 months

As you can see, a wide variety of data can be collected. After you have determined what data you will use, do the following:

1. Open your spreadsheet program and create a draft worksheet that includes columns and rows of your data. Include column and row titles.
2. Review the features demonstrated within Figures 3.6 and 3.10 from Scenarios 1 and 2.
3. Format your new document with as many of the features demonstrated in those figures as possible. Use Table 3.1 as a checklist to guide your efforts.

Table 3.1 Level 1 Workout and Practice Checklist
Creating and Formatting a Spreadsheet

Spreadsheet Content	
	___ Data was organized (rows and columns) in a clear, logical manner.
	___ Cell content is free from spelling errors.

Document Format	
	___ A new worksheet within the spreadsheet program was created.
	___ Column and row headings were inserted, aligned, and formatted appropriately.
	___ Cells were populated with data.
	___ Column widths were sized appropriately so that titles and data could be easily read.
	___ Gridlines were incorporated.
	___ Formulas were incorporated to analyze the data.
	___ Selected rows, columns, or cells were colored and/or shaded.
	___ Charts of the data were created and included within the spreadsheet document.
	___ Charts were easy to read and included titles, a legend, and gridlines (if applicable).
	___ Charts were formatted to highlight the data and the chart itself (e.g., use of shading, colors).

Level 2: "What If's. . ." and Other Good Stuff

What should you be able to do?

In this section we want you to learn to recognize and use additional spreadsheet features, as well as to understand how to use the **Help** feature of the software effectively. With this instruction, you should be able to create, edit, and format several original data sets into a spreadsheet format and use formulas to compare, analyze, and summarize the data.

Getting some Help

Similar to the other Office programs, there is also Help in MS Excel and most other sophisticated spreadsheet software. To use **Help,** click the **Help** button on the tab bar of the main ribbon.

Clicking the Help button opens the Help window. From here you can browse general Help topics, bring up a general table of contents of all Help topics, complete a search for a specific question that you might have, and so on.

| Home | Insert | Page Layout | Formulas | Data | Review | View | Developer | Add-Ins | ⓘ |

Excel Help button

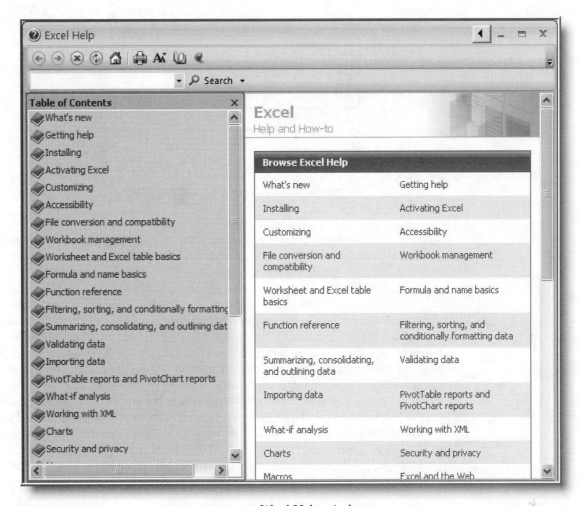

Word Help window

By typing in key words or even a full question, Help will respond with a variety of potential answers for you to investigate. Help generally *does not* have all of the answers—but it will have a lot of them. Make sure you become familiar with how it works and how often it can be of assistance.

Scenario 3: "The Store"

Barry Pfleger couldn't believe what he had just been "volunteered" for. As an assistant soccer coach, he was "asked" to take charge of the Woodrow High School "Gotta Have It" Spirit Store. Originally the store's inventory had been helpful in getting students to purchase and use items like pencils, paper, flags, and clothing—all with the school Whippoorwill logo engraved or embossed. Additionally, the extra revenue, although not great, had been used to purchase a few extra pieces of equipment for various "Fightin' Whipper" athletic teams.

Over the course of the last couple of semesters, however, the inventory had gotten old, products weren't ordered correctly, and the store hadn't been open for regular "business." Barry was a pretty good English teacher, but he wasn't too sure about learning the retail business. Luckily, Olivia, one of his senior soccer players, noticed his anxiety and offered her help. She explained that her parents owned a small pet store and she was always helping her dad with his books.

"First," she began, "you really need to determine where you are. So, let's get a couple students into the Gotta Have It Store and together we can count everything that it contains. We'll need to get a record of what every item is, how many there are, and if possible the original cost of each." She quickly drew a grid on her coach's clipboard (see Figure 3.13) and labeled the rows "*Item*" and the columns "Cost" and "Quantity"

Figure 3.13 Starting of a simple inventory spreadsheet

After an afternoon of sorting, counting, and looking through old receipts, Coach Pfleger and Olivia reviewed their completed inventory sheet. Olivia then suggested that the next step would be to recreate it as an electronic spreadsheet. She explained that with the inventory in an electronic format, a formula could be used to calculate the wholesale subtotal. In addition, she suggested adding some columns, such as one for the subtotals for how much the inventory was worth now (wholesale price × the quantity of a specific item) and columns for the subtotals if there were markups of 25%, 50%, or even higher. Olivia explained that as the inventory changed over the next few months, it would be easy to then update the changes on the electronic spreadsheet and the totals would automatically be calculated.

We aren't going to explain exactly how to do each, but we will give you the example of the feature and critical questions you can think about and investigate (via Help or Office Assistant) to find the needed answers. In addition, mentoring videos have been created, and can be accessed on the text's Web site, that will guide you through the use of each of these features (see **www.prenhall.com/newby** >>> **Chapter 3** >>> **Mentor Video**).

Feature	Steps to Get It Done
Using formulas and functions	**Information about and procedure for creating and inserting:** Excel Help • Key word: **Formula.** • Select *Create a simple formula with constants and calculation operations* and follow the given procedure. • Select *Create a formula with functions* **Key features to note, explore, and try out:** • As shown in Features 7, 8, and 9 in Scenario 1 of this chapter, you can create your own simple formula and insert it within a cell. For simple calculations, this is often the quickest and easiest method. • For more advanced calculations, it may be more efficient to click on the Formula bar button (see Figure 3.2) to produce the Insert Function dialog box (see Figure 3.9). Within this box you can select the functions that have already been developed within Excel. The function wizard will guide you through selecting the correct cells to reference.
Inserting graphics or pictures	**Information about and procedure for accessing and inserting:** Excel Help • Key word: **Insert picture.** • Select *Insert clip art* and follow the given procedure (note that you can also select to insert pictures from the Web, a file, and so on).

Feature	Steps to Get It Done
	Key features to note, explore, and try out: • Once a picture or clip art has been inserted into your spread-sheet, you can click on it and a box and handles will appear around it. You can use the handles to alter the size of the picture or you can click, hold, and drag the picture to a new location. • Once the picture is selected, the contextual **Picture Tools/Format tab** appears. Within the set of tools you can adjust the picture (e.g., contrast, color), add various border styles, crop it, or alter its size.
Word wrap within cells	**Information about and procedure for allowing:** Excel Help 🔘 • Key word: **Word wrap.** • Select *Wrap text automatically* and follow the given procedure **Key features to note, explore, and try out:** • Highlight the cells where you want the text to be wrapped. • Go to **Home tab** >>> **Alignment** group >>> **Word wrap button**
Freeze panes to lock rows or columns	Because spreadsheet can become very long or very wide (thus the name spreadsheet), it often becomes difficult to see and remember specific important information (e.g., column titles) when that info has been scrolled off the screen. At times, it is helpful to "freeze" an important row (e.g., the row with all of the headers for the columns) so that when scrolling occurs, that specific row (or column) remains in the same position. **Information about and procedure for accomplishing:** Excel Help 🔘 • Key word: **Freeze panes.** • Select *Freeze or lock rows and columns* and follow the given procedure. • Also select *Split panes to lock rows or columns in separate worksheet areas* **Key features to note, explore, and try out:** • Select a row below or a column to the right of where you want the freeze to occur. • Go to **View tab** >>> **Window group** >>> **Freeze pane** drop-down gallery. • Select the option that you desire. • To unfreeze, return to the **Freeze pane** drop down gallery and you will notice that there is now an *Unfreeze Panes* option. **Note:** A similar effect can also be achieved by *splitting the pane*. This is done by pointing your mouse cursor to the split box located at the top of the vertical scroll bar (used to split the pane horizontally) and to the right of the horizontal scroll bar (used to split the pane vertically). As you go over the split box your pointer will change into a two-headed arrow. Click and drag the split bar down or to the left. When you no longer want the split pane, simply double click anywhere on the split bar.
Renaming work-sheets	When you create a workbook, Excel automatically names the work-sheets as *Sheet1, Sheet2, Sheet3,* and so on. To be more descriptive, you may want to rename those sheets. This is very easily accomplished: • Double click on the sheet tab of the worksheet you want to rename. See Figure 3.2 in the lower left corner.

continued

Feature	Steps to Get It Done
	• Simply type in the new name. 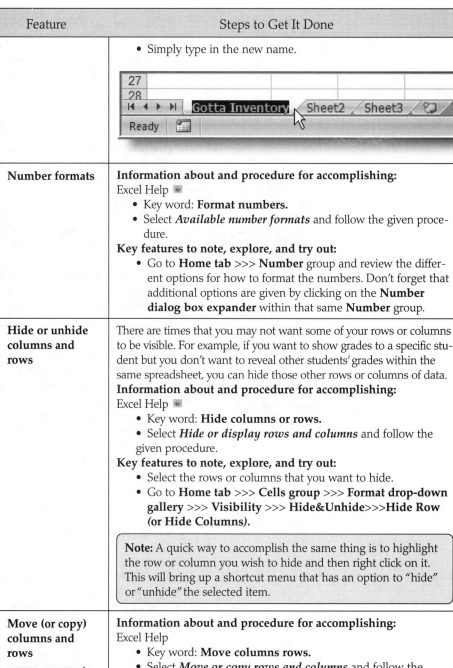

Number formats	**Information about and procedure for accomplishing:**
	Excel Help
	   • Key word: **Format numbers.**
	   • Select *Available number formats* and follow the given procedure.
	Key features to note, explore, and try out:
	   • Go to **Home tab** >>> **Number** group and review the different options for how to format the numbers. Don't forget that additional options are given by clicking on the **Number dialog box expander** within that same **Number** group.

Hide or unhide columns and rows	There are times that you may not want some of your rows or columns to be visible. For example, if you want to show grades to a specific student but you don't want to reveal other students' grades within the same spreadsheet, you can hide those other rows or columns of data.
	Information about and procedure for accomplishing:
	Excel Help
	   • Key word: **Hide columns or rows.**
	   • Select *Hide or display rows and columns* and follow the given procedure.
	Key features to note, explore, and try out:
	   • Select the rows or columns that you want to hide.
	   • Go to **Home tab** >>> **Cells group** >>> **Format drop-down gallery** >>> **Visibility** >>> **Hide&Unhide**>>>**Hide Row (or Hide Columns).**
	
	Note: A quick way to accomplish the same thing is to highlight the row or column you wish to hide and then right click on it. This will bring up a shortcut menu that has an option to "hide" or "unhide" the selected item.

Move (or copy) columns and rows
 	
	Information about and procedure for accomplishing:
	Excel Help
	   • Key word: **Move columns rows.**
	   • Select *Move or copy rows and columns* and follow the given procedure.
	Key features to note, explore, and try out:
	   • Select the row or column that you want to move (or copy).
	   • Go to **Home tab** >>> **Clipboard** group >>> **Cut** (or **Copy**).
	   • Right click on the row below or the column to the right of where you want your respective row or column to be moved. The right click will bring up the shortcut menu. On that menu, select **Insert Cut Cells** (or **Insert Copied Cells**).
	
	Note: A common mistake is to attempt to move or copy a row or column by using the **Paste (Home tab** >>> **Clipboard** group) instead of the **Insert Cut (or Copied) Cells**. However, if **Paste** is used, you will find out that you have *replaced* the destination row or column content with that which you wanted to move or copy. Be careful in what you are doing.

Feature	Steps to Get It Done
Printing	Often when it comes to printing your work, it saves time, paper, and ink if you first preview what will be printed. Through the Print Preview process, you are able to make needed changes prior to the hard copy being produced. **Information about and procedure for accomplishing:** Excel Help ⬛ • Key word: **Print Preview.** • Select *Preview worksheet pages before printing* and follow the given procedure. **Key features to note, explore, and try out:** • Go to **Print Preview** by clicking on the **Microsoft Office Button** >>> **Print** >>> P**rint Preview**. Print Preview will allow you to review what the worksheet will look like when it is printed. • From within **Print Preview** you can select **Page Setup**. Page Setup allows you to control these (and other) options for your worksheet: • Orient (and print) the page in **Portrait** or **Landscapes**. • Scale the page (reduce it proportionally) so that it fits to an exact size (i.e., this allows you to make sure a worksheet that is a bit too big to be printed on a single page can be quickly resized to fit and print on one page). • Set the **Margins** for the printed page(s). • Add a **Header/Footer** to the printed page(s). • Control the order in which the pages are printed.

Figure 3.14 "Gotta Have It" Inventory

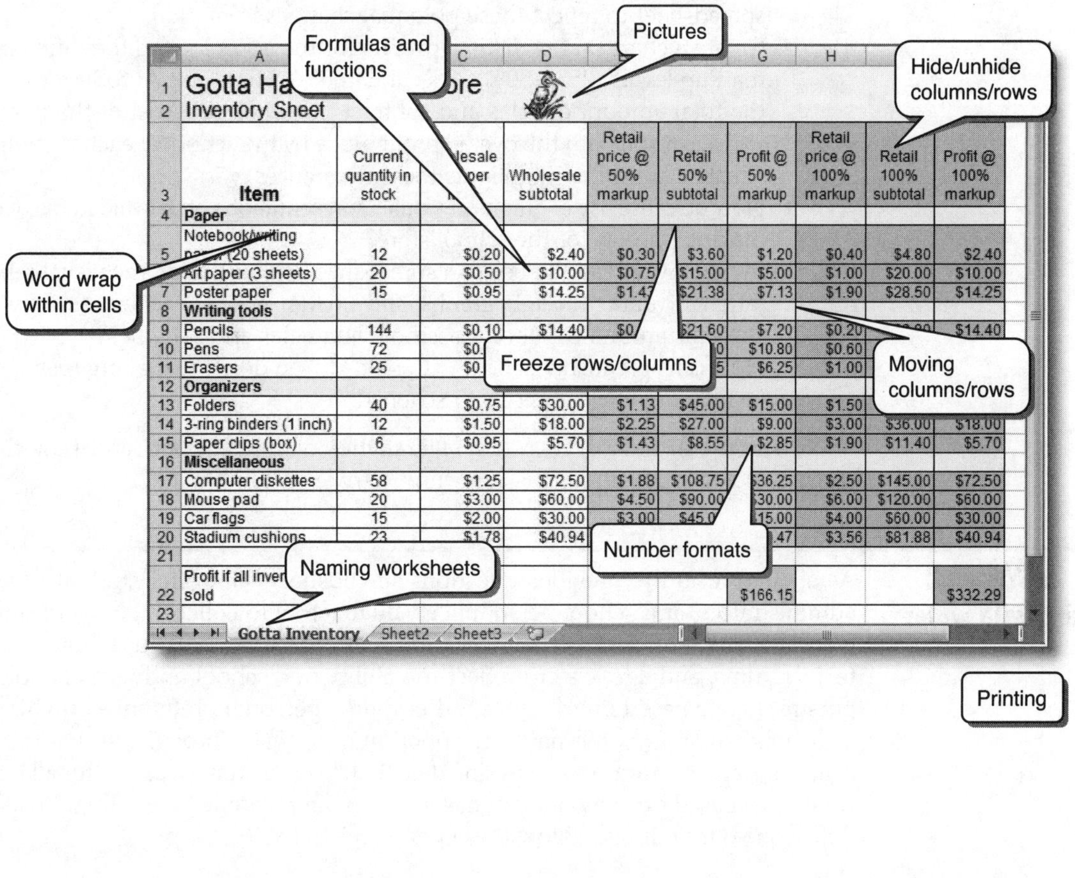

Level 2a Workout: Practice using additional Excel features

Before moving on to your own work, it might be wise to try a few exercises with the Gotta Have It Store.

1. Go to the text's accompanying Web site and open the unfinished version of Gotta Have It Store (**www.prenhall.com/newby** >>> **Chapter 3** >>> **Level 2a Workout** >>> **gottastore**).
2. Try to do the following. If you have difficulty, review the procedures given in both the step-by-step procedures of the Level 1 scenarios, and the suggestions for accessing Help, and the information provided with Scenario 3 and Figure 3.14.

   a. Create additional columns for the different markup retail prices, and so on.
   b. Add formulas to calculate the projected markup prices, the subtotals, and grand totals. If easier, try using the insert function dialog box to add the needed formulas.
   c. Move the columns and/or rows from one location to another.
   d. Complete formatting of the worksheet by:

   - Naming your worksheet
   - Word wrapping the cells that have overly long titles, and so forth.
   - Adding color to highlight and organize the data
   - Adding relevant pictures, clip art, and so on.

   e. Hide and then unhide specific rows or columns.
   f. Freeze panes and/or split panes to work with the expanded spreadsheet.

   > **Note:** Each of these key features is demonstrated on the mentoring videos within the text's accompanying Web site. Go to the **www.prenhall.com/newby** >>> **Chapter 3** >>> **Mentor Videos**.

3. Answer the following questions and/or complete the following tasks:
   - What if the markup was 25% or 75%? Create two additional columns in your spreadsheet to reflect these potential changes in markup.
   - Create a chart that compares **profits** for the school given the different retail markup levels (25%, 50%, 75%, and 100%). Hint: Use AutoSum to tabulate the total amount of sales and subtract the wholesale cost of the items. This will leave you with the overall profit made by the school at each markup level. Create a chart that highlights these differences.
   - How does the use of graphs or visual representations of data aid in the decision-making process for the school store?
   - In what ways can the use of a spreadsheet (in particular, the visual representation of data through graphs and charts) assist teachers as they assess students and reflect upon classroom strategies and activities?
   - How can spreadsheets help with data-driven decision making (using data to justify or confirm choices) in schools?

   Now that you have seen a few of examples of spreadsheets and how they are constructed and formatted, it is your turn to try your hand at it.

Level 2b Workout: Working with water

As alluded to in the previous questions spreadsheets can offer students, teachers, administrators, and school personnel a valuable tool to collect, aggregate, and analyze data. The term *data-driven decision making* is frequently used in educational texts, forums, and agencies to reflect the ability of a school and its stakeholders to pursue change based on evidence rather than a personal preference or whim.

In this workout, you'll have an opportunity to walk through the basic steps of collecting, aggregating, and analyzing data that has a universal context for all humans: water use. Based on the data you collect and manipulate, you will then be asked to reflect on your findings. Follow these next steps to begin.

Step 1: As a means to demonstrate data collection, aggregation, and analysis, your initial task is to chart your household's water use. Pick a 5-day period of time when most members are at home and collect the frequency of the following activities:

- Baths
- Showers
- Teeth brushing
- Hand and face washing
- Face or leg shaving
- Dishwasher
- Dishwashing by hand
- Loads of laundry (machine)
- Toilet flushes
- Glasses of water (for drinking)

There are several ways to tally the frequency of these activities: a household journal in a common location, sticky-notes posted throughout the home (next to the kitchen sink, for example) to allow participants to self-report, and so on.

Step 2: Create an Excel spreadsheet to calculate the total use of the household AND the number of gallons of water used per person.

- All calculations MUST be done with formulas.
  - Be sure to use the following formulas: basic multiplication of cells, division of cells, and SUM.
  - *Note:* Showers are the only item that must be multiplied by frequency and length of time.
- Format the cells for visual clarity. Use color and font choice to clearly present your data.
- Use the following data rates to calculate the water use. The rates are PER USE:

Bath: 50 gallons	**Dishwasher:** 20 gallons per load
Shower: 2 gallons per 1 minute	**Dishwashing by hand:** 5 gallons per load
Teeth brushing: 1 gallon	**Clothes washing (machine):** 10 gallons per load
Hands and face washing: 1 gallon	**Toilet flush:** 3 gallons
Face/leg shaving: 1 gallon	**Water to drink :** 8 ounce glass = 0.0625 gallon

Data rates are courtesy of the U.S. Geological Survey (USGS) Web site at http://ga.water.usgs.gov/edu/sq3.html

Step 3: Using the data you have collected, create a chart (design of your choice) to represent the water use by the household. Clearly label the components of your chart. Include a descriptive title and legend.

Step 4: Create a MS Word document that includes the chart and incorporates the following discussion components:

- Include a title for the "report."
- Compose an introductory paragraph that describes the data collection process.
- Include the chart in the MS Word document.
- Within the body of the report, address the following questions:
  - Which activity used the most water for your household? Which used the least amount of water?
  - What is the average number of gallons each member of your household used?
  - What other water-using activities occurred in your household that we did not calculate?

- Conclude the report by reflecting upon the following questions:
  - The USGS reports that the average U.S. citizen uses 80 to 100 gallons of water per day. Based upon this rate, does it seem that your household is above or below the national average of water use? Why do you think that is?
  - Looking at the data you have collected, what steps might members of your household take to further reduce the amount of water used?

Table 3.2 Level 2b Workout and Practice Checklist Working with Water

Spreadsheet Content	___ Content is accurate.
	___ Content is free from spelling and grammatical errors.
	___ Totals for the total water use for the household and the number of gallons of water used per person are calculated and reported.
	___ Proper formulas (e.g., basic multiplication and/or division of cells, SUM) were used within the spreadsheet.
	___ Proper data rates were used to calculate the water usage.
	___ Proper citation was given for the data rates that were used.
Spreadsheet Format	___ A new worksheet within the spreadsheet program was created.
	___ Column and row headings were inserted, aligned, and formatted appropriately.
	___ Cells were formatted for visual clarity (i.e., gridlines, color, font color, size and style, and so on, were used to add clarity and not distract from the data).
	___ Column widths were sized appropriately so that titles and data could be easily read.
	___ A clearly labeled chart was created from the data that represents water use by the household.
Report Content and Format	___ A clearly written, word processed report that includes a discussion of the data, chart, and overall household water use was completed.
	___ The report is free of grammatical and spelling errors.
	___ The content of the report should include a description of the water use in the household (e.g., which activity uses the least or most water, number of gallons each member used, what additional water using activities should have been included in the report but were not, better ways to monitor water use).
	___ The report concludes with recommendations of ways to further reduce the amount of water used within a household.

Level 3: Integration and Application in the Classroom

What should you be able to do?

Here is where you get to actually use this software to help yourself and your students. This section is to help you begin to see all of the many applications that are possible with using the spreadsheet. You should be able to use these examples as a springboard to launch ideas on ways to improve levels of student learning and your personal productivity.

Introduction

For many of us, thinking of spreadsheets generally conjures up thoughts of a fancy grade book. That's fine. However, it's time for you to expand on this a bit—and perhaps to see this as a tool for a wide variety of tasks, as well as a tool to help your students learn. Read and reflect on the examples given in this section. Think about ways you can integrate spreadsheets into your life and your curriculum. There will be times when integrating Excel or some similar spreadsheet will enhance the overall learning of the student.

Spreadsheet integration

Creating the enhanced learning experience: A partial lesson plan

Topic: A study of the people, places, and cultures of an African country.

Overview: As explained in Chapter 2 ("Word processing"), Mr. Carpenter is an eighth-grade social studies teacher at Lowell Middle School and he is beginning a unit of study on the African country of Zimbabwe. One of his past students, Jonathon Rogers is a graduate student working on an internship for an international health and education organization located in Zimbabwe. During the next school year, Mr. Carpenter wants his students to gather and exchange information about the Zimbabwean people and country with the help of Jonathon. Through Jonathon's work assignment, he will be visiting many schools, as well as health facilities. Hopefully, Mr. Carpenter's classes will be able to contact Jonathon through both the postal service and e-mail to gather their desired information.

One goal of the instructional unit is for the students to discover what life is like in another country and culture. Through various discussions, Mr. Carpenter's classes identified several relevant points of interest that they wanted to examine and make comparisons.

Specific Learning Task: One specific area of interest was of the types and amounts of food eaten by similarly aged students in the two countries. The goal was to gather data from students in both countries on what they commonly eat. Once gathered, cross-country comparisons could be examined, as well as comparisons with governmental nutritional guidelines.

Sample Learning Objectives: Students will be able to do the following:

1. Describe the most common foods eaten by the sample of students from the two different cultures.
2. Identify and describe foods common between the two cultures.
3. Based on the collected data, identify potential discrepancies between U.S. governmental nutritional needs of students in both countries.

Procedure:

1. Subdivide each of Mr. Carpenter's eighth-grade classes into three research groups.

   - Research Group A: This group will gather and report data on common food eaten by a sample of students in Mr. Carpenter's class.
   - Research Group B: This group will work with Jonathon and gather data on common food eaten by a similar sample of same-aged Zimbabwean students.
   - Research Group C: This group will research government suggested nutritional information on the types and amounts of food that should be eaten by similarly aged students.

2. Create small data journals to collect data on foods eaten. Each journal should have a place to record the type and amount of food eaten during the morning, afternoon, and evening of each day for a 14-day time period. Also include instructions for the students to describe foods that individuals from other cultures may not recognize.

3. Randomly select 10 students (5 girls and 5 boys) from Mr. Carpenter's class and contact Jonathon to see if he can likewise get 10 participants from one of his schools he's working with.

4. Have Jonathon review the data journals and ask for any needed clarification on food types, and so on, and then mail the completed journals to Lowell Middle School. Members of Groups A and B will examine their respective journals and enter the data received.

5. Group C will record the suggested governmental types and amounts of food.

6. Students will compare the data from the two countries and the suggested governmental standards and

   a. Determine most common food eaten within each country
   b. Determine foods commonly eaten by students in both countries
   c. Determine general nutritional value of the common foods eaten by the individual students in both countries
   d. Present a data chart that illustrates the comparisons between countries and the standards

7. Write a short paper about a proposed visit to Zimbabwe and what types of food they could expect to encounter. Use the data chart to identify which foods they would be excited about trying and what foods they probably would try to avoid.

Questions about Spreadsheet Integration

This lesson could be completed in a number of ways. One specific method would be to use a spreadsheet, such as Excel, to help gather, analyze, and report the results of the collected data. Use these reflective questions to explore the value of potentially integrating a spreadsheet within such a lesson as outlined by Mr. Carpenter.

- How can spreadsheets be used by the teacher and the students within this lesson plan? Provide at least two examples of use for each.
- What could be added to a spreadsheet to further compare the nutritional value of the food consumed? In other words, what type of a column could be included to provide students with a means to rank the nutritional value of the reported types of food consumption?
- After you have entered such a column as just described (nutritional value), which features or tools of Excel could be used to manipulate and analyze the data?
- In addition to nutritional value, what other types of data on food consumption could be collected to assist in the cultural comparison?
- Which type of chart would be most helpful in providing a cultural comparison based upon food consumption? Would more than one chart be necessary? Explain.
- How could this data (numerical and via charts) be used to aid the students in creating long-term predictions regarding the health of all groups of students?
- How could this data (numerical and via charts) be used to make recommendations for dietary change?
- What types of follow-up activities could accompany this lesson plan? What types of projects (individual or class) could be built upon this data collection and analysis? Describe at least two distinct, student-centered learning projects.
- What if a teacher does not have access to a colleague in Zimbabwe? What are some alternative methods or resources for gathering a similar set of comparative data?

Level 3a Workout: Integrating spreadsheets

This is a good time for your practice. First, reflect on the partial lesson plan given earlier. Next, think about the use of spreadsheets within applied classroom settings. Finally, work through each of the following steps.

1. Read each of the following situations. Imagine being directly involved in the planning for each of these projects. Select one (or more if you wish) for further consideration.

Favorite Color

A third-grade teacher at Johnson Elementary asked his kids to tell him which color was the most preferred. To investigate, he had his students go out after school for 10 consecutive days and identify and record 20 different human-made items that they encountered (e.g., vehicles, houses, clothes). They were to report each item and its main color. From their findings they were to determine which was the most recorded color, the least used color, and if certain items were colored more frequently one color than another.

Holiday Wrap

For a school project, the seventh-grade students of Mayflower Middle School have decided to open a gift wrapping business at one of the small center shops in the local mall. They need to project their costs for the coming months of September through December. They also need to show how many volunteers need to be working at any one time for all of the shifts. Additionally, they need to show the amount of projected money they will earn based on the number of boxes wrapped, size of the box, and time required to wrap. Last, they need to consider if competition from other gift wrapping stores should be considered and what can be done to impact their overall prices.

Utilities Manager

How much raw sewage is processed each day at the local water or sewage treatment plant? Which days of the week produce the highest and lowest amounts of sewage? Are there typically high and low months or weeks of the year? Based on charts of processed sewage, identify potential causes of the fluctuations in the amount of sewage that is treated.

Growth Rate

Is there a way to compare the population growth rate of different countries of the world and then predict which ones may have problems in the future based upon rapid, stagnant, or decreasing growth rates? Which areas of the world would you predict would have the greatest amount of worry in the next few decades based on their current level of population growth?

2. Based on your selected project, consider the following questions that concern the integration of word processing. Mark your response to each question.

Integration assessment questionnaire (IAQ)

Will using **SPREADSHEET** software as a part of the project	
Broaden the learners' perspective on potential solution paths and/or answers?	__Yes __ No __ Maybe
Increase the level of involvement and investment of personal effort by the learners?	__Yes __ No __ Maybe
Increase the level of learner motivation (e.g., increase the relevance of the to-be-learned task, the confidence of dealing with the task, and/or the overall appeal of the task)?	__Yes __ No __ Maybe
Decrease the time needed to generate potential solutions?	__Yes __ No __ Maybe
Increase the quality and/or quantity of learner practice working on this and similar projects?	__Yes __ No __ Maybe
Increase the quality and/or quantity of feedback given to the learner?	__Yes __ No __ Maybe
Enhance the ability of the student to solve novel but similar projects, tasks, and problems in the future?	__Yes __ No __ Maybe

3. If you have responded "Yes" to one or more of the IAQ questions, you should consider the use of a spreadsheet to enhance the student's potential learning experience.

4. Using the example lesson plan, develop a lesson plan based on your selected project. Within the plan, indicate how and when the learner will use a spreadsheet. Additionally, list potential benefits and challenges that may occur when involving this software within the lesson.

Level 3b Workout: Exploring the NETS Standard connection

Developing and executing a lesson plan that integrates the use of spreadsheets directly addresses several of the Standards (NETS) for both teachers (NETS*T) and students (NETS*S). See the Appendix for a full listing of the standards.

Part A: Generally the main purpose for learning and using application software is to increase one's level of production—that is, to do things faster, better, or both. NETS standards (NETS'T Standard V and NETS'S Standard 6.b) help us focus on these productivity objectives for both teachers and students. There are other technology standards, however, that may also be potentially addressed through one's knowledge and use of spreadsheet software. Reflect on the following questions and consider the potential impact of spreadsheet integration (refer to the Appendix to review the full sets of standards):

- How could the integration of spreadsheets improve the collection, analysis, and assessment of data collected by the teacher and/or the students? Explain how these enhanced data collection and analysis capabilities increase levels of problem solving. (NETS'T IV.B. and V.B.; NET'S 3 and 4)
- How can the use of spreadsheet software help to develop students' higher order skills and creativity? Is there something about the use of spreadsheets that may enhance the exploration of alternative problem analyses, data comparisons, predictions, and ultimate solutions? How does the "what if . . ." capabilities afforded by spreadsheets allow for increased levels of creative problem solving? (NETS'T III.C.; NETS'S 1 AND 4)
- In what ways could spreadsheets be used to facilitate the communication and collaboration between teachers, students, parents, and subject matter experts on specific projects that ultimately impact student learning? Are there alternative means of displaying data (e.g., charts) that would allow for diverse audiences to better grasp the meaning of the information? (NETS'T V.D. and VI.B.; NET'S 2)

Part B: Go to the ISTE Web site http://cnets.iste.org. Within that site, select to review either the student or the teacher NETS Standards. Once you have selected the standards to review, select either the student or teacher profiles and look for the corresponding scenarios. Review the scenarios and determine how spreadsheets could be used within several of those situations.

While visiting the ISTE Web site and exploring the scenarios, go to the lesson plan search area and select a number of different lesson plans of interest. Review those and determine the role (if any) of spreadsheets within the development, implementation, and assessment of the lesson. Note this from both the perspective of the teacher developing the lesson and the perspective of the student participating in the implemented lesson.

Further ideas on using the spreadsheet as a learning tool

Note: These ideas are to help you generate your own thoughts of what can be done. Don't let it bother you if they're not the right content or grade level; use the idea and adapt it to be helpful within your own situation. These are meant to be a stimulus for additional ideas.

Here are a few ideas that may help you see how a spreadsheet might be beneficial:

1. Give or generate a set of data and have students analyze and summarize the data by developing different formulas (e.g., means, standard deviations) to compare the results.
2. Have the students develop a survey, then collect, record, and analyze the data using statistical functions within the spreadsheet. Moreover, use the chart feature to report the data that they collected.
3. Collect, store, and compare monthly temperature averages for key cities in strategic locations of the world. Compare those averages with the average temperatures of the students' hometown.
4. Have the students collect data on the growth (e.g., height, loss of teeth) of their classmates over the course of a school year. Compare that data with students in other classes, other grades, other schools, or other countries.
5. Have the students compare the amount of soda, juice, and water that is purchased from the school's vending machines during different times of the day, days of the week, and/or months of the year. They could also calculate the amount of money earned by the school from these machines given the cost of the repair and maintenance.
6. Have students develop a personal budget for their current level of living. Also have them budget for when they enter college, the military, or the work force.
7. Have students create a sign-up chart for using specific items within the classroom (e.g., a special learning center, the computer, a special place to sit and read).
8. In a business class, have students monitor the price of specific stocks and note trends that may suggest optimal buying or selling times.
9. In a physical education class, have students create a spreadsheet that collects and analyzes weekly efforts in speed, endurance, strength, and so on.
10. Have students maintain a statistical record of their favorite professional sports star and compare performance levels across several years.
11. Have students design a judge's rating sheet for a club or sport (e.g., gymnastic, dancing, skating, diving)
12. Have students guess what the most popular color of cars or truck is, and then have them count the different colors that pass on a street near the school during a 20-min time period. Also have them count and record colors of M&M candies (or any other multicolored candy), socks, eyes, whatever, and analyze what they find.
13. Using the rows and columns of a spreadsheet, have the students design a sign-up sheet for use of the computer lab. This could also be converted to be used as a work assignment sheet for various jobs in the classroom on different days of the week.
14. With the rows and columns as a guide, have students develop crossword puzzles covering key words in a history, geography, science, or other school subject lesson.

Additional ideas for using a spreadsheet as an assistant

1. **Grade book.** Student scores can be recorded, edited, sorted, summarized, and reported with relative ease.
2. **Life organizer.** With all of those columns and rows, a spreadsheet is a good tool to develop a calendar or a daily meeting or work schedule. If you need to develop a set schedule for the lab, the spreadsheet can easily be formatted to display the times in a clear manner. It also works well to create quick and easy seating charts.
3. **Estimator.** Use it to record the current state and progress and then estimate where goals should be set. For example, a teacher in a high school weight lifting class can record a student's name, current weight, lifting capabilities, and then project what future goals for lifting should be set. The charting function allows for these goals to be shown in a visual manner. *Note:* This is also a good thing for personal weight

management programs (those things we refer to as "diets" and "watching our weight").

4. **Personal budgets.**
5. **Calculator.** Calculation of mortgage rates and monthly cost of a home.
6. **Schedules.** Develop time sheets for a small business and the work schedules of the employees. This can also be adapted for work schedules for individuals on school projects.
7. **Money tracker.** Use it to account for all fund-raiser money sales, book order sales, lunch money, and so forth.

Chapter 4

DATA MANAGEMENT

More MS Excel: The Basics of Collecting, Organizing, and Retrieving Loads of Information

Introduction

What should you be able to know and do?

In a world where we have access to a huge amount of information, having a way to organize, store, and retrieve that information is critical. Databases help you select, compare, and/or identify information that can lead to more effective learning and decision making. Within this introduction to databases, we want you to discover

- what a **database** is, what it can do, and how it can help in teaching and learning
- how to justify the use of the database as an effective tool—by knowing when and why it should or shouldn't be used

Terms to know

database	record	field
sort	search	mail merge
filter		

What is a database and what does it do?

Databases are exactly what the name implies—bases for specific data. They are specialized storage bins where one can place information and then later recall it. The trick is knowing how to get the information into the database so that it can later be located and recalled. Databases are incredibly important in a society that needs access to all kinds of information. How that information is organized is very important—or finding it can become a very arduous task.

A familiar example of an old and new database can be found in many libraries. Years ago (although it really hasn't been that long ago), most libraries had a large catalogue of 3- by-5-inch cards that contained information about each of the books in the library. To find a book, you first went to the card catalogue and looked for a card by either the book's title, author, or subject. Once you located an appropriate card, you could get information about the topic to access the book on the proper library shelf. Today, most of those card catalogues have been replaced by a computerized database. Using the same organizational structure, the computer can be used to search the library's database based on a specific book's author, title, or subject.

What are some commonly known databases?

- Microsoft's Access
- FileMaker Pro
- Corel's WordPerfect Office X3 Paradox
- Sun Microsystems' StarOffice Base
- dBASE

Can you use something else instead (i.e., Excel)?

Yes, many of the basic functions of the database can be accomplished by using a spreadsheet program such as Microsoft's Excel. That is, if you know spreadsheet basics, you may already know most of the needed functions to have it serve to manage your data. For this reason, we are going to concentrate on Excel as a tool that can be used to carry out simple data management functions.

> **Note:** There are times when a commercial database program is needed. If the amount of data you are working with is huge or if you need specialized forms to enter the data and/or to retrieve it, then you may want to consider learning and using a commercial database program. Our contention is that most teachers and students don't need that kind of power (and the accompanying headaches) for most of the tasks they will use a database for.

> **Important Note**: We made the determination that for most teachers, a thorough knowledge of a commercial database would not be as needed as other forms of software (e.g., PowerPoint, Word, Excel). This decision came about because of our experience in working with teachers and students and how they commonly use the computer within the school setting. However, we recognize that there may be some of you who really would like to know about the basics of a "normal" database. Therefore, we have developed Level 1 and Level 2 for Microsoft Access and placed it on this text's accompanying Web site (**www.prenhall.com/newby** >>> **Chapter 4** >>> **MS Access**). If you desire to learn and have an experience working with Access, please feel free to access and use it.

Why bother learning how to use a database?

- **Organization is the name of the game.** A database can help you organize vast amounts of information. If you have access to lots of information, organization is important.
- **Sorting with lightening speed.** Databases allow you to **sort** information automatically in a number of different ways. For example, an electronic student database can be sorted to produce an alphabetical list of all students. However, with the right information, you can also sort to list all students in alphabetical order based on their grade, gender, color of eyes, and shoe size if you desire. Multiple sorts can add to the power of the database.
- **Speed searches.** By using the **search** mechanism, you can have the computer find information you seek in a fraction of the time and effort needed to do it manually. Have it find one specific student and his or her associated information. Or have it find all instances of a specific characteristic for a data set (e.g., all students who have birthdays in October).
- **Boolean searches.** These types of searches allow you to search for specific information that contains specific words, letters, numbers, and so forth, but also to ignore other bits of information that you really don't want. For example, search for information on Lincoln, *not* Nebraska.
- **Grasp overwhelming amounts of information.** Using the combined features of search and sort, you can identify specific bits of important information that allow you to "see" relationships that may not have been readily apparent—for example, noting the elective courses frequently taken by high school students who are successful at gaining entrance into prestigious colleges.
- **Make comparisons.** Wouldn't it also be nice if you could pull out information and have it compare it for you? That is, search the electronic recipe database and have it identify and print all recipes that (1) use chicken, (2) feed up to six people, and (3) can be prepared in 20 minutes or less.

- **Multiple uses.** It isn't too difficult to begin to think about databases teachers might find helpful. Student information, books I own, books students have borrowed, lesson plans, supplies I have on hand versus supplies that are needed, electronic portfolios, quotes, references, pictures—the list goes on. These are all things that could be referenced, stored, searched, sorted, compared, and retrieved—if you have a knowledge of databases and how to use them to your advantage.

How are databases used at school? A brief list of ideas	By the teacher:	By the student:
	• Student information	• References for a research paper
	• Lesson plans	• Compare information on jobs, cities, businesses, weather
	• Mail merge data	• Addresses of friends and relatives
	• Articles, books, software, and so on in a personal library	• Compiled record of all work completed
	• Electronic student and personal portfolios	• Information on scholarships, grants, loans for college

Orientation

What's the workspace look like?

Figure 4.1 is an example of a database of information on books pertaining to copyright and plagiarism. This database was created in Microsoft Excel and should be familiar from our work in Chapter 3 (Spreadsheets). Instead of a focus on using the spreadsheets' capabilities with numbers, here we are using its rows and columns to store specific text information. Similar to the workspace when Excel was used as a spreadsheet, there are command tabs, each containing groups of related commands, as well as ways to adjust the cells, columns, and rows.

What commands can be used?

As we pointed out in Chapter 3 for Excel spreadsheets—and the other MS Office applications (e.g., MS PowerPoint, MS Word)—there is a ribbon of tools that runs across the top of the work screen. Within each ribbon various *command tabs* (e.g., Home, Insert, Page Layout, References) can be selected, which then reveal an associated command set or group. Once a command tab has been selected this specific group remains visible and ready for use. Items within the set may appear as individual items or as a *gallery* of related items. For example, selecting the Data tab (see Figure 4.2) in Excel reveals a group of commands that deal specifically with sorting and filtering data, as well as other things.

For more information about the Excel ribbon and command tabs, please review the Excel Orientation video on the text's accompanying Web site (**www.prenhall.com/ newby >>> Chapter 3 >>> Mentor Video**).

Databases, records, and fields

Remember the last time you went to a new doctor or dentist? On that initial visit the office administrator had you fill out some forms. The forms asked for your name, address, phone number, as well as your insurance company, policy number, and health history.

Ever wonder what happened to that form you filled out? In most cases, the form was taken back and put into a folder with your name on it. Then it was placed in a filing cabinet with other patient folders. The filing cabinet that holds all of the patients' files is known as a *database* and the individual file or form that you filled out is your *record*. On that record you filled in bits of information (address, medications you currently take, and so forth), and each bit of information is known as a *field*.

Figure 4.1 View of Microsoft Excel work area used to organize and manage textbook data

Office button – contains the file commands (e.g., new, save, print)

Command tabs – (e.g., Home, Insert, Page Layout, Formula) that allow access to groups of commands

General Work Area – Data is entered here and edited

Scroll bars

	A	B	C	D	E	F	G
1	Author	Book Title	Pub date	Publisher	Pub Location		
2	Buranen, L., & Roy, A. M., (eds.)	Perspectives on Plagiarism and Intellectual Property in a Postmodern World	1999	State University of New York Press	Albany, NY		
3	Butler, R. P.	Copyright for Teachers and Librarians	2004	Neal-Schuman Publishers, Inc.	New York		
4	Center for Intellectual Property, University of Maryland University College	College, Code, and Copyright: The Impact of digital Networks and Technological Controls on Copyright and the dissemination of Information in Higher Education	2005	Association of College and Research Libraries	Chicago		
5	Crews, K. D.	Copyright Law for Librarians and Educators: Creative Strategies and Practical Solutions	2006	American Library Association	Chicago		
6	Heller, J. S.	The Librarian's copyright Companion	2004	William S. Hein & Co., Inc.	Buffalo, NY		
7	Hoffman, G. M.	Copyright in Cyberspace 2: Questions and Answers for Librarians	2005	Neal-Schuman Publishers, Inc.			
8	Jensen, M. B.	Does Your Project Have a Copyright Problem? A Decision-Making guide for Librarians	1996	McFarland & Co, Inc.			
9	Judson, H. F.	The Great Betrayal: Fraud in Science	2004	Harcourt, Inc.	Orlando, FL		
10	Mallon, T.	Stolen Words: The Classic Book on Plagiarism	1989	Harcourt, Inc.	Orlando, FL		
11	Robin, R.	Scandals & Scoundrels: Seven Cases that Shook the Academy	2004	University of California Press	London, England		
12							
13							
14							
15							

Figure 4.2 The ribbon holds the command tabs, command groups or sets, and individual commands

Electronic databases are set up exactly the same way. The database holds numerous records and each record has specific fields of information. From our example in Figure 4.1, the database consists of all of the combined books listed. Each row indicates a specific record of one of those books. Each record is made up of several *fields* of information (e.g., the author, title, publication date of a specific text).

Here is another example: Suppose your high school dance team is raising money by conducting a dance clinic for the area elementary school students. On the registration form you ask the students for their name, address, grade level, gender, T-shirt size, and years of dance experience. As the registrations come in, you develop an electronic record for each student by inputting the individuals' fields of information (e.g., name, address, grade level, and soon.) for each student. Your database is the full set of all individuals who have registered. There is an individual record on each participant and you have a set number of fields of information about each participant (e.g., grade level).

What can be in a field?	Plenty. It could hold a letter of the alphabet, a name, a number, a picture, an audio or video clip, or even a whole chapter of a textbook. Some databases allow you a huge amount of space to put whatever you want within the field. In Excel, for example, in one cell (field) you can put as much as 32,000 characters of text. That is similar to about a chapter of text from a normal high school text.

The power of "sort and filter"	The power of the database is that it allows you to quickly sort and **filter** information it holds. For example, you can sort all of the records based on any or all fields contained within the records. Thus, you can sort each of the records alphabetically based on the name field (or gender field, or address field, or any other field) that is common within all of the records.

Even more powerful is the ability to search for a subset of the records based on a specific field. That is, you have the database quickly search all the data for specific information and filter out only that which is desired. So if you want to find out how many participants in your dance clinic are male, you could filter based on the gender field and bring out only those records of male participants.

You can see the real power of this information when you think about a doctor who wants to examine the records of all patients aged between 50 and 60, who have had an office visit in the last 5 years and have been diagnosed with diabetes. Or perhaps the teacher who desires to search from her database of hundreds of lesson plans to identify and filter out any and all that deal with science experiments involving copper for fourth- and fifth-grade students. Instantaneously, this information could be filtered and delivered. |

Orientation Workout: Explore the territory 	Turn on the computer and launch MS Excel or a similar program. Once it appears on the screen, try the following:

1. Create a new Excel spreadsheet.
2. Explore the various tabs on the ribbon and examine the different command groups.
3. On the new spreadsheet, practice entering information by clicking on any cell in the workspace.

   • Enter a word or series of words.
   • Highlight some or all of the words you enter.
   • Click on various command tabs, groups, and individuals commands tools. Note how your highlighted words change based on the tool that you have selected to use.

4. Review Chapter 3, Level 1, on how items are formatted within the spreadsheet. The same formatting can be used when Excel is used as a database. Attempt to set up headings, expand the width of the columns, and adjust the word wrap to achieve some sense of how data can be inserted in this tool.
5. Play with it for a short while to get a feeling for what can be done and how easy it is to use. |

Level 1: Revisiting the Recycling Project

What should you be able to do?	At this level, your focus is on using various tools and techniques to store data in a database and make the data retrievable in various forms.

What resources are provided?

Basically, Level 1 is divided into a common scenario, selected solutions, and a practice exercise (i.e., Workout). The scenario has been constructed to allow you to examine a common situation and how it could be addressed through the use of this software. To do this, we have provided the following:

a. Draft spreadsheet documents (see the text's accompanying Web site—**www.prenhall. com/newby** >>> **Chapter 4** >>> **Workout Level 1** that you can use to practice and review how the features are used to address the problems presented within each scenario.

b. Quick reference figures (see Figures 4.3–4.5), which identify the key features that have been incorporated within the solution presentation. These allow you to rapidly identify the key features and reference exactly how to include such features within your own work.

c. Step-by-step instructions on how to incorporate all highlighted features within your work.

d. Video mentoring support that will guide you through the integration of each of the highlighted features (see the text's accompanying Web site: **www.prenhall.com/ newby**).

e. Workout exercises that allow you to practice identifying and selecting which software features to use, when to use those features, how they should be incorporated, and to what degree they are effective.

How should you proceed?

If you have <u>little or no experience</u> with MS Office 2007 and particularly Excel, then we suggest you do the following:

1. Read and review Scenario 1.
2. Examine the quick reference figures (Figures 4.3–4.5) and all included features.
3. With the step-by-step directions provided, use the software and practice creating the database and completing a sorting and filtering of the data.
4. If you have any confusion or difficulty with these processes and tools, access the videos and monitor the features as they are demonstrated and discussed within the short video clips.
5. Once you feel comfortable, go to the Workout and work through the problem and exercises as it outlines.

If you have <u>experience</u> with Excel 2007, you may want to review the scenario and the quick reference examples first. If sorting and filtering are unfamiliar, then you may wish to access and use the step-by-step procedures, as well as the mentoring support videos. Once the review has been completed, then move directly to the Workout exercise and create your own database by incorporating similar elements as shown in these figures.

Scenario 1: The recycling project workers

Remember from the Level 1 exercise within Chapter 3 ("Spreadsheets"), John Rena's science classes worked on a spring semester aluminum can recycling project. John found it helpful during that time to have contact information for each of his students involved in the project. Using his spreadsheet program as a database, John created a record for each of his students (e.g., address, phone, parent's names) and put it within the same workbook as the data from the recycling project. The rows and columns on this worksheet/database are not to be calculated; however, they can be manipulated. Note Figure 4.3 is a screen shot of a sample of John's full student database with all of the rows representing individual student records and the columns representing the specific fields of information found within each record. Note also how the data in this fashion can now be manipulated by sorting it in a specific way (Figure 4.4 reveals students based on the class periods when they take science) and by filtering it (Figure 4.5 reveals only those who participated as leaders in the recycling project) in order to get quick, specific information from the overall data.

Figure 4.3 A sample of Mr. Rena's database of student information

	A	B	C	D	E	F	G	H	I	J
1	Last Name	First name	Class period	Leader	Phone	Address	City	State	Zip	Parents
2	Barrymore	Cade	5	no	478-5211	134 South 300 North	Lafayette	IN	47905	Mr. & Mrs. Barrymore
3	DeFore	Alexis	3	yes	472-4578	11439 US Hwy 245	Lafayette	IN	47908	Beverly DeFore
4	Drury	Landon	3	no	447-0999	2393 W. 100 N	Lafayette	IN	47905	John and Dee Drury
5	Jeski	Robert	4	no	472-8356	4839 W. 100 N	Lafayette	IN	47905	Mr. & Mrs. Jeski
6	Moreno	Elizabeth	2	yes	424-2252	3147 St. Rd. 39	E. Lafayette	IN	47902	Barry and Elana Swartz
7	Packard	Dale	1	no	472-6854	5214 Autumn Ln.	Lafayette	IN	47905	Mr. & Mrs. Packard
8	Polk	Madison	4	yes	472-7531	434 W. Monty St.	Lafayette	IN	47908	Roberta Thomas
9	Primm	Kenny	1	no	421-0990	200 Ferry St.	Lafayette	IN	47905	Jacob and Bernice Pietro
10	Sanchez	Valerie	1	yes	538-7732	2905 Holly Hill Dr.	Lafayette	IN	47905	Louis and Claudia Sanchez
11	Saterwaite	Kimberly	5	yes	424-6587	106 Meridian St.	E. Lafayette	IN	47902	Mr. & Mrs. Tim Saterwaite
12	Scherrer	Mark	2	no	572-8876	3626 Debbie Drive	E. Lafayette	IN	47902	David Scherrer
13	Smith	Fiona	4	no	424-9921	2561 Midline Ct.	E. Lafayette	IN	47902	Andrew Smith
14	Trager	Carlie	5	no	472-7753	2340 yeager Rd.	E. Lafayette	IN	47902	Bonita and Charles Welcher
15	Washington	Violet	2	yes	478-3321	300 Main St.	Lafayette	IN	47905	Suzy and Dave Washington
16	Weingram	Ralph	3	yes	443-9090	452 Rockhill Dr.	Lafayette	IN	47905	Terra and Bill Weingram
17										

Can data   **Student Info**

Figure 4.4 Mr. Rena's sample database *sorted* based on his student's class period

	A	B	C	D	E	F	G	H	I	J
1	Last Name	First name	Class period	Leader	Phone	Address	City	State	Zip	Parents
2	Packard	Dale	1	no	472-6854	5214 Autumn Ln.	Lafayette	IN	47905	Mr. & Mrs. Packard
3	Primm	Kenny	1	no	421-0990	200 Ferry St.	Lafayette	IN	47905	Jacob and Bernice Pietro
4	Sanchez	Valerie	1	yes	538-7732	2905 Holly Hill Dr.	Lafayette	IN	47905	Louis and Claudia Sanchez
5	Moreno	Elizabeth	2	yes	424-2252	3147 St. Rd. 39	E. Lafayette	IN	47902	Barry and Elana Swartz
6	Scherrer	Mark	2	no	572-8876	3626 Debbie Drive	E. Lafayette	IN	47902	David Scherrer
7	Washington	Violet	2	yes	478-3321	300 Main St.	Lafayette	IN	47905	Suzy and Dave Washington
8	DeFore	Alexis	3	yes	472-4578	11439 US Hwy 245	Lafayette	IN	47908	Beverly DeFore
9	Drury	Landon	3	no	447-0999	2393 W. 100 N	Lafayette	IN	47905	John and Dee Drury
10	Weingram	Ralph	3	yes	443-9090	452 Rockhill Dr.	Lafayette	IN	47905	Terra and Bill Weingram
11	Jeski	Robert	4	no	472-8356	4839 W. 100 N.	Lafayette	IN	47905	Mr. & Mrs. Jeski
12	Polk	Madison	4	yes	472-7531	434 W. Monty St.	Lafayette	IN	47908	Roberta Thomas
13	Smith	Fiona	4	no	424-9921	2561 Midline Ct.	E. Lafayette	IN	47902	Andrew Smith
14	Barrymore	Cade	5	no	478-5211	134 South 300 North	Lafayette	IN	47905	Mr. & Mrs. Barrymore
15	Saterwaite	Kimberly	5	yes	424-6587	106 Meridian St.	E. Lafayette	IN	47902	Mr. & Mrs. Tim Saterwaite
16	Trager	Carlie	5	no	472-7753	2340 yeager Rd.	E. Lafayette	IN	47902	Bonita and Charles Welcher
17										

Can data   **Student Info**

Figure 4.5 Mr. Rena's database *filtered* to show only those students who performed the role of leaders on the recycling project

	A	B	C	D	E	F	G	H	I	J
1	Last Nam ▼	First nar ▼	Class peri ▼	Leader ▾	Phone ▼	Address ▼	City ▼	Sta ▼	Zi ▼	Parents ▼
4	Sanchez	Valerie	1	yes	538-7732	2905 Holly Hill Dr.	Lafayette	IN	47905	Louis and Claudia Sanchez
5	Moreno	Elizabeth	2	yes	424-2252	3147 St. Rd. 39	E. Lafayette	IN	47902	Barry and Elana Swartz
7	Washington	Violet	2	yes	478-3321	300 Main St.	Lafayette	IN	47905	Suzy and Dave Washington
8	DeFore	Alexis	3	yes	472-4578	11439 US Hwy 245	Lafayette	IN	47908	Beverly DeFore
10	Weingram	Ralph	3	yes	443-9090	452 Rockhill Dr.	Lafayette	IN	47905	Terra and Bill Weingram
12	Polk	Madison	4	yes	472-7531	434 W. Monty St.	Lafayette	IN	47908	Roberta Thomas
15	Saterwaite	Kimberly	5	yes	424-6587	106 Meridian St.	E. Lafayette	IN	47902	Mr. & Mrs. Tim Saterwaite
17										

Can data   **Student Info**

No.	Feature	Steps to Get It Done
1	**Create and populate a new database**	1. Launch Excel. If a new worksheet does not appear, click on the Office button and select "New" from the drop-down menu. 2. Select the Blank Workbook and click on the Create button. A new, blank worksheet should appear and you can begin entering data.

continued

No.	Feature	Steps to Get It Done
		3. Go to Chapter 3 ("Spreadsheets") and review Steps 2–6 in Level 1. These steps will guide you in the following: • Insert, align, and format column headings • Enter data • Adjust columns and rows • Add gridlines • Format cells
2	**Sort the records**	1. Click anywhere within the database. 2. Go to **Data tab** >>> **Sort & Filter** group >>> **Sort** command button. The **Sort** dialog box (see Figure 4.6) will appear. You can also get this same Sort Window by clicking **Home tab** >>> **Editing** group >>> **Sort & Filter** command button >>> and then select the **Custom Sort** option. 3. Within the **Sort** dialog box, click the down arrow in the "Sort by" section (if you don't see a "Sort by" section, click on the "Add Level" button and the "Sort by" section will appear). A list of the column headings will appear. Select the field you want to base the sort on (e.g., Mr. Rena selected "Class period" as the column [field]). 4. Click OK and the sort will be completed. 5. To really get a hang of this, try sorting a number of different ways and use descending as well as ascending orders. **Figure 4.6** Sort window **Note:** In the **Sort** dialog box you can also select whether you have a header row on your database. This tells the database or spreadsheet to consider the first row as a listing of headings or as a record of data. In this case, we have a header and thus it needs to be marked as such.
3	**Create a comprehensive sort**	There may be times when you want to complete a sort of several different kinds of data at once. For example, in the database of students for the recycling project, you may find it helpful to see the database of students grouped by the city in which they live and then, within those cities, grouped by whether they were a leader in the recycling project. Such comprehensive sorts are completed in the following manner. 1. Click anywhere within the database and get the "Sort Window" to appear (**Data tab** >>> **Sort & Filter** group >>> **Sort**). 2. In the "Sort by" section, click on the drop-down arrow and click on the field (column header) that you want the first or primary sort to be based. 3. Click on the "Add Level" button and a new sort selection row ("Then by") will appear.

No.	Feature	Steps to Get It Done
		4. In the "Then by" section, click on the drop-down arrow and click on the field (column header) that you want the second sort to be based upon (see Figure 4.7). 5. Continue to add levels as needed for the comprehensive sort. 6. Once you have selected all of the levels and sort columns, then click OK and the sort will be completed. **Figure 4.7** Sort window with an added level 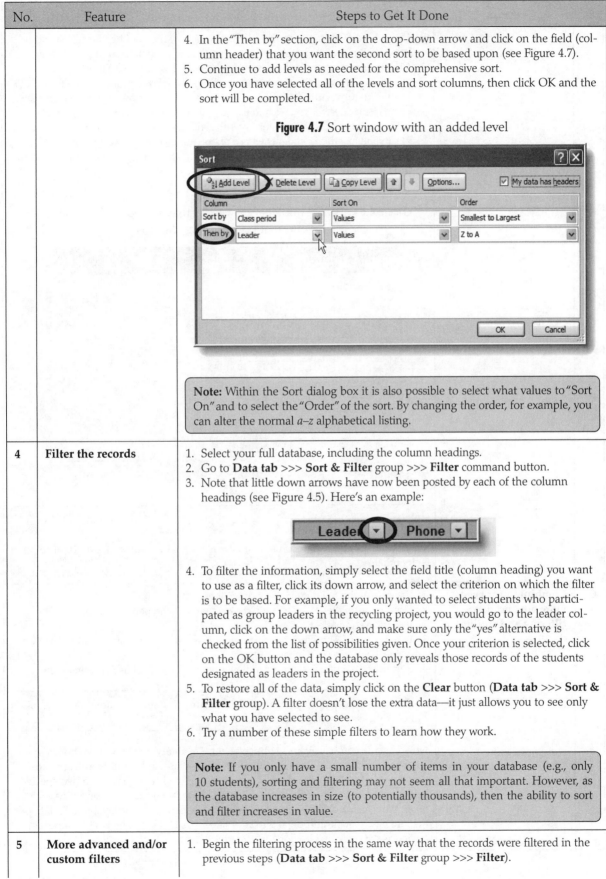 **Note:** Within the Sort dialog box it is also possible to select what values to "Sort On" and to select the "Order" of the sort. By changing the order, for example, you can alter the normal *a–z* alphabetical listing.
4	**Filter the records**	1. Select your full database, including the column headings. 2. Go to **Data tab** >>> **Sort & Filter** group >>> **Filter** command button. 3. Note that little down arrows have now been posted by each of the column headings (see Figure 4.5). Here's an example: Leader ▼ Phone ▼ 4. To filter the information, simply select the field title (column heading) you want to use as a filter, click its down arrow, and select the criterion on which the filter is to be based. For example, if you only wanted to select students who participated as group leaders in the recycling project, you would go to the leader column, click on the down arrow, and make sure only the "yes" alternative is checked from the list of possibilities given. Once your criterion is selected, click on the OK button and the database only reveals those records of the students designated as leaders in the project. 5. To restore all of the data, simply click on the **Clear** button (**Data tab** >>> **Sort & Filter** group). A filter doesn't lose the extra data—it just allows you to see only what you have selected to see. 6. Try a number of these simple filters to learn how they work. **Note:** If you only have a small number of items in your database (e.g., only 10 students), sorting and filtering may not seem all that important. However, as the database increases in size (to potentially thousands), then the ability to sort and filter increases in value.
5	**More advanced and/or custom filters**	1. Begin the filtering process in the same way that the records were filtered in the previous steps (**Data tab** >>> **Sort & Filter** group >>> **Filter**).

continued

No.	Feature	Steps to Get It Done
		2. Once the down arrows are positioned by each of the field headings, select the key criterion that you desire by selecting the appropriate column. 3. Click the down arrow for the selected column and select **"Text Filter"** and then **"Custom Filters. . . ."** A **Custom AutoFilter** dialog box will appear (see Figure 4.8). 4. In the **Custom AutoFilter** dialog box, use the down arrow button to select the comparison operator you wish to use (e.g., equals, contains, and so on). In the box next to the comparison operator, enter the criterion you wish to compare. For example, to find just those students whose phone numbers begin with the prefix 472, select the comparison operator of "begins with" and type in the "472" in the box to the right. 5. Click OK and note how the filter has worked. **Figure 4.8** Custom AutoFilter dialog box that is used to access specific information within the database 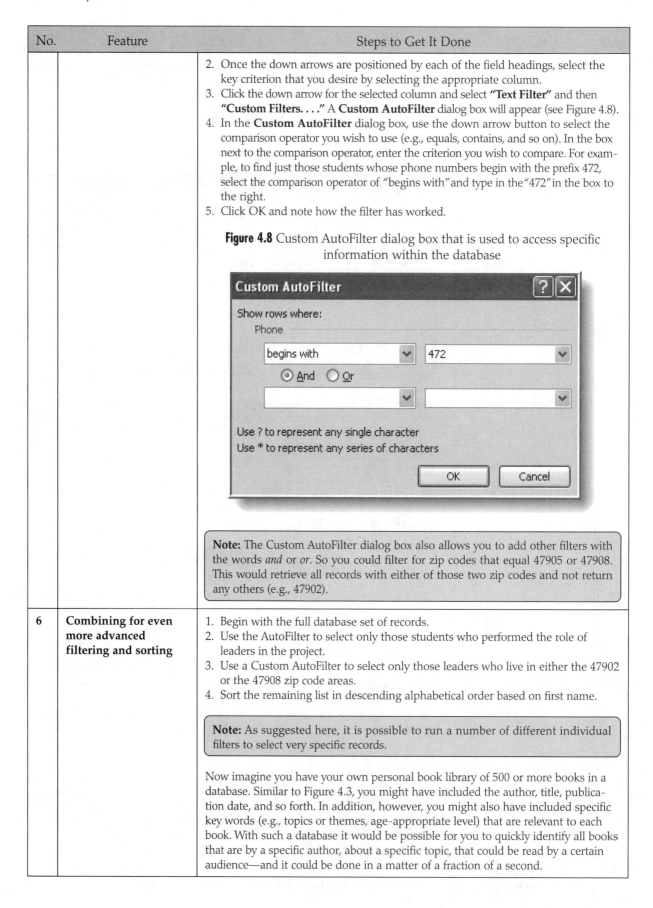 **Note:** The Custom AutoFilter dialog box also allows you to add other filters with the words *and* or *or*. So you could filter for zip codes that equal 47905 or 47908. This would retrieve all records with either of those two zip codes and not return any others (e.g., 47902).
6	**Combining for even more advanced filtering and sorting**	1. Begin with the full database set of records. 2. Use the AutoFilter to select only those students who performed the role of leaders in the project. 3. Use a Custom AutoFilter to select only those leaders who live in either the 47902 or the 47908 zip code areas. 4. Sort the remaining list in descending alphabetical order based on first name. **Note:** As suggested here, it is possible to run a number of different individual filters to select very specific records. Now imagine you have your own personal book library of 500 or more books in a database. Similar to Figure 4.3, you might have included the author, title, publication date, and so forth. In addition, however, you might also have included specific key words (e.g., topics or themes, age-appropriate level) that are relevant to each book. With such a database it would be possible for you to quickly identify all books that are by a specific author, about a specific topic, that could be read by a certain audience—and it could be done in a matter of a fraction of a second.

Level 1a Workout: Practice using the basic database features

For you to feel comfortable using a database, you really need to practice developing and playing with a set of data in this format. With this first workout, we want you to review all that was presented in the step-by-step procedures. However, there are many other things that were not touched on within this chapter, so as you work on this exercise, please explore and try some of the new aspects you encounter. In addition, you may need to refer to Chapter 3 ("Spreadsheets") to recall and use some of the basic Excel features.

Here is a basic outline of what you need to do:

1. Review Figures 4.3–4.5.
2. Either open the existing version of student database on the text's accompanying Web site (**www.prenhall.com/newby**) >>> **Chapter 4** >>> **Level 1 Workout** >>> **Student-Info**), or if you like, you can open a new worksheet and enter the information yourself. Once opened (or once you have typed it in), your worksheet should look something like Figure 4.3.
3. Using that database, complete the following:

   a. Add an additional field of information (e.g., favorite subject in school, sports he or she plays, total cans contributed) by inserting a new column heading and filling in an estimate of the data for each of the students.
   b. Add records for several other students to the list and fill in all of the relevant fields of information.
   c. Save the newly revised spreadsheet or database to your hard drive, flash drive, and so on. Use a specific name that you can remember and access at a later time.
   d. Select a field of information and sort the data based on that field.
   e. Select one of the cities listed and filter the data so that only those students living in that specific city are listed.
   f. Complete an advanced filter by having the database only reveal those students who live in the city of Lafayette with a last name that begins with either a *W* or a *B*.

> **Note:** Refer to specific feature numbers and the given step-by-step procedures as needed. Additionally, use the mentoring videos to help guide you through any specific procedure that needs additional clarification.

Level 1b Workout: Creating your own database

We all work and interact with databases. In this workout, identify something in your life that you can develop into a simple database. It might include a list of the music you own (a compilation of all of your CDs and MP3 files), electronic games that you have mastered, collections you have assembled (e.g., stamps, coins, Beanie Babies), family medical records, or articles assembled for a literature review.

For the Level 1b Workout, create a database that includes your own data. Your database should include a minimum of 10 records with a minimum of 5 fields of information for each record.

As you can see, there is a variety of the type of data that can be collected. After you have determined what data you will use, do the following:

1. Open your spreadsheet program and create a draft worksheet that includes your columns and rows of your data. Include column titles.
2. Review Scenario 1 and all of the sorting and filtering features demonstrated within Figures 4.3–4.5.
3. Print a copy of the full database as you have completed it.

4. Complete a sort of the full database and print a copy of the newly sorted data.
5. Filter the database in some relevant manner and print a copy of the filtered data.
6. On the full database, complete an advanced filter with an additional sort and print the results.
7. Compare all of the printouts and note the potential value of each of the sorted and filtered data.

Use Table 4.1 as a checklist to guide your efforts.

Table 4.1 Level 1 Workout and Practice Checklist Creating, Sorting, and Filtering a Database of Information

Database Content	___ Records were organized in a clear, logical manner.
	___ Relevant fields of data were included.
Database Sort	___ The full database was sorted based on a selected field of information.
	___ A comprehensive sort was completed using a minimum of two levels of information fields.
	___ A specific subset of data was generated through a simple filtering of the data based on a selected field of information.
	___ An additional subset of data was identified through the use of a custom filter that employed a minimum of one comparison operators.
	___ A final subset of data was created that included data that was both sorted and filtered.

Level 2: Mail Merge and Other Good Stuff

What should you be able to do?

A real time saver comes with being able to use the data stored within a database. One of the best examples of such a use is the *mail merge*. In this section, we want you to develop a database file of information and merge it with a form letter. This will require you to effectively use the Help feature of Excel.

Getting some Help

As shown in Chapter 3, Help is an important element of the Excel and similar software programs. To use it, click the Help button on the tab bar of the main ribbon.

Clicking the Help button opens the Help window. From here you can browse general help topics, bring up a general table of contents of all Help topics, complete a search for a specific question that you might have, and so on.

| Home | Insert | Page Layout | Formulas | Data | Review | View | Developer | Add-Ins | ⑦ |

Excel Help button

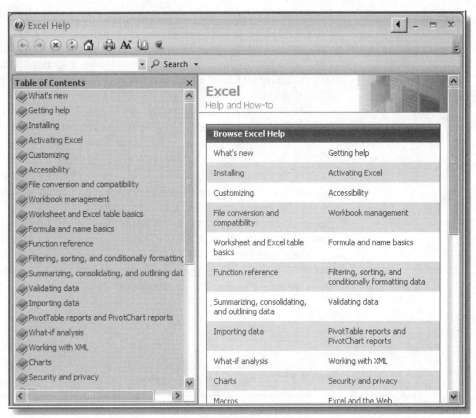

Word Help window

By typing in key words or even a full question, Help will respond with a variety of potential answers for you to investigate. Help generally does not have all of the answers—but it will have a lot of them. Make sure you get a sense for how it works and how often it can be of assistance.

Scenario 2: "Thanking those who helped"

Let's imagine that John Rena is still using his spreadsheet/database for his recycling project. Now that the recycling program has come to a successful conclusion at the end of the school year, he feels it necessary to send out some thank you notes to his students and their parents for all of the time and effort they put into making the project work. To do this, he is going to use the database of information that he has on all of his students. With that information, he can access names, addresses, parents' names, and even the names of those who served in leadership roles within the project.

With so many students involved, it could take quite a bit of time to handwrite all the needed notes. As we learned from Chapter 2, a word processor could help by writing a single letter and then entering different names and addresses for each of the students and printing each individual letter—but that also would take a lot of time for all of his students. With the data from the project collected within his spreadsheet and all of his student information data within his database, it is now possible for John to create one letter that grabs the needed information from the database to automatically personalize each letter. So even though he writes just one letter, this process will create a letter for each student that is addressed to each individual and that contains data relevant to that individual (e.g., personal address, data from his or her specific class period, parents' names). (*Note:* This is the same process used for the "personalized" junk mail you receive.) By allowing the computer to merge information from the database with a letter composed on a word processing program, John will save a lot of time. Letters, forms, mailing labels, and so on can be created to interactively use data from a selected database. The end result is the best of both worlds: a single document is created that magically pulls specific information from the database so that it appears written specifically for each student. This is known as a *mail merge*.

Within Level 2 of this software application, we want you to explore how to create a form letter or mail merge document, and then have you create one for your own use. Take a close look at the word processed letter (see Figure 4.9). We have left _____ spaces where the merged information is to go. (See Figure 4.10 with the merged fields inserted.) Once the information is merged with this form letter, then output such as Figure 4.11 can be created with very little additional effort. Note that only a single word document has been created, but when printing the documents, as many as needed can be produced, each with the _____ filled in with personally relevant information drawn from the database.

If you need any of these features and procedures to be demonstrated, access the text's Web site and view the mentoring videos for support (see **www.prenhall.com/newby** >>> **Chapter 4** >>> **Mentor Video**).

Figure 4.9 Sample letter that indicates where merging will occur

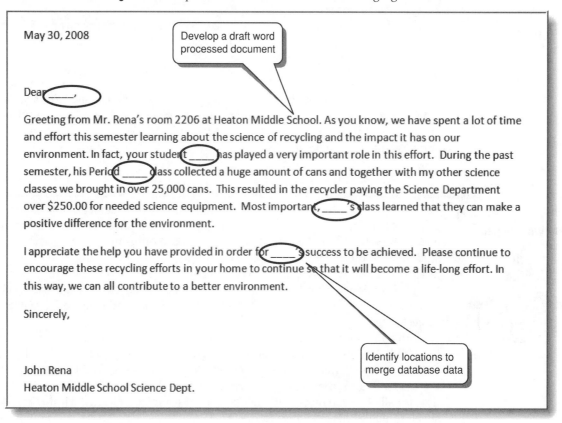

Figure 4.10 An example letter with merged fields inserted

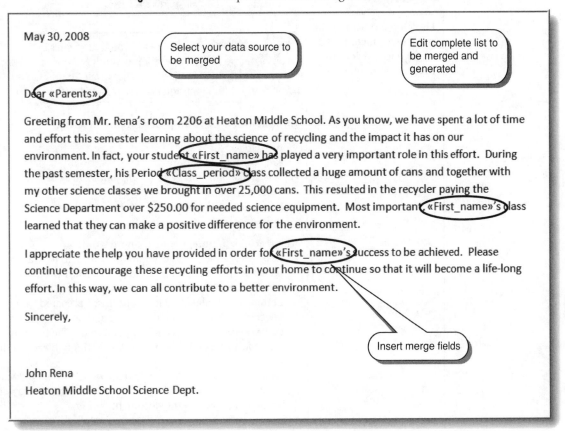

Figure 4.11 An example mail merge letter with actual student data inserted

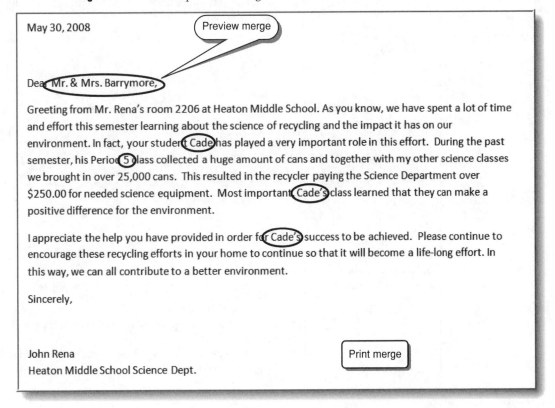

Feature	Steps to Get It Done
Develop a draft word processed document with placeholders for data to be merged	**Important note**: In most cases, you'll find it easier to complete the mail merge from within MS Word or similar word processing software. Likewise, the best Help to guide you through the merging process is found within Word. **Information about and procedure for creating:** Word Help ![] • Key word: **Mail Merge.** • Select *Use mail merge to create and print letters and other documents*. • Select *Set up the main document* and follow the given procedure. **Key features to note, explore, and try out:** • To begin the mail merge, within MS Word go to **Mailings tab >>> Start Mail Merge** group **>>> Start Mail Merge** (see Figure 4.12). From the drop-down gallery, select **Letters**. If you already have a document prepared, you can select to navigate to that document and open it. In addition, you can also select at this point to use the **Step-by-step Mail Merge Wizard** to walk you through each of the various steps of the merge. • Similar to Figure 4.12, create a draft word processed document. As you create it, think of how the database data will be integrated within the document. • You may find it convenient at this point to leave placeholders or spaces in locations where data will be merged. • Review the step-by-step procedures given within Scenarios 1 and 2 of Chapter 2 ("Word Processing"). Those procedures will guide you through the process of setting up and formatting a draft document.

Figure 4.12 Mailings tab with merge command groups

Select your data source to be merged	**Information and procedure:** Word Help ![] • Key word: **Mail Merge.** • Select *Use mail merge to create and print letters and other documents*. • Select *Connect the document to a data source* and follow the given procedure.

Feature	Steps to Get It Done
	Key features to note, explore, and try out: • Once your document has been created, it's time to connect it with the source of data that will be merged into it. Within MS Word, go to **Mailings tab** >>> **Start Mail Merge** group >>> **Select Recipients** (see Figure 4.12). • If you have already created the database, you can select the alternative for "Use existing list . . ." and navigate to that spreadsheet or database. **Note:** If your selected database or spreadsheet has multiple worksheets, you will need to select which worksheet contains the data you wish to merge. **Important note:** You can only merge data into a document from one data worksheet. If your data is on more than one worksheet, create a new single data worksheet that includes all the needed "to-be-merged" data, then connect your word processed document to that newly created data source.
Edit the list to be merged	**Information and procedure:** Word Help ▣ • Key word: **Mail Merge**. • Select *Use mail merge to create and print letters and other documents.* • Select *Refine the list of recipients or items* and follow the given procedure. **Key features to note, explore, and try out:** • Once the data source has been selected, you can click on the **Mailings tab** >>> **Start Mail Merge** group >>> **Edit Recipient List** (see Figure 4.12). This will bring up the Mail Merge Recipients dialog box. From this box you can refine your list via sorting, filtering, finding, and eliminating duplicates, and so on. You can also go directly to your data source (e.g., dbase1.xls) and edit the data.

continued

Feature	Steps to Get It Done
Insert merge fields	**Information and procedure:** Word Help 🔲 • Key word: **Mail Merge.** • Select *Use mail merge to create and print letters and other documents.* • Select *Add placeholders, called mail merge fields, to the document* and follow the given procedure. **Key features to note, explore, and try out:** • In your word processed document, place your cursor where you want the data to be inserted. • Go to the **Mailings tab** >>> **Write & Insert Fields** group >>> **Insert Merge Field** (see Figure 4.12). • A drop-down gallery of the potential fields of information that can be inserted will appear (these are the column heads from your source database or spreadsheet). Select the category you wish to merge at that point in your document. • A placeholder (e.g., <<Parents>>) with the title of the merged category will be inserted in your document where your cursor was located. • Repeat this procedure and insert placeholders for all needed merges within your document.
Preview and print results	**Information and procedure:** Word Help 🔲 • Key word: **Mail Merge.** • Select *Use mail merge to create and print letters and other documents.* • Select *Preview and complete the merge* and follow the given procedure. **Key features to note, explore, and try out:** • Go to the **Mailings tab** >>> **Preview Results** group >>> **Preview Results** (see Figure 4.12). • Check to see that the document now has the correctly inserted merged data for your first recipient. • You can click through all of the database and see each of the merged documents. • Once you are satisfied with your results, click on the **Mailings tab** >>> **Finish** group >>> **Finish & Merge** (see Figure 4.12). • From the drop-down gallery of options, select to print. A small dialog box will appear that will allow you to select which of the documents you wish to send to the printer.

Level 2a Workout: Practice using additional database features

Before moving on to your own work, it might be wise to try a couple of exercises with Mr. Rena's class's database.

1. Go to the text's accompanying Web site and open Mr Rena's database that includes information on some of his students (**www.prenhall.com/newby**>>> **Chapter 4** >>> **Level 2a Workout** >>> **recycle students**).

2. Using the information provided within the Level 2, Scenario 2, of this chapter, create a simple word processed document and insert data from the recycle students

database of information. Make sure when you merge you do a minimum of the following:

- Include at least four or five merged fields within your document.
- Review, edit, and select four or more final documents to be printed with different data merged on each document.
- Create envelopes or mailing labels for each of the letters that you created using the same mail merge process and data source.

> **Note:** For additional support, each of these key features is demonstrated on the mentoring videos within the text's accompanying Web site. Go to **www.prenhall.com/newby** >>> **Chapter 4** >>> **Mentor Videos.**

Level 2b Workout: Create your way to manage data

With this information and example, create a database (from Microsoft's Excel) that you can use. Keep it simple at first. Perhaps it can be for your CD collection, your book collection, your Christmas card address book, a bibliography of special articles, inventory of school items you have in your storage place at school, your special medications—something pertinent to your life.

Adapt the database so that it contains something you can use. Practice sorting and looking at different views of the database through the use of various filters. Finally, save your database, close it, and then open MS Word. Complete a mail merge using a new document you create and the data from the records within your database. Examine each of the merged documents, pat yourself on the back, and then begin to imagine all of the ways that this little tool might be able to help you with various bits of data that you have laying around.

Use Table 4.2 as a checklist to make sure you have included a number of key features that have been highlighted within Scenarios 1 and 2 of this chapter (see Figures 4.3–4.5 and 4.9–4.11).

> **Note:** Invoke Rule 2—Save your work!

Table 4.2 Level 2 Workout and Practice Checklist Completing a Mail Merge

Data Source	___ A database of relevant information was created.
	___ All data fields are clearly labeled and organized.
Original Document Content	___ A new word processed document was created.
	___ The document has been clearly written, with no spelling or grammatical errors.
	___ The document has been formatted for efficient and effective reading and comprehension.
	___ Placeholders for the "to-be-merged" data have been inserted.
	___ A final subset of data was created that included data that was both sorted and filtered.
Merged Document	___ Data from data source was properly merged into new merged document.
	___ Copies of the merged document, with different data within each copy, were produced.

Level 3: Integration and Application

What should you be able to do?

It's important for you to picture how the use of a database can be relevant to both you and your students. This section is to help you see all of the many applications possible that involve a database. You can use these examples as a springboard to launch ideas on ways to improve levels of student learning and your personal productivity.

Introduction

Within Levels 1 and 2 of this chapter, we focused on database management from the perspective of your learning to use it. But to extend its use, you need to think about data management as a means to enhance the learning experience of students. There are times when integrating databases within a learning situation may actually improve the learning opportunities and possibilities of the learners. However, there are other times when such integration would be more of a hassle than the potential benefits warrant. Learning to tell the difference can help you be successful in what you develop and use in your classroom.

Database management integration

Creating the enhanced learning experience: A partial lesson plan

Topic: A study of the people, places, and culture of an African country.

Overview:

Mr. Carpenter (as explained in Chapters 3 and 4) is a middle school social studies teacher determined to help his students expand their understanding of various countries of the world. For this school year, his classes have the opportunity to work with Jonathon Rogers, a university graduate student who is on an internship working for an international health and education organization in the African country of Zimbabwe. With Jonathon's help, Mr. Carpenter's eighth graders are able to obtain first-hand information about the country, people, and culture of Zimbabwe.

Through research, the students have learned that Zimbabwe is a country with many exotic animals. In fact, much of its total economy is based on the tourist industry. People from all over the world travel to this African country to see elephants, tigers, and giraffe in their natural habitats.

Specific Learning Task:

Zimbabwe is a country of national parks that have been set aside to protect the animals and habitats found there. Each of the parks is noted for unique animals and plants. Members of the class are to research the parks and obtain information about the location and size of the park, the types of animals and plants that reside there, and the major problems inherent with protecting, operating, and maintaining each park.

Sample Learning Objectives:

Students will be able to do the following:

1. List and describe (e.g., animal and plant life, geographical features) several national parks within Zimbabwe.
2. Plan a safari through Zimbabwe to photograph and videotape exotic animals in their natural habitats.
3. Describe the problems and challenges that administrators and governmental officials face as they attempt to preserve the wildlife and habitats of the national parks of Zimbabwe.

Procedure:

1. Examine the following list of National Parks within Zimbabwe; Chimanimani National Park, Chizarira National Park, Kazuma Pan National Park, Mana Pools National Park, Zambezi National Park.
2. Divide the class into groups, and have each group complete Internet and library research on their selected national park.
3. Have each group answer the following questions about their national park:

    a. Where is their park located (i.e., in what part of Zimbabwe)?
    b. What is the size of the park?
    c. What types of animals and plants are found within the park?
    d. What are some unique characteristics of the park? That is, if you were to visit this park, what are some key things you should really do and see?
    e. What are the chief problems or challenges facing the park in today's world?

4. Contact Jonathon to see if he can obtain any further information about the parks (e.g., Has he visited one? Has he any stories? Can he suggest anyone to contact to get further information? Does he have any pictures?)
5. Have the students compile a report and/or presentation on their selected park.
6. Following the presentations, facilitate a discussion focused on the challenges facing the parks today. Potential lead questions could be as follows: (a) Should a poor country such as Zimbabwe be investing money in the parks at this time when the level of poverty of the people is so high? Should outside (richer) countries help to take care of the parks and wildlife found within Zimbabwe?

Question of Database Integration:

This activity could be completed with or without the use of database software. Use these reflective questions to explore the value of potentially integrating database software within such an activity as outlined by Mr. Carpenter.

- What benefit would there be to compiling the information on the national parks in a database? How could such a database be used in a classroom setting?
- How could such a database be used to compare and contrast various elements of the individual parks?
- Could a database be used to organize resources for a research project?
- How could a national parks database aid in teaching students about (1) identifying issues that face the parks and (2) suggesting potential solutions for these issues?
- How could a lesson (from a future teaching area or grade level) that uses databases to promote critical thinking be described briefly?

Level 3a Workout: Integrating database management

Using the example lesson plan as a guide, follow the steps in this workout as you think about the potential use of databases within various applied settings.

1. Read each of the following situations. Imagine being directly involved in the planning for each of these projects. Select one (or more if you wish) for further consideration.

Bird Watchers

A fourth-grade teacher wants her students to learn how to categorize. On a field trip to the local zoo, she has her students record all of the different types of birds that they see and that are identified within the zoo. Once back into the classroom, the students begin to list the different characteristics of the birds (types of food they eat, country of origin, feather colors and markings, distances and speed of flight, color and size of eggs, and so on). Once the list has been gathered, students are given novel examples and are asked to group the bird with those from the list that are most similar based on various critical characteristics.

Internet Web sites

Do the types of favorite Internet sites frequently visited by individuals differ based on gender, age, or racial background? This was a question posed by a high school psychology teacher. To measure the potential differences, a survey was created for all elementary, middle, and secondary students in the school district. Responses asked for students to indicate what were their top three favorite Internet sites, what were the top three most useful, and how much time they spent weekly on the Internet.

Theme Park Comparisons

What are the "best" theme or amusement parks in the world? Mr. Ramollo wants his fifth-grade students to compare various theme or amusement parks around the world to see which ones would be rated the very best. Students needed to develop a list of key characteristics for the theme parks and then use the Internet to investigate which theme parks achieved the highest ranking for each of the categories.

Internet Cafés

An investor wants to know where would be the best place to make an investment in an Internet café. Such cafés are used throughout the world as places individuals can visit to rent time on a computer to use e-mail and surf the Internet. The cafés seem to have their greatest success in those countries that have high populations, relatively low income, and poor postal systems. How can this investor determine some locations throughout the world that may be prime areas for such an investment?

2. Based on your selected project, consider the following questions that concern the integration of database management software. Mark your response to each question.

Integration assessment questionnaire (IAQ)

Will using **DATABASE MANAGEMENT** software as a part of the project:			
Broaden the learners' perspective on potential solution paths and/or answers?	___Yes	___ No	___ Maybe
Increase the level of involvement and investment of personal effort by the learners?	___Yes	___ No	___ Maybe
Increase the level of learner motivation (e.g., increase the relevance of the to-be-learned task, the confidence of dealing with the task, and/or the overall appeal of the task)?	___Yes	___ No	___ Maybe
Decrease the time needed to generate potential solutions?	___Yes	___No	___ Maybe
Increase the quality and/or quantity of learner practice working on this and similar projects?	___Yes	___No	___Maybe
Increase the quality and/or quantity of feedback given to the learner?	___Yes	___No	___Maybe
Enhance the ability of the student to solve novel but similar projects, tasks, and problems in the future?	___Yes	___No	___Maybe

3. If you have responded "Yes" to one or more of the IAQ questions, you should consider the use of database management software to enhance the student's potential learning experience.
4. Using the sample lesson plan, develop a lesson plan based on this project. Within the plan, indicate how and when the learner will use a database. Additionally, list potential benefits and challenges that may occur when involving this software within the lesson.

Level 3b Workout: Exploring the NETS Standard connection

Developing and executing a lesson plan that integrates the use of database management software directly addresses several of the NETS for both teachers (NETS*T) and students (NETS*S). See the Appendix for a full listing of the standards.

Part A:

Generally, the main purpose for learning and using application software is to increase one's level of production—that is, to do things faster, better, or both. NETS standards (NETS*T Standard V and NETS*S Standard 6) help you focus on these productivity objectives for both teachers and students. There are other technology standards, however, that may also be potentially addressed through one's knowledge and use of database software. Reflect on the following questions and consider the potential impact of database management integration:

- How could the integration of database software improve the collection, organization, analysis, comparison, and assessment of data collected by the teacher and/or the students? Could an enhanced capability of searching and sorting data lead to increased levels of analysis, synthesis, and creative problem solving? (NETS*T III.C. and IV.B.; NET*S 3 and 4)
- In what ways could the use of database management software facilitate the higher order skills of comparison, synthesis, and evaluation between large sets of information? Would higher order learning of specific content area materials be increased as one develops, organizes, and populates a database system? (NETS*T IV.A. and V.B.; NETS*S 1 and 4)
- Could a database be used (e.g., mail merge) to facilitate the communication and collaboration between teachers, students, parents, and subject matter experts on specific projects that ultimately impact student learning? (NETS*T V.D. and VI.B.; NET*S 2)

Part B:

Go to the ISTE Web site http://cnets.iste.org. Within that site, select to review either the student or the teacher NETS Standards. Once you have selected the standards to review, select either the student or teacher profiles and look for the corresponding scenarios. Review the scenarios and determine how databases could be used within several of those situations.

While visiting the ISTE Web site and exploring the scenarios, go to the lesson plan search area and select a number of different lesson plans of interest. Review those and determine the role (if any) of databases within the development, implementation, and assessment of the lesson. Note this from both the perspective of the teacher developing the lesson and from the perspective of the student participating in the implemented lesson.

Further ideas on using data management as a learning tool

Note: These ideas are to help you generate your own. Don't let it bother you if they aren't the right content or grade level—use one and adapt it to be helpful within your own situation. These are meant to be stimuli for additional ideas.

Here are a few ideas that may help you see how a database might be beneficial:

1. Give the students a table for them to investigate and fill out. The table might include comparative fields of information about countries, people, places, and so forth. Help the students see trends in the data by sorting or filtering based on specific criteria. For example, have them collect data on weather patterns for various geographic regions around the world. Based on a comparison of average temperatures, what could the students predict about the type of agriculture that can be produced for that region?
2. Have the students collect data within a specific experiment. For example, using different degrees of acid-based water for plants, measure the growth rate of different

types of plants. With the database compare various acid levels and predict what the impact of acid rain would be on plant life given certain concentrations of acid within the rain.

3. Have the students create a database of the world's most recognized scientists during the 17th, 18th, 19th, and 20th centuries. Have them categorize the type discoveries made and the country of origin. Have the students examine, sort, and filter the data to see from which parts of the world the most notable discoveries came and if there are specific trends based on location, century, and so on.

4. Have the students create a reference database of research articles (including author, title, full publication information, key words, and short annotated bibliography) and then merge the information into the reference section of a research paper you have assigned.

5. Using this reference list database, have students cooperatively create a database of articles about a specific topic (e.g., cyber ethics) and combine their efforts together into a single large database for students to use on a related research project.

6. Have the students develop a database about their favorite animal (or state, or national park, or relative). Have them list all of the salient features of their animal (name, what it looks like, color) and then have them all combine their efforts into a single database of information. Have the students then search and sort based on specific characteristics and note the common elements of the different selected animals.

7. Have the students identify different symptoms of various ailments or conditions. Also have them include the name of the ailment and potential prescriptions to overcome the problem. Give the students specific scenarios that require them to filter their database based on symptoms and determine possible prescriptions for solutions.

8. Develop databases about different types of governments from countries of the world. Include information about population, average income, religious affiliations, and so forth. Filter to compare the type of government expected given specific religions, affiliations, such as of the respective country's population.

Additional ideas for using data management as an assistant

1. **Organizer.** For the classroom teacher, databases are frequently used to help organize information. For example, if you have a personal book collection, it would be wise to have a database that lists all of the relevant information about the books, their locations, and so on. You can even get fancy and indicate which of the books has been borrowed and by whom. This is a great way to avoid buying multiple copies of the same book and to know where they are all located.

2. **Label maker.** Create all kinds of folder labels. In your filing cabinets you have all kinds of folders with different lesson plans, activities, and so forth. A database of these titles with the ability to mail merge labels allows you to quickly print off labels for those folders.

3. **Label maker II.** On the first day of class (or when you are going on a field trip, dividing kids into special activity groups, for example), create name tags via a label mail merge with your student info database.

4. **Mailing lists.** Create info sheets of all of your students, parents, and possible others. You can keep specific information about each of your students and use that to sort, filter, or merge within personalized letters.

5. **Lesson plans.** List all of your lesson plans based, for instance, on content, type of learner, instructional methods, and media.

6. **Electronic portfolios.** Create a database that allows you to know what is in each of your students' portfolios, assessment information, location of the pieces, and so forth. With electronic means you can even save and duplicate versions of the students' work when needed.

7. **Examples.** Use a database to list all of your examples of your past students' work, what lesson plan the project relates to, key words about it, and where it is located so that you can find it again to show other students.

Chapter 5

PRESENTATION SOFTWARE
MS PowerPoint: The Basics of Creating Presentations, Handouts, and Much, Much More

Introduction

What should you know about presentation software? 	Presentation software (e.g., Microsoft's PowerPoint) is designed to help you get your message across to others and look good in the process. This software can become one of the most interesting, enjoyable, and fruitful for both students and teachers to learn. Within this introduction, we want you to discover the following: • What a presentation program is, what it can do, and how it can help in teaching and learning • How to justify the use of the presentation program as an effective tool—by knowing when and why it should or shouldn't be used

Terms to know	slide	normal view	action button
	slide sorter view	slide show view	Master slide
	animations	template	

What is presentation software and what does it do?	Presentation software is a computer application that allows you to do just what the name implies—create and deliver presentations. As a teacher and/or student a great deal of learning focuses on presentations of some kind—thus this application is one that should become a regular in your learning arsenal. Review Figure 5.1 and note the three slides that have been created as part of a presentation about computer hardware. With relative ease, you can build individual slides and then sequence them together into a full **slide** show. On each slide you can put text, pictures, Internet links, audio clips, **animations**, video clips—the list goes on. Plus you can instruct this program to create handouts and run itself automatically if you want the "no-hands" approach. With all of these benefits, it's also a great tool to have students use as they design and create their own presentations.

What are some commonly used presentation-type software?	• Microsoft's PowerPoint • Apple's Keynote • Corel's WordPerfect Presentations • Lotus's Freelance Graphics • Sun Microsystems' StarOffice/OpenOffice Impress • GoBe Productive

Figure 5.1 Three individual slides or screens in a PowerPoint presentation

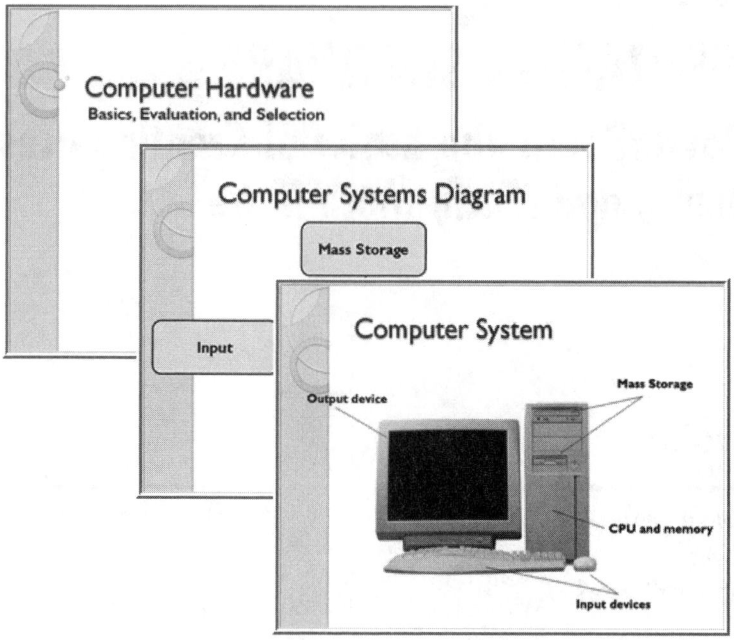

Computer Hardware
Basics, Evaluation, and Selection

Computer Systems Diagram

Mass Storage

Input

Computer System

Output device

Mass Storage

CPU and memory

Input devices

> **Note:** We focus on MS PowerPoint (PPT). However, **all of what we present can be done in most of these other presentation programs listed**. So if you don't have access to MS PPT, don't be alarmed — you can still complete the projects and learn the basic skills.

Why bother learning how to use PPT or other forms of presentation software?

- **Quality shows.** (PPT) allows you to create presentations that will pleasantly surprise you. Suddenly your work can look better and your message will be cleaner and clearer for your audience.
- **It's fast.** Because many of the processes within this program are automated, you can learn to develop presentations in very quick order. You can brainstorm using an outlining function within the program and immediately turn the outline into a basic set of presentation slides. This helps when time is important (and when is time *not* important?).
- **It's easy to adapt.** Once you have the basics of a presentation completed, you can easily adapt and change it to fit a new audience. It also works well with other programs. If you have a graph in Excel and want it included—PPT can do that. Or if you have a poem in a word processed file, a simple cut and paste and it's now in your presentation.
- **Ease of adding multimedia.** Sometimes a picture can say a 1000 words—so here's the chance to use visuals, audio, video clips, additional Web sites, and so forth, to enhance your presentation. All can be added with relative ease and speed.
- **Two (or three) things at once.** Guess what? As you are working to develop your presentation slides, PPT automatically creates handouts you can print, copy, and

have ready to distribute. Likewise, as you finish your presentation, if you want to "put it on the Web"—it is ready to go. Such features allow you to look like you put in more effort than actually needed.

- **Helps with learning.** Often we hear "The teacher actually learns the most." You can use this to the benefit of your students by having them develop presentations.
- **It's not just for oral presentations any more.** PPT can be a very effective and efficient way to create individualized instruction. For example, PPT can be used to set up learning centers that allow learners to select the sequence of information, give responses, and receive feedback on their efforts.
- **Creates its own backup system.** Suppose you go to a convention to deliver your presentation and they don't have the computer setup that you need. You can simply print your slide and copy it as a transparency to be used on a normal overhead machine. Also, the handouts can be used if the bulb in the overhead burns out.

How are presentation programs used at school? A brief list of ideas	**By the teacher:**	**By the student:**
	• Lectures and presentations • Individual tutorials • Parent–teacher nights • Classroom handouts • Staff development	• Student-made presentations • Oral reports • Electronic portfolios • Group projects • Science experiments

Orientation

What's the workspace look like?

Figure 5.2 shows the workspace of a common presentation program (MS PowerPoint). This figure depicts an example of a presentation currently being developed. Note the use of the outline area to quickly add content, and the note area used to add notes for the speaker. To view this example presentation (Computer Hardware), go to the text's accompanying Web site (**www.prenhall.com/newby** >>> **Chapter 5** >>> **Example Presentation** >>> **Computer_hardware**).

What commands can be used?

As in all MS Office applications (e.g., MS Word, MS Excel) there is a ribbon of tools that runs across the top of the work screen. Within each ribbon the actual tools that can be used to develop presentations are grouped together under the various command tabs (e.g., Home, Insert, Design, Animation). Selecting a specific tab reveals an associated command set or group. Once a command tab has been selected, this specific group remains visible and ready for use. Items within the set may appear as individual items or as a gallery of related items. For example, selecting the Design tab (see Figure 5.3) in PPT reveals a group of commands that deals specifically with the orientation of the slides, selecting or creating themes for the slide backgrounds, and how items can be arranged and grouped within the presentation.

The tabs have been developed to make your life easier. No longer do you have to go through hundreds of potential drop-down menu items to find the needed tool; the tabs allow you quick access to related groups of commands.

It should be noted that there are additional commands that will occasionally be needed. These contextual commands appear when a specific object like a picture, graphic, table, or chart is selected.

> **Note:** These command tabs have been developed to correspond directly with how you sequentially create a presentation in PPT. That is, as you start the development of a presentation, the key commands for creating and working on your first slide are found under the first tab (Home); as you develop a number of slides and need to add additional content, pictures, and so on, then the needed group is found by selecting the Insert command tab. Next, as you begin to bring all of the slides together to form a coherent presentation, the commands within the Design command tab are easily accessed.

Figure 5.2 Normal view of the workspace used to create PPT presentations

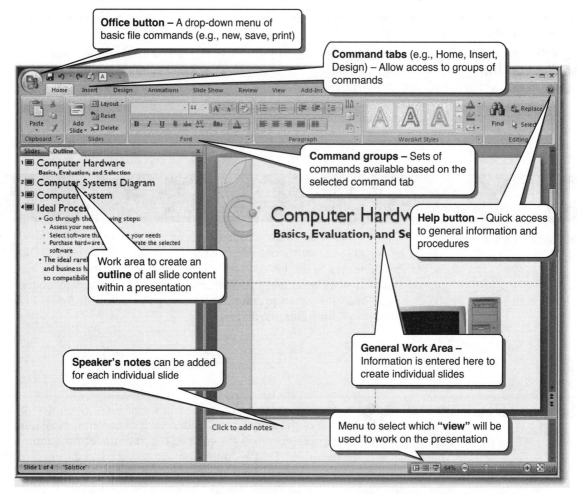

Figure 5.3 The ribbon holds the command tabs, groups, and individual commands

For more information about the PPT ribbon and command tabs, please review the Mentor Videos on the text's accompanying Web site (**www.prenhall.com/ newby >>> Chapter 5 >>> Mentor Video**).

Orientation Workout 1: Explore the territory

Turn on your computer and attempt the following:

1. Launch the PPT software.
2. Create a new PPT presentation with a blank first slide.
3. Explore the various tabs on the ribbon and the different command groups.
4. Create three or four new slides
5. On the various practice slides

   • Add text
   • Change the text's format (e.g., size, style)
   • Change the slide layout
   • Adjust the design templates
   • Add text to the speaker's notes
   • Switch between different views of the slides (e.g., normal vs. slide sorter vs. presentation)

Key features

Views   To work effectively within PPT, there are different ways that you can view your workspace. To select one of these views, click on the PPT ribbon's **View tab** and select from one of the views in the **Presentation View** command group. In addition, there's a **View** bar generally located on the lower right portion of the workspace in PPT that looks like ⊞ ⊞ ⊟. Clicking on these will also change the workspace view.

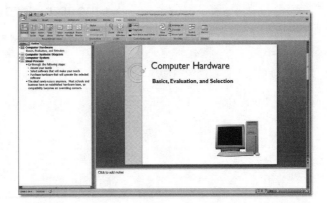

NORMAL View. ⊞ ⊞ ⊟

Note that you can view and work in the outline on the left, the slide itself (main work section), and enter in any speaker notes directly below the slide. This is generally the view used to complete most work. Figure 5.2 is a larger versions of this.

> **Note:** When you are creating a number of slides and entering a large amount of text *or* even when you are brainstorming a potential presentation, click on the Outline tab and work in that view. You can expand this view to a majority of the workspace; it's very similar to working in MS Word outline. This can facilitate the development of your presentation.

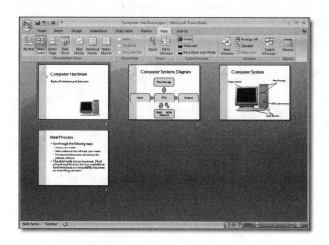

SLIDE SORTER View.

When you have a number of slides created, it often becomes difficult to change their order, to quickly see where a new slide needs to be inserted, or to delete a slide no longer needed. This is where the slide sorter view comes to the rescue. This view allows you to see all of your slides in smaller version that can easily be grabbed and moved, deleted, added, and sequenced to your specifications. You will also find that this is a good view to use if you are adding transitions between slides.

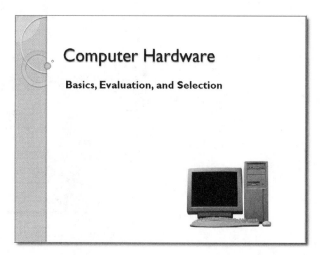

SLIDE SHOW View

This is the view that you use to present your slide program. Within this view, the slide takes up the full screen and no toolbars or other features are displayed. You should also note that within this view all of the animations, action buttons (more on those later) will be executed when selected to do so.

Slide Layouts   PPT has a number of different "premade" layouts that may match what you need for the slide you are about to create. Each layout already has inserted placeholders that may contain pictures, tables, titles, bulleted lists, and so forth. If one of these premade layouts matches your needs, it can be quickly selected, and then information can be automatically formatted to meet the specifications of your slide. You "point and click" and let the PPT layout do the work instead of taking the time to create the layout yourself. This can be a real time saver!

If you don't like the way it looks once you have used a layout, you can adapt it directly or select a different auto layout and have it reformat automatically for you.

How do you access the slide layouts?   Either create a new slide or go to the slide where you want to change the layout. Click the **Home tab** and then select the **Layout button** within the **Slides** group (**Home >>> Slides** group **>>> Layout**). Once the Layout button has been clicked, the slide layout gallery will appear (see Figure 5.4).

MAC USERS   Whenever a new slide is created, the "Slide Layout" window will appear. You can make a selection of the layout at that point. If you desire to change the layout at any time, **Format >>> Slide Layout . . .** will bring back the Slide Layout window.

Figure 5.4 New slide with Slide Layout gallery exposed

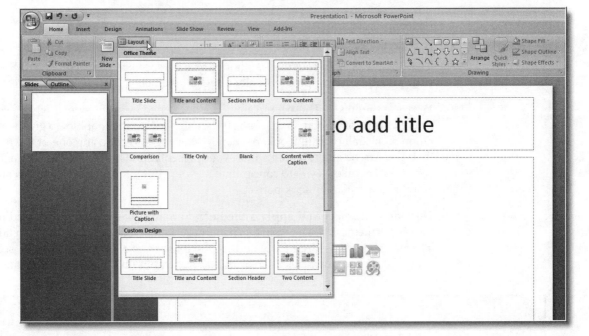

How does the slide layout work?   First, you select the layout of your choice (scroll through the Layout Gallery and click on your selection). The new slide will immediately be adapted to the type of layout you have selected (instructions to "Click to . . ." within dashed line boxes will indicate the placeholder). As you insert content or pictures, in your slide, you simply click in the area where you want to work. All spacing, fonts, and formatting have been done for you. Figure 5.5 is an example of a new slide with a slide layout that has been set up to allow for a title, text, and other elements such as tables, charts, pictures, video, to be quickly inserted. Again, a great way to speed the process along.

Figure 5.5 New slide with a selected slide layout

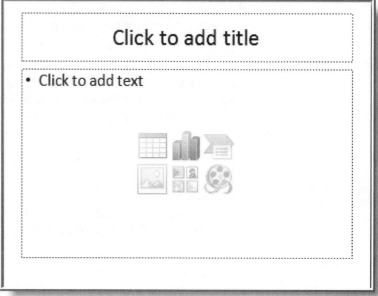

Themes

What is a theme?   Themes are already completed design settings that can be selected and applied to your presentation to give it a specific, consistent look. PPT comes with a large variety of professionally designed themes.

Why use themes?   These templates were developed by professionals who have considered the color combinations, font styles, and background graphics to give a presentation an overall polished look. By merely selecting and choosing one of the themes, that look can be incorporated within your presentation without any further effort on your part. This allows you to concentrate on your content for the presentation and not worry about making it look perfect.

How do you select and apply a theme?   Simply click the **Design tab** and review the various themes shown within the theme gallery of the **Theme** group (**Design tab** >>> **Theme** group >>> **Theme**). Note that there are extra themes that can be selected using the up and down selection arrows found within the Theme group section.

Other interesting notes about themes:

1. **Preview:** You can preview how a specific theme will look by simply moving your mouse cursor over a targeted theme. The preview lets you see what your slide will look like without actually making the formal change.

2. **Adapting themes:** If you like a specific theme format but prefer to adapt the color scheme, the font styles, or even the special effects, this is easily done by selecting from the color, font, and effects galleries (**Design tab** >>> **Theme** group >>> **Colors** (or **Fonts** or **Effects**).
3. **Changing a theme:** If you ever desire to change a theme, repeat the process and select a new theme. Once applied, it will automatically replace the previously selected theme.
4. **Applying themes for different slides:** A theme can be applied to a single slide or an entire presentation of slides. To make this selection, right click on any selected theme and make your selection of how it should be applied from the menu options presented.
5. **Additional theme options.** If you would like additional options for various types of themes, go to the Microsoft Office PowerPoint Help and type the key word: Theme. A Web site will be accessed that will allow you to download from various theme options.

(MAC USERS)   To apply the Slide Design: **Format >>> Apply Slide Design** and a window will appear that will help you select and apply the design. Likewise, if a change is needed, this is the procedure to make the slide design changes.

Masters

What is a "Master" slide?   A "Master" is a background that repeats on all slides, notes, or handouts of a presentation. It can contain text, graphics, automatic slide numbers, action buttons, and so on.

Why use Masters?   Masters are real time savers. There are situations in which you will want some element of a slide to be consistently presented on all slides of a presentation (e.g., the same colored background, the school logo, your name, the date, a set of action buttons, slide numbers). The master allows you to create it *once* and it automatically appears on all slides in the presentation (except for the ones you indicate you don't want it to appear on). This can help with keeping the slides looking consistent.

Are there different kinds of masters?   Yes, besides the slide master, there is also a master for the **Handout** page and one for the **Notes** page. In this way you can control how all of the pages for your handouts look and/or how the speaker's notes are designed and published.

How do you access the Masters?   Simple. On the PPT ribbon, go to the **View tab** >>> **Presentation Views group** >>> **Slide Master (or Handout Master or Notes Master).**

How do you use the Masters?   Review Figure 5.6. This is a Slide Master that has some suggested elements already set up for you. In the left-hand column, there are different **master slide** layouts from which to select. Once a layout has been selected, simply click on any of the different elements within the workspace (e.g., title). You can

Figure 5.6 The Slide Master

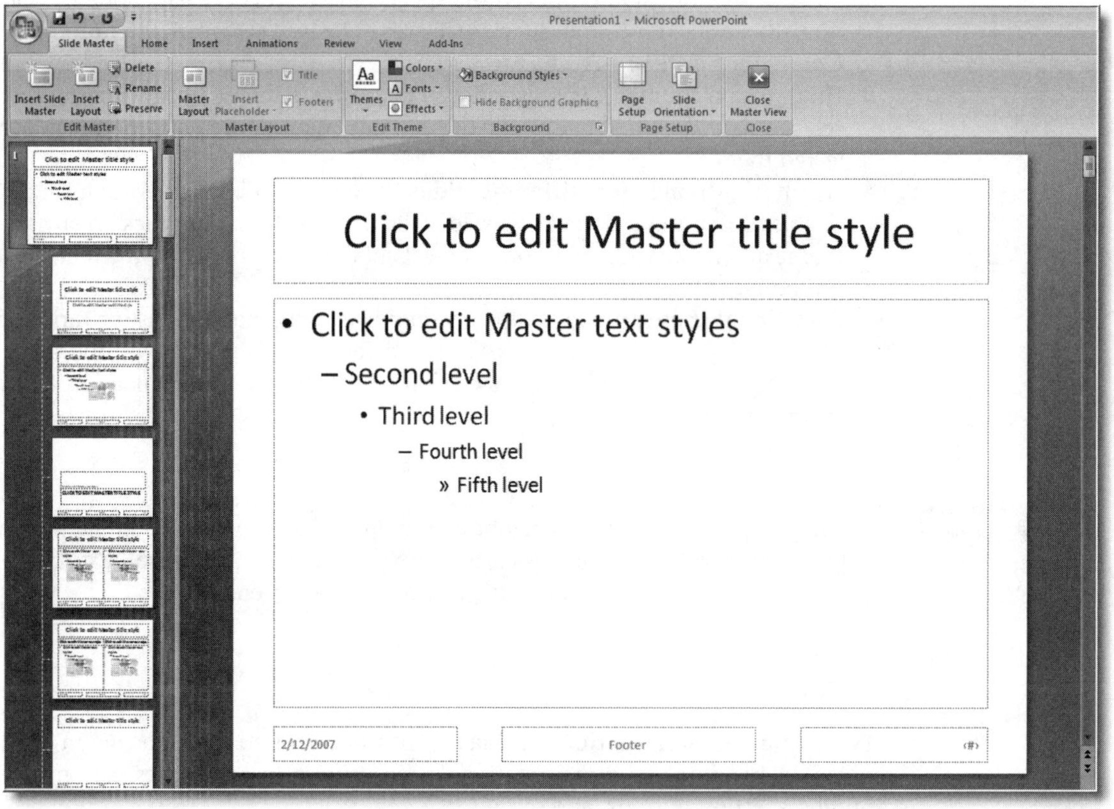

adjust and add to this Master just as you would to any other PPT slide. With the Slide Master tab selected, you can adjust what is already there (e.g., change the style, size, font of the heading) and this will automatically be applied to all slides currently in your presentation or that will later be added to your presentation. If you don't like your changes, you can always change it back—nothing is permanent. When you are finished working with the Slide Master, click on the Close Master View button and you will return to the normal slides of your presentation.

For a guided tour of these key features, please review the ***PPT Key Feature*** video on the text's accompanying Web site (**www.prenhall.com/newby** >>> **Chapter 5** >>> **Mentor Videos**.)

Orientation Workout 2: Explore the key features

While in PPT:

1. Open the Computer Hardware PPT slide show. You can find it on the accompanying Web site to this text (**www.prenhall.com/newby** >>> **Chapter 5** >>> **Example Presentation** >>> **Computer_hardware**).
2. Add a new slide to the end of that presentation (**Home tab** >>> **Slides** group >>> **New Slide**).
3. Select a layout for the new slide (**Home tab** >>> **Slides** group >>> **Layout**). Fill in the placeholders with information relevant to the elements of the layout. Apply the theme to all slides in your Computer Hardware presentation.
4. Change the theme for this slide show (**Design tab** >>> **Theme** group >>> **Theme**). Preview various themes, then select and apply the one that you desire. Once you have applied the theme, alter the color and/or font scheme.
5. Open the Slide Master (**View tab** >>> **Presentation Views** group >>> **Slide Master**) and alter some feature on the Slide Master (e.g., add your name to the bottom of the Slide Master.)

6. Return to your slides and switch to the slide sorter view. Rearrange the order of the slides by clicking and dragging one or more of the slides.
7. Change to the slide presentation view and examine all slides as if it were an actual presentation.

To view a demonstration of how to complete this Workout, review the **PPT Explore the key features** video at the text's accompanying Web site (**www.prenhall.com/newby** >>> **Chapter 5** >>> **Mentor Videos**).

Level 1: Creating Presentations to *Teach*

What should you be able to do?

Given specific guidelines and step-by-step procedures, you will be able to use various tools, techniques, and features of an electronic presentation program (specifically PPT) to design, create, and deliver a presentation.

What resources are provided?

Basically, Level 1 is divided into common teaching scenarios, selected solutions, and practice exercises (i.e., Workouts). The scenarios have been constructed to allow you to examine common problems and how they can be addressed through the use of this software. To do this we have provided the following:

a. Completed PPT presentations (see the text's accompanying Web site: **www.prenhall.com/newby** >>> **Chapter 5** >>> **PPT Examples**) that you can review, compare, and learn how the features are used to address the problems presented within each scenario.
b. Quick reference figures that identify (via visual callouts) all of the key features that have been incorporated within the solution presentation. These allow you to rapidly identify the key features and reference exactly how to include such features within your own work.
c. Step-by-step instructions on how to incorporate all highlighted features within your work.
d. Video mentoring support that will support and guide you through the integration of each of the highlighted features (see the text's accompanying Web site: **www.prenhall.com/newby** >>> **Chapter 5** >>> **Mentor Videos**).
e. Workout exercises that allow you to practice identifying and selecting which software features to use, when to use those features, how they should be incorporated, and to what degree they are effective.

How should you proceed?

If you have little or no experience with MS Office 2007 and particularly PPT, then we suggest you do the following:

1. Read and review Scenario 1,
2. Review the finished PPT presentation for that scenario (see the text's accompanying Web site: **www.prenhall.com/newby** >>> **Chapter 5** >>> **PPT Examples** >>> **Differ1**),
3. Examine the quick reference figures (Figures 5.7, 5.8, and 5.9) and all of the highlights,
4. With the step-by-step directions given for each highlighted feature, use the software and practice using each of the features,
5. Access the videos that explain each of the features and how they are accomplished within the software (**www.prenhall.com/newby** >>> **Chapter 5** >>> **Mentor Videos**),
6. Once you feel comfortable with these features, go to Scenario 2 and repeat these same steps with the new features introduced for that scenario in both the actual

Figure 5.7 Presentation slide that demonstrates use of titles, graphics, themes, fonts, and so on.

Figure 5.8 An additional presentation slide showing use of graphics and animated lists.

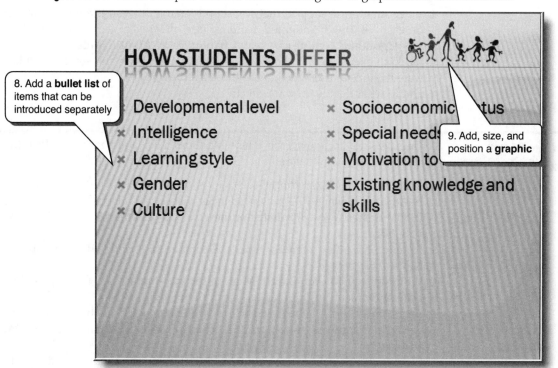

Figure 5.9 Incorporating hyperlinks and altering backgrounds within a presentation slide.

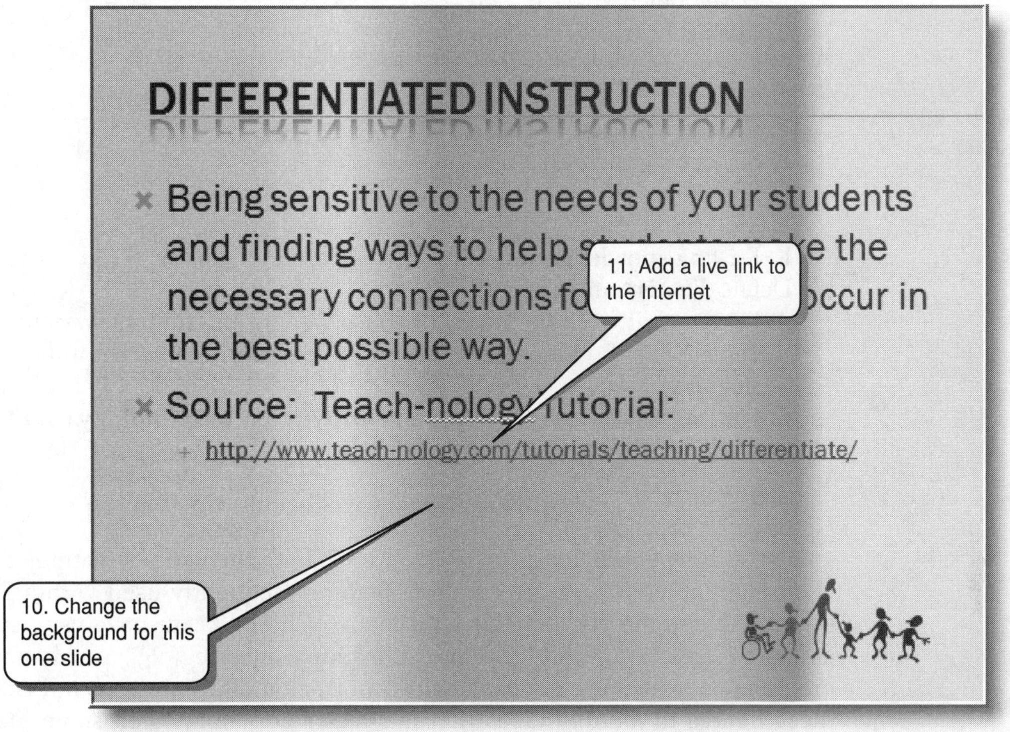

presentation (**www.prenhall.com/newby** >>> **Chapter 5** >>> **PPT Examples** >>> **SciMethod**) and the quick reference figure (Figures 5.11, 5.12, and 5.13);

7. After both scenarios have been reviewed, go to the Workout and work through the problems and exercises as it outlines.

If you have <u>experience</u> with PPT 2007, you may want to review the scenarios and the quick reference figures first. If any of the features are unfamiliar, then use the step-by-step procedures as well as the mentoring support videos. Once the review has been completed, then move directly to the Workout exercise and create your own PPT presentation by incorporating many of the highlighted features.

Scenario 1: How students differ

Janice, another eighth-grade teacher and one who is viewed as the computer "expert" in the school, comes to you with a request. She has been asked by your principal to give a series of short in-service lessons on integrating technology in the classroom. This week's is designed to focus on how technology can address individual student differences. She explains that she needs your help in reviewing the common differences of students faced by teachers and then she will follow with what can be done with technology to address those issues.

Even though you feel this is one more thing to add to your "to-do list," you quickly remember all the times Janice has rescued you in the computer lab with her suggestions and practical help. So you smile and hear yourself enthusiastically reply, "Sure, I'd be happy to."

After a day or two of thinking about it (and a little research), you develop the following short outline and send an e-mail to Janice to get her thoughts and approval:

I. Introduction: How students differ
    A. Begin with a story about how two students differ in the way they approach a problem.

II. Highlight how students differ
   A. Developmental level
   B. Intelligence
   C. Learning style
   D. Gender
   E. Culture
   F. Socioeconomic status
   G. Special needs
   H. Motivation
   I. Existing knowledge and skills

III. Define differentiated instruction:
   A. Being sensitive to the needs of your students and finding ways to help students make the necessary connections for learning to occur in the best possible way.
   B. Source: Teach-nology Tutorial: **http://www.teach-nology.com/tutorials/teaching/differentiate/**

Later that day, she sends you back an e-mail with three attached PPT slides (see Figures 5.7, 5.8, and 5.9)

As you look over Figures 5.7, 5.8, and 5.9, note the various features that have been highlighted. These are common features frequently used within PPT presentations. You may be familiar with many of them if you have used such programs before. In addition, other application software (e.g., word processing) programs may also use similar features (e.g., changing font size and color). Use these figures to identify areas that may be new or may need some practice to renew your skills.

To fully appreciate and understand all the features within this short presentation, open the actual program on this text's accompanying Web site: (**www.prenhall.com/newby** >>> **Chapter 5** >>> **PPT Examples** >>> **Differ1**) and view it as a slide show. Use Figures 5.7–5.9 to highlight all the key features that have been implemented within the show.

If you find some of the features new or that you need additional experience using, create a new slide in PPT and follow the step-by-step procedure for that specific feature. If you need additional guidance on how it can be completed, go to the text's Web site, **www.prenhall.com/newby** and access the **Mentor Video** for that feature. The video will walk you through exactly how to use the feature.

No.	Feature	Steps to Get It Done
1	**Create a new slide**	1. Start PPT and create a new PPT presentation (**Office Button** >>> **New**). 2. When the New Presentation window appears, click on the **Blank Presentation** icon and then the **Create** button (**Blank Presentation** >>> **Create**). 3. A new presentation should be opened with one slide. The slide will have a layout similar to a title slide.
2	**Add a title to the slide**	1. Click on the area in the new slide designated for the title. Type in the title of this slide (e.g., *Individual Student Differences . . .*). 2. Click on the subtitle area of the slide and type in the subtitle (e.g., *Technology Integration . . .*). Note how the slide autolayout controls the location, font type, and size.
3	**Change location of different elements of the slide**	1. To move any element on a slide, click once on the item you want to move and "handles" (little boxes) with a line around the item will appear. 2. Move your cursor directly over the line and it will turn into a four-way arrow. 3. Click, hold, and drag the item to the new location on the slide and then release the button.

No.	Feature	Steps to Get It Done
		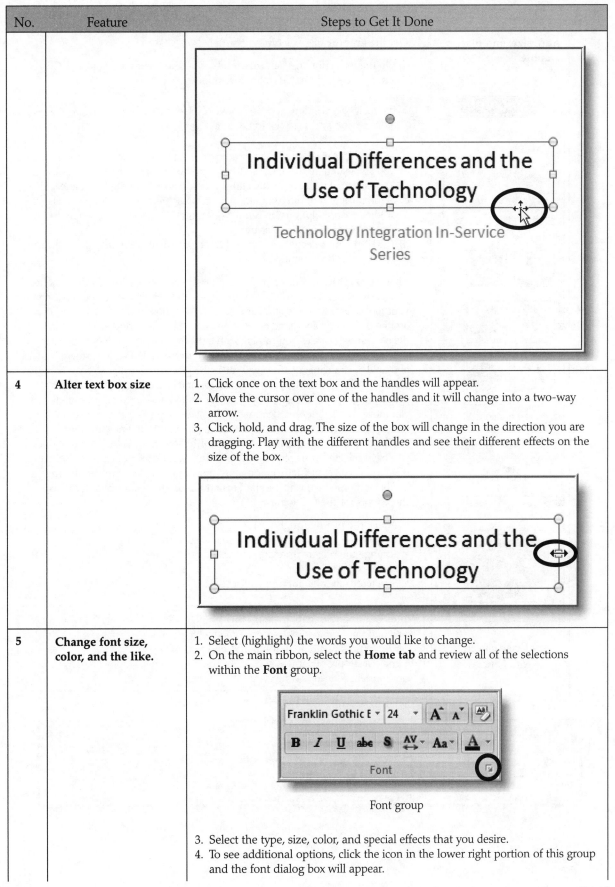
4	**Alter text box size**	1. Click once on the text box and the handles will appear. 2. Move the cursor over one of the handles and it will change into a two-way arrow. 3. Click, hold, and drag. The size of the box will change in the direction you are dragging. Play with the different handles and see their different effects on the size of the box.
5	**Change font size, color, and the like.**	1. Select (highlight) the words you would like to change. 2. On the main ribbon, select the **Home tab** and review all of the selections within the **Font** group. Font group 3. Select the type, size, color, and special effects that you desire. 4. To see additional options, click the icon in the lower right portion of this group and the font dialog box will appear.

continued

No.	Feature	Steps to Get It Done
6	**Add, size, and place a graphic** 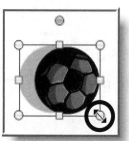 Clip Art task pane Selected clip art with handles	1. **Get the graphic** (e.g., picture, clip art). a. On the main ribbon, click **Insert tab** >>> **Illustrations** group >>> **Clip art.** . . . The Clip Art task pane will appear. The Clip Gallery window appears. Make a selection from this gallery or choose to go online and select from additional choices. b. In the Clip Art task pane, enter a key word that describes the type of clip art you are searching for (e.g., "sports") and then click on the **Go** button. Various small versions of the clip art should appear in the task pane. c. Scroll through the different alternatives presented in the task pane. Use the "Other Search Options" to refine your search if needed (e.g., where to search, types of media to search for). d. Click on your selected clip art and the picture will automatically be inserted within your document. 2. **Size the graphic.** If your inserted clip art is the perfect size for your document—great, leave it as it is. However, in many cases, the size will not be perfect. So point your mouse at the picture and left click once. You should note that a box is drawn around the picture and handles are placed at each of the corners and in the middle of each of the sides. You can grab a handle by putting your mouse pointer on the handle (note that your pointer changes into a double-headed arrow), left click, and hold it. Dragging a handle will cause the picture to be altered. Try different handles and see what happens to the shape and size of the picture. 3. **Place the graphic.** Once your picture is inserted and sized appropriately, you can move it to a different location on the slide by putting the mouse on top of the graphic, clicking, holding, and then dragging it to the new location. 4. **Adapt or adjust the quality of the graphic.** You should also note that once you have selected your picture (the picture has the box around it with the handles) a special set of **Picture Tools** becomes available (look for the **Picture Tools** tab immediately above the **Format** tab on the main ribbon). You can use these tools for the following: • Adjust the picture (brightness, contrast, color) • Change the picture style (border, shape, special effects) • Arrange the picture in relation to other items (bring to the front, send to the back) • Size (crop, alter height and width) **Note:** Working with clip art and other graphic files may take a bit of practice. You'll find that some don't look very good when their size is changed to a drastic degree—others work great. You'll also find that access to the Internet gives you an endless supply of various clip art, pictures, and other graphics. that you may want to use and insert within your documents.

Picture Tools

No.	Feature	Steps to Get It Done
7	**Add a theme**	1. On the main ribbon, click on the **Design tab** and review all of the themes within the **Theme** group. By moving your mouse over the different themes, you can preview how they would look once they have been applied. Click on the theme you want applied to your presentation. If you need to change the theme, just make a different selection, click, and the new theme is applied. 2. Once a theme has been applied, you can use other commands within the Theme group to alter the color, font, and/or the effect within your selected theme. In this way, you can personalize each of these professionally de-signed themes.
8	**Add list of items that can be introduced (animated) one at a time: Custom Animation**	1. Insert a new slide (**Home tab** >>> **Slide** group >>> **New Slide**). 2. Select a layout for the new slide that will allow for a list of items to be entered. Here is an example that could be selected from the list within the layout gallery. Select one that you think will work well. 3. Click in the placeholder for the title and enter your title for the slide. 4. Click in one of the columns and add your content for each of the bullets (e.g., Developmental level, Intelligence). 5. Go to the main ribbon and select the **Animation tab** >>> **Animation** group >>> **Custom Animation** button. The Custom Animation task pane will appear. 6. Click on your bulleted list of items that you have inserted on your slide. 7. On the Custom Animation task pane, click and hold the "Add Effect" button. 8. From the revealed menu, select how you want the items in the list to appear during the slide show (Entrance) and any other effects that you would like to try. There are several options to choose from and you may want to experiment with each to see what fits best with your presentation.

continued

No.	Feature	Steps to get it done

9. You may also want to select if you want your list of items to be emphasized in any way, how you want them to exit the slide, and/or if you want them to move across the slide and show motion in some way. All of these effects are selected within this **Add Effect** area.
10. Each of the effects can be modified (when to occur, to what degree, and so forth) within the **Modify** area of the **Custom Animation** task pane.
11. Once you have selected one or more effects, view what the effects will look like by clicking on the **Play** button at the bottom of the task pane. If alterations are needed, return to the "Modify" selections.
12. To remove an effect, simply select the element (e.g., the list) and click on the Remove button.

This is a fun feature to work with. Spend some time trying different effects and different ways to time those effects.

> **Note:** Not only can you do these custom animation effects with bulleted or numbered lists of items, it also works for any element (e.g., clip art, words, word art) that you select on the slide. By selecting the elements, you can also determine the sequence and the timing for the animation.

MAC USERS

Although you don't use task panes, the procedures for custom animations (and the results) are very similar. Use the **Slide Show** >>> **Animations** >>> **Custom . . .** menus and the custom animation window will appear. Make your selection for the type of effect, as well as the order and timing.

No.	Feature	Steps to get it done
9	**Add, size, and position a graphic**	This is basically a repeat of what we learned in Step 6. Notice how you can use a graphic in a smaller version as a logo or theme within other PPT slides.
10	**Change the background of a specific slide**	1. In some cases you may want one (or more) of your slides to vary from your selected theme carried by the other slides in the presentation. To alter the background of one slide, make sure you begin by going to that slide in the presentation. 2. On the main ribbon, click on the **Design tab** >>> **Background** group >>> **Background Styles**. The Background Styles gallery will appear and you can preview how the slide's background can be changed. 3. If you desire a change different from that offered in the gallery, click on the **Format Background** button and a dialog box will appear with more choices.
11	**Insert a hyperlink to the Internet**	1. Type the text you would like to serve as the link. If you choose to use the Web address as the text that appears, simply type in the address and press the space bar. The link is automatically created for you, and the font and style changes to indicate its link to the Web.

No.	Feature	Steps to get it done
		2. If you would prefer to use customized text for the link, insert the text, select it, click the **Insert tab** >>> **Links** group >>> **Hyperlink button**. The **Insert Hyperlink** window will appear. 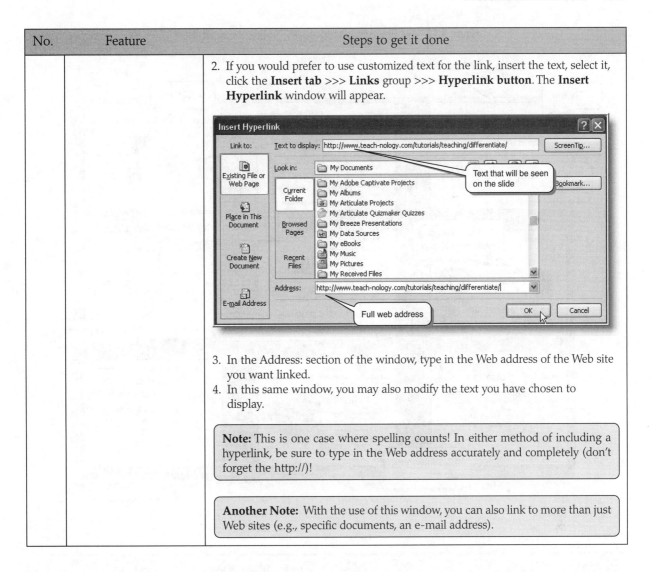 3. In the Address: section of the window, type in the Web address of the Web site you want linked. 4. In this same window, you may also modify the text you have chosen to display. **Note:** This is one case where spelling counts! In either method of including a hyperlink, be sure to type in the Web address accurately and completely (don't forget the http://)! **Another Note:** With the use of this window, you can also link to more than just Web sites (e.g., specific documents, an e-mail address).

**Scenario 2:
The Scientific Method**

Getting ready for the school Science Fair offers a number of challenges. One of the biggest is persuading parents to buy into the project. For Roberta Andrews, educating the parents of her students about the different elements of the project hadn't always been consistent and hadn't produced reliable results in the past. One key element that had often led to confusion—but critical to the projects—is "The Scientific Method."

This year, Roberta decided to do something different. Early within the school year—in fact, during her school's "Meet the Teacher Night,"—she decided to introduce the topic to the parents. To do this effectively, she thought of using a PPT presentation. This would allow her to present the material in a professional manner and efficiently create handouts that the parents could take home and discuss with their kids. Later, she might actually reuse the presentation as an introduction to the Science Fair projects for her students and give them the handouts to take home to remind the parents of what they had heard during her presentation.

Go to the text's Web site and review Roberta's presentation **www.prenhall.com/ newby** >>> **Chapter 5** >>> **Example Presentation** >>> **SciMethod.** As you go through it, note how it was constructed and the different elements presented. Several will be similar to those reviewed within Scenario 1. Review the quick reference Figure 5.10, the coordinated step-by-step procedures, and the video mentoring guides to learn how to use each of the features.

Figure 5.10 The Scientific Method PPT slide presentation

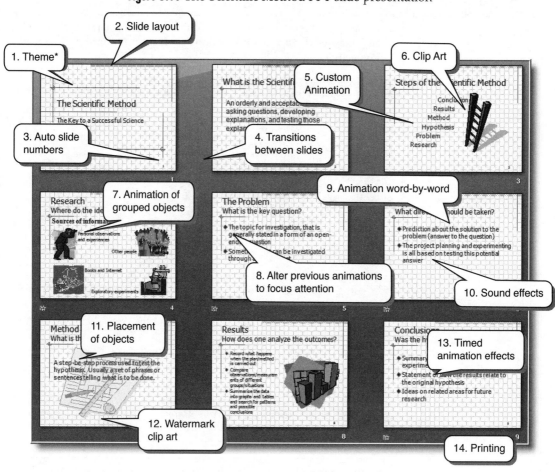

No.	Feature	Steps to Get It Done
1	**Select the theme for the presentation**	1. Different themes for a presentation can be readily accessed (**Design tab** >>> **Theme** group). 2. Review pages 122–123 for a discussion of the value of themes, their application, how to preview, and so forth. 3. Review Feature 7 of Scenario 1 (page 131) for the steps to incorporate a theme.
2	**Select a slide layout**	1. Altering a slide layout can be quickly accomplished (**Home tab** >>> **Slides** group >>> **Layout** gallery). 2. From the gallery, select the layout that will work best with the content that you want in the slide. There are layouts that can be used for text lists, charts, tables, clip art, movies, and so on. 3. Review page 121 for a discussion of the value of slide layouts, their application, how to use, and so forth.
3	**Auto page numbers**	1. Click **Insert tab** >>> **Text** group >>> **Slide Number** or **Header & Footer.** 2. In the pop-up window, select the options you would like to use. To add slide numbers, place a check in front of the "Slide number" option. Then click "Apply to All." **Note:** Following these same steps you can place page numbers (as well as other header and footer information) on slides, note pages, and handout pages.

No.	Feature	Steps to Get It Done
		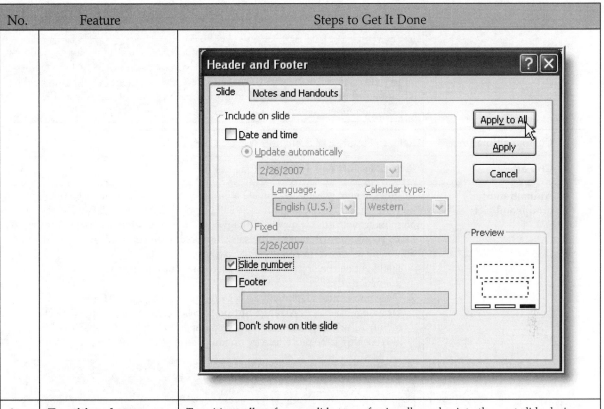
4	**Transitions between slides**	Transitions allow for one slide to professionally evolve into the next slide during a presentation. For example, as the first slide fades, the next slide emerges from the center of the screen.

1. Go to the slide where you want the transition to occur.
2. Review all of the possible transitions from the transitions gallery (**Animations tab** >>> **Transitions to This Slide** group >>> **More button** (to reveal the full gallery).
3. Preview the transitions by moving your cursor over the gallery selections.
4. Click on the effect you desire.
5. In this same group of commands, you can also select the speed of the transition, whether to add a sound effect, as well as how to advance the slide (e.g., on the click of the mouse or by some predetermined amount of time).

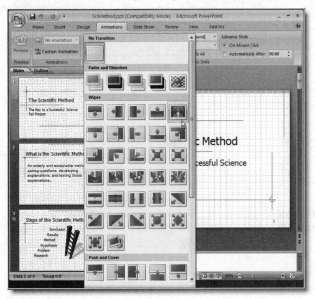

continued

No.	Feature	Steps to Get It Done
		Note: These steps show you how to create transitions one at a time for each slide (this can become quite burdensome if you have a lot of slides). By first going into the slide sorter view, however, you can select any number of slides at a single time and then create the same transition between all of the selected slides. A much more efficient method!
5	**Custom animation**	Refer to Feature 8 of Scenario 1 (page 131).
6	**Clip art**	Refer to Feature 6 of Scenario 1 (page 130).
7	**Animation of grouped objects**	At times, you may want to animate a group of objects simultaneously. Depending on how you set up the animation, it will be possible for you to begin a series of animations with simply a click of the mouse. A simple way is to first group the items you want to animate at the same time and then complete a simple custom animation as shown in Feature 8 of Scenario 1. 1. Highlight all the objects you would like to group together within the animation. 2. Once one group is highlighted, click on the "group" button (**Home tab** >>> **Drawing** group >>> **Arrange button** >>> select from the **Group Objects** menu). All selected items will now be grouped together as a single item. You can also use this same procedure to "ungroup" a set of previously grouped items. 3. Once all of the different groups of items have been formed, open the **Custom Animation** task pane (**Animations tab** >>> **Animations** group >>> **Custom Animation button**). 4. Select the grouped item that you want to appear first and then click on the **Add Effect** button. Select the type of entrance you desire for the grouped item to be animated, as well as the direction and the speed that it should enter. If you want the grouped items to be emphasized in some way or to exit the slide when needed, this is the place to create this type of animation (all using the **Add Effect** button). 5. Repeat this process for each of the grouped items that you wish to animate. 6. Click the **Play** button to review what you have created. If you wish to alter the animations, use the custom animation task pane to select the animation that needs to be altered, and then alter when it occurs, how it occurs, how fast it occurs, and so on.
8	**Alter previous animations;**	You can alter an animation in a number of ways. This is often done to add emphasis or to draw attention to specific parts of the presentation. Use the following steps to alter previous animations, animate word-by-word, and add sounds.
9	**Animate word-by-word; and**	

No.	Feature	Steps to Get It Done
10	**Add Sounds**	1. After applying an animation, make sure the **Custom Animation** task pane is showing (**Animations tab** >>> **Animations** group >>> **Custom Animation button**). 2. From the list of animated objects in the custom animation task pane, select the animation you would like to modify. (You can select more than one by clicking and holding down the shift key on your keyboard.) 3. Right mouse click on your selection and then select **Effect Options**. 4. The **Effect Options** window will appear. Click on the **Effect tab** and then you can do any or all of the following under the **Enhancements** section: a. **After animation:** Select how the text that has already appeared will look once a new animation enters the slide (e.g., change color, fade). b. **Animate text:** to select how the text should initially enter the slide (e.g., all at once, by word, by letter). c. **Sound:** Select sounds that could be included as the text enters the slide (e.g., typewriter, chime, click). 5. Select the enhancements you would like to apply and click OK. 6. Click the **Play** button to review your modification.
11	**Placement of objects**	1. Select the object you would like to move by clicking on the outer edge. 2. Click and drag the object to the location you desire. **Movement Tips** (These work in all MS Office applications!): • **Nudging an object:** To move an item at very small intervals. Select the object. Press the CTRL key on your keyboard while pressing a directional arrow. • **Modify the order of objects:** (e.g., bring to front, send to back, and so forth): Select the object and then select the order (**Home tab** >>> **Drawing** group >>> **Arrange** button >>> **Order objects** menu). • **Rotate or flip an object:** Select the object and then select how you want it rotated or flipped (**Home tab** >>> **Drawing** group >>> **Arrange** button >>> **Position objects** menu >>> **Rotate**).
12	**Watermark backgrounds**	Watermarks (also known as "washouts") are images (e.g., pictures, clip art) that are semitransparent and often used in the background. 1. Add an image from Clip Art. (For more detail, see Feature 6 of Scenario 1, page 130). 2. Select the image. Right mouse click and select **Format Picture**. 3. When the **Format Picture Window** opens, click on the **Picture** button.

continued

No.	Feature	Steps to Fet It Done
		4. Modify the images appearance by adjusting the brightness or contrast scales. 5. Position the watermark (see Feature 11). 6. Send the image "to the back" of the slide (**Home tab** >>> **Drawing** group >>> **Arrange** button >>> **Order objects** menu >>> **Send to Back** button).
13	**Timed animation effects**	There are times when you will want your animations to enter based on time and not on the manual mouse click. 1. After applying an animation, make sure the **Custom Animation** task pane is showing (**Main Ribbon** >>> **Animations tab** >>> **Animations** group >>> **Custom Animation button**). 2. From the list of animated objects in the custom animation task pane, select the animation you would like to modify. 3. Right mouse click on your selection and then select **Effect Options.** **Spiral In** [?] [X] Effect | **Timing** | Text Animation Start: [🕐 After Previous ▾] Delay: [3 ▴▾] seconds Speed: [1 seconds (Fast) ▾] Repeat: [(none) ▾] ☐ Rewind when done playing [Triggers ⬇] [OK] [Cancel] 4. The **Effect Options** window will appear. Click on the **Timing tab.** Select the options for when to start, how long the delay should be between animations, and the overall speed of the animation. 5. Click the OK button when your timing decisions have been made.
14	**Printing**	1. Click **Office** button >>> **Print**. 2. In the Print Window, several standard options appear, such as number of copies, printer location, and collating choices. Unique to PowerPoint is the ability to print a variety of formats of your presentation. Use the **Print what** drop-down list to select the option that meets your needs. 3. If you choose to print handouts, you will have an additional series of choices within the **Handout** section (e.g., how many slides to print per page). 4. It is always good to Preview your choices before printing. The **Preview** button is located in the bottom left-hand corner of the Print Window.

Level 1 Workout: Practice using the basic PPT features

Now you get to actually practice using the features of PPT. You need to create a new presentation and begin to select and integrate the different features within your own work. Here's a basic outline of what you need to do:

Determine what content your program should include. To do this efficiently, go to the accompanying Web site (**www.prenhall.com/newby** >>> **Chapter 5** >>> **Level**

1 Workout >>> Content Outlines) and review the outlines of content that we have already developed for you. You can select the outline that interests you the most and then copy it within the outline view of PPT. Of course, if you have a presentation looming in the near future, you may want to insert your own content and by finishing this workout you may actually have that task nearly completed.

1. Review the previous two scenarios and their step-by-step procedures for each of the displayed features.
2. Develop a set of slides that includes the basic content.
3. Go through the slides and begin to add the needed features to accentuate the relevant elements of the presentation. Use the Level 1 Workout checklist (see Table 5.1), as well as Figures 5.7–5.10, to help you identify all of the features that could be included. Remember this is a practice workout–*practice integrating as many features as possible.*

> **Note:** Refer to specific feature numbers and the given step-by-step procedures as needed. Additionally, use the mentoring videos to help guide you through any specific procedure that needs additional clarification.

Table 5.1 Level 1 Workout and Practice Checklist Designing a Presentation

Project Content	___ Content is accurate and current.
	___ Content is relevant and cohesive throughout the program.
	___ Content achieves the proper "level" for the intended audience.
Presentation Format	___ A new presentation was created.
	___ A theme was used to add cohesiveness and consistency throughout the program.
	___ Slides were numbered consistently throughout the presentation.
	___ Transitions between slides were incorporated.
	___ Various slide layouts, consistent with the needs of the content, were used.
Individual Slide Elements	___ Font size, style, type, and location were adapted as needed within the different slides.
	___ Appropriate graphics (e.g., clip art, pictures, images) were properly selected, sized, and placed on slides.
	___ A watermark was created and placed appropriately in the background of a specific slide.
	___ Animation effects (e.g., various manual and timed entrances and exits, fading of past points, sound effects) for individual and grouped objects were incorporated.
	___ Hyperlinks to specific Internet sites, documents, or other slides were created within the presentation.

Level 2: Creating Presentations to *Learn*

What should you be able to do?

In this section we want you to create, edit, and format several original presentations and sets of individualized instructional materials using advanced PPT features. In addition, you should learn to effectively use the Help feature of the software.

Getting some Help

Similar to Help in Windows, there is also Help in MS PPT and most other sophisticated presentation software. To use Help, click the **Help** button on the tab bar of the main ribbon.

Clicking the **Help** button brings up the Help window. From here you can browse general **Help** topics, bring up a general table of contents of all **Help** topics, review a comparison chart between PPT 2003 and 2007 common commands, and/or complete a search for a specific question that you might have.

PPT Help button

PPT Help window

By typing in key words or even a full question, Help will respond with a variety of potential answers for you to investigate. Help generally *does not* have all of the answers—but it will have a lot of them. Make sure you become familiar with how it works and how often it can be of assistance.

| **Scenario 3: "The Scientific Method" repurposed as individualized instruction** | After successfully using "The Scientific Method" presentation at "Meet the Teacher Night," Roberta Andrews now has other ideas. Using this presentation for the basic content, she quickly adapts it into a self-instructional program that can be used to prepare her students for the development of their science fair projects. Review the program |

on the text's accompanying Web site (**www.prenhall.com/newby** >>> **Chapter 5** >>> **PPT Examples** >>> **SciMeth2**).

In this case, she wants the program to be used by individual students who can control which portions of the presentation they see and be quizzed on what they have read.

Note how the action buttons are used to navigate throughout the program and how they can be used to set up review questions, encourage student interaction, and supply specific feedback.

Here are three slides (Figure 5.11, 5.12, and 5.13) that highlight the key features that have been added within the SciMeth2 version of the Scientific Method presentation. Make sure you examine it first on the text's Web site and then you can examine how these features actually work within a slide presentation.

Once you have reviewed these figures and the actual presentation, review how to find the key information on how to actually develop these features within your projects. In addition, mentoring videos have been created on the text's Web site (**www.prenhall.com/newby**) that will guide you through the use of each of these features.

Figure 5.11

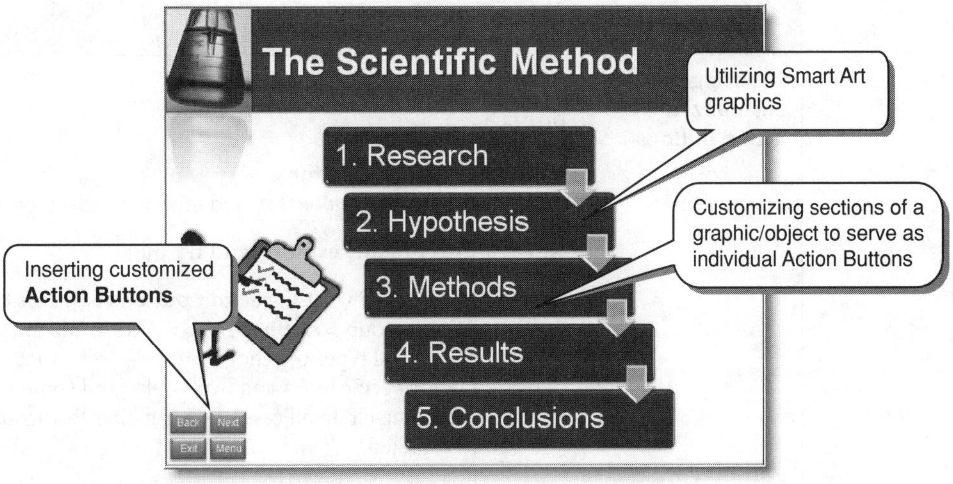

Figure 5.12

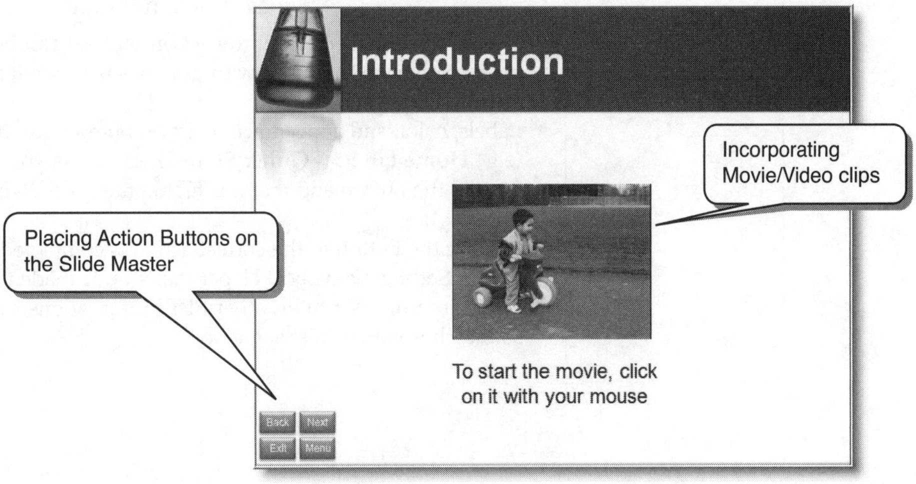

Figure 5.13

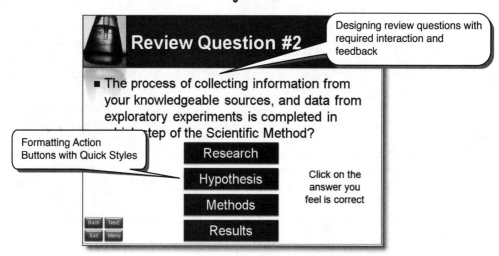

Feature	Steps to Get It Done
Inserting customized action buttons	**Procedure for creating and inserting:** PPT Help 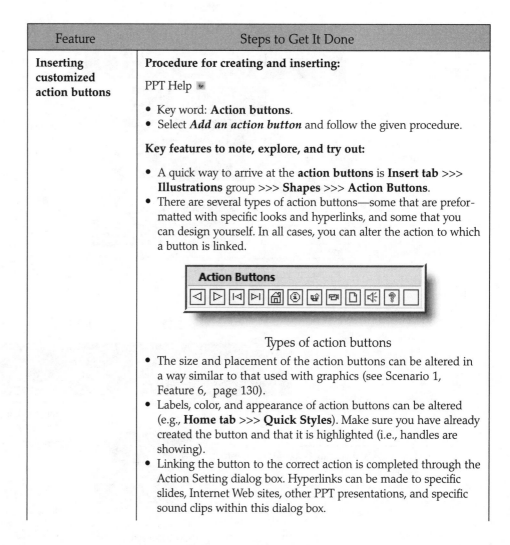 • Key word: **Action buttons**. • Select *Add an action button* and follow the given procedure. **Key features to note, explore, and try out:** • A quick way to arrive at the **action buttons** is **Insert tab** >>> **Illustrations** group >>> **Shapes** >>> **Action Buttons**. • There are several types of action buttons—some that are preformatted with specific looks and hyperlinks, and some that you can design yourself. In all cases, you can alter the action to which a button is linked.

Action Buttons

Types of action buttons

• The size and placement of the action buttons can be altered in a way similar to that used with graphics (see Scenario 1, Feature 6, page 130).
• Labels, color, and appearance of action buttons can be altered (e.g., **Home tab** >>> **Quick Styles**). Make sure you have already created the button and that it is highlighted (i.e., handles are showing).
• Linking the button to the correct action is completed through the Action Setting dialog box. Hyperlinks can be made to specific slides, Internet Web sites, other PPT presentations, and specific sound clips within this dialog box.

Feature	Steps to Get It Done
	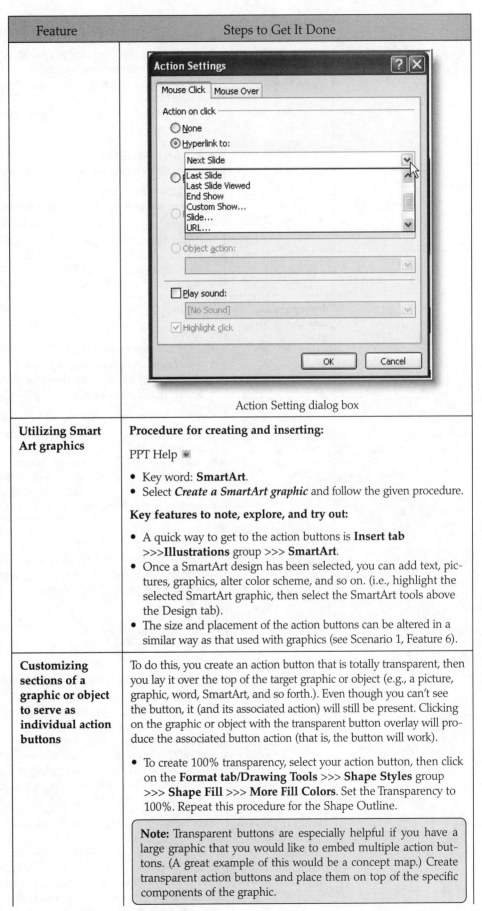 Action Setting dialog box
Utilizing Smart Art graphics	**Procedure for creating and inserting:** PPT Help ⚇ • Key word: **SmartArt**. • Select *Create a SmartArt graphic* and follow the given procedure. **Key features to note, explore, and try out:** • A quick way to get to the action buttons is **Insert tab >>>Illustrations** group >>> **SmartArt**. • Once a SmartArt design has been selected, you can add text, pictures, graphics, alter color scheme, and so on. (i.e., highlight the selected SmartArt graphic, then select the SmartArt tools above the Design tab). • The size and placement of the action buttons can be altered in a similar way as that used with graphics (see Scenario 1, Feature 6).
Customizing sections of a graphic or object to serve as individual action buttons	To do this, you create an action button that is totally transparent, then you lay it over the top of the target graphic or object (e.g., a picture, graphic, word, SmartArt, and so forth.). Even though you can't see the button, it (and its associated action) will still be present. Clicking on the graphic or object with the transparent button overlay will produce the associated button action (that is, the button will work). • To create 100% transparency, select your action button, then click on the **Format tab/Drawing Tools** >>> **Shape Styles** group >>> **Shape Fill** >>> **More Fill Colors**. Set the Transparency to 100%. Repeat this procedure for the Shape Outline. **Note:** Transparent buttons are especially helpful if you have a large graphic that you would like to embed multiple action buttons. (A great example of this would be a concept map.) Create transparent action buttons and place them on top of the specific components of the graphic.

continued

Feature	Steps to Get It Done
Placing action buttons on the Slide Master	Action buttons that you want to appear on all of your slides (e.g., buttons to link to the "next" slide) can be created once and put on the Slide Master. These buttons will then appear on all slides within the presentation. **General information on the Slide Master:** PPT Help • Key word: **Slide Master**. • Select *Create, customize, and apply a Slide Master* **Pages 123–124** of this text's chapter **Key features to note, explore, and try out:** • A quick way to get to the Slide Master: **View tab** >>> **Presentation Views** group >>> **Slide Master**. • Action buttons can be added anywhere on the Slide Master and they will appear in that position on all slides. Therefore, place them in a location that will be free of other items on all slides.
Incorporating movie or video clips	**Procedure for incorporating movies or video clips:** PPT Help • Key word: **Add a movie**. • Select *Add and play a movie in a presentation*. Review the *Overview of movies and animated GIF files* section. • Select the **Add a movie** section and follow the given procedure. **Key features to note, explore, and try out:** • A quick way to get to add a movie is **Insert tab** >>> **Movie clips** group >>> **Movie**. • Movie tools can be accessed by selecting the inserted movie within your slide, then click the Movie Tools button above the Options tab. Movie tools allow you to select when to show the movie, select the volume, size, and arrangement of the movie on the slide.
Formatting action buttons with Quick Styles	Quick Styles allow you to add high-quality formatting to various shapes, SmartArt, or action buttons in a very efficient manner. Accessing the Quick Styles gallery allows you to preview how the shape will look before the formatting is actually applied. **Procedure for using Quick Styles:** PPT Help • Key word: **Quick Styles**. • Select the *Apply or change a Quick Style for shapes* section and the given procedure. **Key features to note, explore, and try out:** • A quick way to access Quick Styles is to select the shape or action button then **Format tab/Drawing tools** >>> **Drawing** group >>> **Quick Styles**. • Quick Styles can add shadows, gradients, line styles, edges, and even 3D perspectives to your shapes. • Before or after Quick Style application, you can size and move your shape. This is similar to moving a graphic as explained in Scenario 1, Feature 6 (page 130).
Designing review questions with required interaction and feedback	With the use of action buttons, it is possible to present the learner with a question and several possible alternative responses on a slide. Having each of the possible responses as an action button allows you to have specific feedback slides linked to each alternative. In addition, the feedback may include information about why the response being made was correct or incorrect and additional information to help the student understand why his or her response was correct or not.

Note: Each of these key features is demonstrated on the mentoring videos. Go to the text's accompanying Web site (**www.prenhall.com/newby** >>> **Chapter 5** >>> **Mentor Video**).

Level 2 Workout: Practice using additional PPT features

Now you try it.

1. Select the content for the presentation. You may use any or all of the following:

   a. Open, adapt, and expand the presentation you created for the Level 1 Workout.
   b. Go to the Level 1 (**www.prenhall.com/newby** >>> **Chapter 5** >>> **Level 1 Workout** >>> **Content Outlines**) sample outlines and develop your own basic presentation using one of the content outlines that have been provided.

   Note: You will have to gather and add more information to these outlines.

   c. A partially prepared presentation has been developed and can be accessed on the text's Web site (**www.prenhall.com/newby** >>> **Chapter 5** >>> **Level 2 Workout** >>> **BlogPresentation.pptx**). It is a presentation that has been created about using blogs in the classroom setting. You can begin with this basic presentation and practice incorporating the advanced features within it.
   d. Review your calendar, school lesson plans, and so on to see when your next presentation will be. Select one that is coming up in the near future. It can be anything (e.g., class discussion on worm segments, proper swimming strokes, visit to the local art museum). Develop a simple outline of content based upon that need.

2. Start PPT and create some slides that cover the key concepts that should be within your presentation.
3. Review the features demonstrated within Scenario 3 of Level 2 (e.g., action buttons, movie clips, SmartArt).
4. Similar to the SciMeth2 presentation (**www.prenhall.com/newby** >>> **Chapter 5** >>> **PPT Examples** >>> **SciMeth2**), create a presentation about your selected content that allows the user the control to navigate through the information (e.g., use of action buttons).
5. Use Table 5.2 as a checklist to make sure you have included a number of key features that have been highlighted within Scenarios 1, 2, and 3 of this chapter.

Table 5.2 Level 2 Workout and Practice Checklist Designing a Learner-Centered Presentation

Project Content	____ Content is accurate and current.
	____ Content is relevant and cohesive throughout the program.
	____ Content achieves the proper "level" for the intended audience.
	____ Appropriate directions were incorporated to help the user understand how to navigate within the program.
	____ Review slides with linked feedback slides were incorporated within the presentation.
Presentation Format	____ A theme was used to add cohesiveness and consistency throughout the program.
	____ Slides were numbered consistently throughout the presentation.
	____ Transitions between slides were incorporated.
	____ Various slide layouts, consistent with the needs of the content, were used.
	____ Slide Master was used to retain common elements throughout all slides.

continued

Table 5.2 Level 2 Workout and Practice Checklist Designing a
Learner-Centered Presentation (*continued*)

Individual Slide Elements	___ Font size, style, type, and location were adapted as needed within the different slides.
	___ Appropriate graphics (e.g., clip art, pictures, images) were properly selected, sized, and placed on slides.
	___ SmartArt graphics was incorporated.
	___ Animation effects (e.g., various manual and timed entrances and exits, fading of past points, sound effects) for individual and grouped objects were incorporated.
	___ Hyperlinks to specific Internet sites, documents, or other slides were created within the presentation.
	___ Appropriate action buttons were created and used to allow individualized navigation by the user.
	___ Quick Styles were used to modify some of the action buttons.
	___ Movie and/or audio clips were incorporated within the presentation.

Level 3: Integration and Application

What should you be able to do?

Here's where you get to actually use this software to help yourself and your students. This section helps you see the many applications possible using PPT (or similar software). You can use these examples as a springboard to launch ideas on how to improve levels of student learning and your personal productivity.

Introduction

The examples given in Levels 1 and 2 coupled with your own development efforts should put you in a good position to begin to see the possibilities for this type of presentation program.

Now we want you to expand your use of this program and think of what you can show and demonstrate to others. Here we give you a number of different ideas, some that you may or may not find helpful, but we hope they are ideas that you can expand upon to make them relevant to your work and those with whom you work.

Presentation software integration

Creating the enhanced learning experience: A partial lesson plan

Topic: A study of the people, places, and culture of an African country.

Overview:

Mr. Carpenter, an eighth-grade social studies teacher at Lowell Middle School, is continuing to search for ways for his students to "explore" Zimbabwe and learn about this African country and its people. Moreover, he wants his students to discover that much can be learned about the people of today by exploring their history and ancestors. With the help of one of his former students, Jonathon Rogers (who now is a university graduate student in Zimbabwe on an internship with an international health and education organization), Mr. Carpenter's hopes to guide his students as they discover the past of this fascinating country.

Through the use of e-mail, regular mail, digital photography, and audio recordings, Jonathon should be able to explore several historically significant sites within the borders of Zimbabwe and then share those with the Lowell social studies classes of Mr. Carpenter.

Specific learning task:

To explore the history of the people of Zimbabwe, the students in Mr. Carpenter's social studies classes were to investigate the ancient city known as the "Great Zimbabwe." Each class was divided into smaller cooperative groups who would be asked to address one of the following sets of questions:

- What was the "Great Zimbabwe?" Who were the people that built it? What did the city look like when it was populated? What caused it to decline and decay?
- If one lived in the Great Zimbabwe, what was life like? What did people do, what did they wear, what did they eat, how did they travel from place to place, what did they believe in, and how did they communicate and conduct business? What were some interesting things about living in this city?
- How were the ruins of the Great Zimbabwe discovered? Who made those discoveries? What was done to the ruins after they were discovered? What is the role of the archeologist in uncovering and understanding a people who no longer are alive? What does the Great Zimbabwe look like today?

Sample learning objectives:

Students will be able to do the following:

1. Identify and describe important elements and events about life during the time of the Great Zimbabwe and how people lived within that society.
2. Examine and explain potential reasons for the rise and fall of great societies such as those who lived within the Great Zimbabwe.
3. Explain the role of archeologists in the discovery of places and people of the past.

Procedure:

1. Break into the groups, examine the assigned questions for study, and brainstorm methods to investigate.
2. Examine Web sites and other reference materials for information about the Great Zimbabwe. For example:

    - Wikipedia: **http://en.wikipedia.org/wiki/Great_Zimbabwe**
    - Riddle of the Great Zimbabwe: **http://www.archaeology.org/9807/abstracts/africa.html**
    - Mystery of the Great Zimbabwe: **http://www.pbs.org/wgbh/nova/israel/zimbabwe.html**

3. Contact Jonathon to see if he has visited this archeological site and/or if he has heard anything about it. Ask for further information if he can find it from individuals who live in the country. If he does visit, have him write his impressions of what it was like and send pictures of what he found.
4. Using the assigned questions as a starting point, create a group presentation about the Great Zimbabwe.
5. Create a follow-up activity that involves the development of learner-focused individualized instruction. Using PPT, create an instructional learning module that individual students can access, navigate, gain information and experience with the content, and be assessed about the information they have experienced.

Questions About the Integration of Presentation Software

This lesson could be completed in a number of ways, including simple oral reports, reenactments or role-plays, or video or live presentations by subject matter experts such as archeologists. In addition, the use of presentation software, such as PPT, can be completed to create overhead slides and handouts to accompany an oral presentation. Use the following reflective questions to explore the value of potentially integrating PPT or another form of presentation software within such a lesson as outlined by Mr. Carpenter.

- How will the small research groups cooperatively brainstorm and plan the presentation? Can presentation software be used to facilitate the planning process?

- Can the development of specific sets of information (e.g., tables or lists of information, charts, and maps) increase the level of understanding for the individual group members?
- Will the presentation involve the use of audio, visual graphics, and/or video clips of some kind? Will these items need to be presented in a way that a large (more than 10 people) group of people can see and hear?
- During and/or following the presentation, can learning be enhanced by the production and distribution of a handout of the presented information? Would such a handout facilitate a group discussion on the topic?
- Will there be a need for the presentation to be stored for later use by other classes, individual students, interested parents, faculty, and so on?

Level 3a Workout: Integrating PPT into the real world of learning

1. Read each of the following situations. Imagine being directly involved in the planning for each of these projects. Select one (or more if you wish) for further consideration.

School Days

The lives of children throughout the world vary based on many different factors. One common element for most is that they go to some form of formal school. But how similar are the experiences that the students have? How does a typical school day in various places of the world compare? What kinds of subjects are studied, how much time is spent on each subject, how much variety is given between the different subjects? How do kids get to school, how long do they stay there, how much homework do they have? How is the learning of the students assessed? After examining all of these different ways of "doing school," what would be an appropriate way to examine and evaluate the similarities and differences between the various school systems? If asked to suggest a plan for the "best" school system, how would the proposal be created and presented?

Pet Care

Third-grade students were learning about pets. In separate groups they focused on different common family pets. They studied the types of food needed, the care needed, the living space, and even the amount of play and exercise that the animal needed. Together they decided to make a program that would help other students learn about the care of family pets. They wanted to assemble all of their information and produce a resource for other students to use when they had a question about a pet they might own or might be thinking about owning.

Invention Evolution

Over time, good ideas have a tendency to evolve. Transportation, for example, has evolved from riding animals to riding in spaceships. As inventions have been used and evaluated, changes naturally occur. In what ways have some of our common tools (the dishwasher, vacuum cleaner, computer, light bulb, television) evolved over time?

Marketing a Business

A new start-up company has come to your company and asked you to make a presentation about marketing one of its new products. The product is a new form of software that companies use to monitor and report all Web activity by their employees. It helps companies make sure employees are properly using the Internet during office hours. How can the new company be convinced that you have the knowledge and capabilities to market their new software?

2. Based on your selected project, consider the following questions that concern the integration of presentation software such as PPT. Mark your response to each question.

Integration assessment questionnaire (IAQ)

Will using **PRESENTATION** software as a part of the project:	
Broaden the learners' perspective on potential solution paths and/or answers?	__ Yes __ No __ Maybe
Increase the level of involvement and investment of personal effort by the learners?	__ Yes __ No __ Maybe
Increase the level of learner motivation (e.g., increase the relevance of the to-be-learned task, the confidence of dealing with the task, and/or the overall appeal of the task)?	__ Yes __ No __ Maybe
Decrease the time needed to generate potential solutions?	__ Yes __ No __ Maybe
Increase the quality and/or quantity of learner practice working on this and similar projects?	__ Yes __ No __ Maybe
Increase the quality and/or quantity of feedback given to the learner?	__ Yes __ No __ Maybe
Enhance the ability of the student to solve novel but similar projects, tasks, and problems in the future?	__ Yes __ No __ Maybe

3. If you have responded "Yes" to one or more of the questions, you should consider the use of PPT to enhance the student's potential learning experience.
4. Develop a lesson plan based on this project. Within the plan, indicate how and when the learner will use PPT. Additionally, list potential benefits and challenges that may occur when involving this software within the lesson.

Level 3b Workout: Exploring the NETS Standard connection

Developing and executing a lesson plan that integrates the use of presentation software such as Microsoft's PPT directly addresses several of the NETS Standards for both teachers (NETS·T) and students (NETS·S). See the Appendix for a full listing of the standards.

Part A: Generally, the main purpose for learning and using application software is to increase one's level of production—that is, to do things faster, better, or both. NETS Standards (NETS·T Standard V and NETS·S Standard 6) help us focus on these productivity objectives for both teachers and students. There are other technology standards, however, that may also be potentially addressed through one's knowledge and use of presentation software. Reflect on the following questions and consider the potential impact of the integration of such software (refer to the Appendix):

- When designing a presentation, how can the use of the outlining feature within PPT (and similar presentation programs) increase brainstorming for creative thinking? Can this feature also be used to increase collaborative planning between groups of individuals during the planning process? (NETS·T III.B. and III.C.; NETS·S 1 and 2)
- In what ways could the use of linked graphics, as well as video and audio clips, be integrated to increase levels of learning for diverse audiences? (NETS·T VI B. and VI.C; NETS·S 2 and 5)
- By using action buttons to produce individualized instructional materials, in what ways can the use of linked activities, Web sites, and other information be used to manage the students' learning environment? (NETS·T II.E)

- Presentation software was created to help disseminate information. How could the use of such software improve the communication skills developed by both teachers and students (NETS•T V.D.; NETS•S 2)

Part B: Go to the ISTE Web site **http://cnets.iste.org.** Within that site, select to review either the student or the teacher NETS Standards. Once you have selected the standards to review, select either the student or teacher profiles and look for the corresponding scenarios. Review the scenarios and determine how presentation software could be used within several of those situations.

While visiting the ISTE Web site and exploring the scenarios, go to the lesson plan search area and select a number of different lesson plans of interest. Review those and determine the role (if any) of presentation software within the development, implementation, and assessment of the lesson. Note this from both the perspective of the teacher developing the lesson and the perspective of the student participating in the implemented lesson.

Further ideas on using PPT as a learning tool	When using presentation software such as PPT, people often think immediately about how to use it merely for verbal presentations. The first few examples are ideas based on such presentations—but then look beyond to see other possibilities for this software and how individuals can adapt and use it to learn.

> **Note:** These ideas are to help you generate your own ideas of what could be done. Don't let it bother you if they aren't the right content or grade level—use the idea and adapt it to be helpful within your own situation. These are meant to be a stimulus for additional ideas.

1. Classroom demonstration: With the use of scanned pictures, imported videos, sound, and other media, you can readily demonstrate concepts, procedures, and so on to a group of individuals.
2. Have students create their own reports and practice verbal skills by making presentations to the class (e.g., book reports).
3. Have the students create and deliver a group project where the presentation is the central product they create. For example, have groups of students create science fair oral presentations about their group projects.
4. Develop a debate between two or more groups of students. Each "side" could develop their own key points and present them to a panel of judges via presentation software.
5. Use the outlining feature within PPT to have groups of students brainstorm certain concepts and how they would be presented for logical explanations.
6. Using action buttons, have the students create interactive presentations that link with the Internet and specific Web sites for additional information, media, and activities.
7. Create a preview or review quiz or test for students that allows them to make a selection and receive feedback on their performances.
8. Create an interactive calendar that allows students to click on the day and receive information on what will occur, homework assignments, links to various activities, student jobs, and so forth.
9. Create an interactive book club where students can click on any book (active button) listed and find out something about the book, read student critiques about the book, and perhaps even send questions via e-mail to the author.
10. Create a map of the city (or of the world, or of the human body, and so on) and have transparent action buttons that allow students to click on certain sections and further information will be given about that section.

11. Create a flier for advertising some product or announcement—for example, simple fliers using graphics to promote a school dance, someone's birthday, or a special award.

12. Develop a comparison table that lists the pros and cons to a specific issue (e.g., building a new power plant in a nearby location). Each cell could be hyperlinked to other slides explaining the pros and cons issue in more detail.

13. Create an interactive timeline based on some period in history. Along the timeline have action buttons that will activate relevant graphics, videos, text, or audio media revealing important elements of that point in history.

14. Have students create a presentation on a proposal for a major course project. Perhaps this can be a presentation about a future science fair project, a major English, history, and math integrated project, and so forth. Have them create handouts of their work and defend their ideas and overall proposal.

15. Create a WebQuest (see **http://webquest.sdsu.edu/webquest.html**) using PPT and hyperlinks as the software instead of a Web development editor.

16. Have students create a self-instructional, automatic presentation. Have the program play music in the background as it demonstrates and explains the steps involved in some type of procedure (e.g., how a paleontologist outlines and evaluates a potential dig site, how a farmer tills the ground, the processes used to refine petroleum, how potatoes are processed into potato chips).

17. For a geography, social studies, or history lesson, have each student in a class create a slide about a specific place, people, or time period. Put all of the slides together to form one slide show. Each of the students can then discuss his or her contribution.

Additional ideas on using PPT as an assistant

1. **Handouts.** Several of the key slides can be quickly printed as handouts for the students. These can then be used while the presentation is being made so that students can concentrate on what is being said versus trying to write down key concepts of the presentation. These also serve as very good advance organizers and as reviews following the presentation.

2. **Notes pages.** Often presentations are given on several occasions or for different classes. With the notes page, it is possible to create a version of the presentation that also has your notes of what you should say and explain for each of the slides presented. These notes can also be helpful to students who missed the presentation or who may not have caught everything said at the time of the presentation.

3. **Templates.** Many individuals find that a good presentation can be readily "repurposed" and adapted for another audience. By using the saved presentation as a **template**, a few changes can quickly be made and a "new" presentation is created.

4. **Storage places.** This is a little different, but individuals have been known to use certain presentations on specific topics as a good place to "hold" important Web sites, pictures, ideas, and so on. For example, within a specific science presentation, an individual may find it convenient to create a resource page or slide of other related Web sites addresses that can readily be found and used if a later need on this topic is discovered or when an update of the presentation is needed. This same idea may hold for specific pictures, graphics, ideas, or sound clips.

5. **Graphics.** Use the draw function in this program to create all kinds of charts, procedures, and other learning aids that students can see and follow. A seating chart or even an organizational chart, for example, can be quickly created. A job aid (simple procedure to follow) could be created in a matter of seconds (e.g., fire drill procedures, steps to follow to check out a book in the library, steps to completing a proper serve in tennis).

6. **Awards.** Create certificates for extra effort and merit.

Chapter 6

DESKTOP PUBLISHING
MS Publisher: The Basics of Desktop Publishing
(written in cooperation with Cindy York)

Introduction

What should you know about desktop publishers?	Desktop publishing (e.g., Microsoft's Publisher) is designed to help you and your students create professional looking publications. You need to know a few of its basics so that you can use it effectively. In this opening section, we want you to know the following: • what a desktop publisher program is, what it can do, and how it can help in teaching and learning • how to justify the use of the desktop publisher program as an effective tool—by knowing when and why it should or shouldn't be used

Terms to know

font	graphic	WordArt
text box	border	table
border art	fill color	
boundaries/guides		

What is a desktop publisher and what does it do?	Desktop publishers are computer applications that allow you to design and produce professional-looking publications at home or school. Using desktop publishing is very similar to using a word processing program and allows you to create print publications, e-mail publications, or Web publications. Desktop publishing allows for manipulation of the size and shape of print publications, allowing for things such as a one-page flyer, wall banner, index card, or greeting card, just to name a few. Microsoft's Publisher provides many templates and ideas as well as blank publications that allow you to choose the page layout such as postcard, index card, business card, full page, tent card, side fold card, top fold card, and so on. This provides for flexibility and creativity on your part.

Types of publications	There are many different types of publications. The most common you'll find is print publications. These could be advertisements, signs, note cards, business cards, labels, and so forth. Within MS Publisher there are also e-mail publications and Web publications. E-mail publications consist of e-mail newsletters, event or activity announcement, product announcement, and so on. Web publications can consist of the same things as e-mail publications, as well as just about anything else someone would want to create on a Web site.

What are some commonly used desktop publishers?	• Microsoft's Publisher • Quark, Inc.'s QuarkXPress • Adobe's PageMaker • Adobe's InDesign • Adobe's FrameMaker • Broderbund's Print Shop Deluxe • Corel's CorelDraw Graphics

> **Note:** We focus on Microsoft's Publisher in this text. However, **all of what we show you can be done in any of the other desktop publishers listed**. So if you don't have access to Publisher, don't be alarmed—you can still complete the projects and learn the basic skills.

Why bother learning how to use desktop publishing?

- **Save money and time.** Professional publications can be expensive and time-consuming. Publishing from your computer allows for quick and easy modifications to any document.
- **Quality publications.** Desktop publishing allows the use of clip art and professional-looking fonts. Desktop publications look much more professional than handwritten ones. A quality publication will grab someone's attention much better than a casually created publication.
- **Themes—templates, font schemes, color schemes.** "Design sets" allow you to keep a theme throughout different documents such as letterhead, envelope, and label. Publisher offers many templates, publication design ideas, color schemes, and **font** schemes.
- **Multiple uses.** It's easy to see how many different types of publications you can create using this software. From award certificates, to labels, to newsletters—you can create just about anything you might need.
- **Learning tool.** Desktop publishing can be integrated into various lessons, for example, the history of publishing. This lesson could begin prior to the printing press and lead into today's newspaper and magazine publishing.

How can desktop publishing be used at school? A brief list of ideas

By the teacher:

- Newsletters
- Flyers
- Signs or banners
- Calendars
- Nameplates
- Award certificates
- Class Web site

By the student:

- Classroom newspapers
- Book reports
- Club announcements
- School event flyers
- Family trees
- Greeting cards
- Brochures
- Personal Web portfolio

Orientation

What's the workspace look like?

Figure 6.1 is an example of the workspace of a common desktop publisher (MS Publisher). Note where you can enter in your information and some of the common toolbars, buttons, and menus located around the workspace. You should note that unlike other Microsoft Office 2007 applications (e.g., Excel, Word), Publisher uses toolbars that include a main menu of tabs with associated drop-down menus. Most tools that you use within Publisher can be found on these various drop-down menus.

Figure 6.1 View of a Microsoft Publisher desktop publishing work area

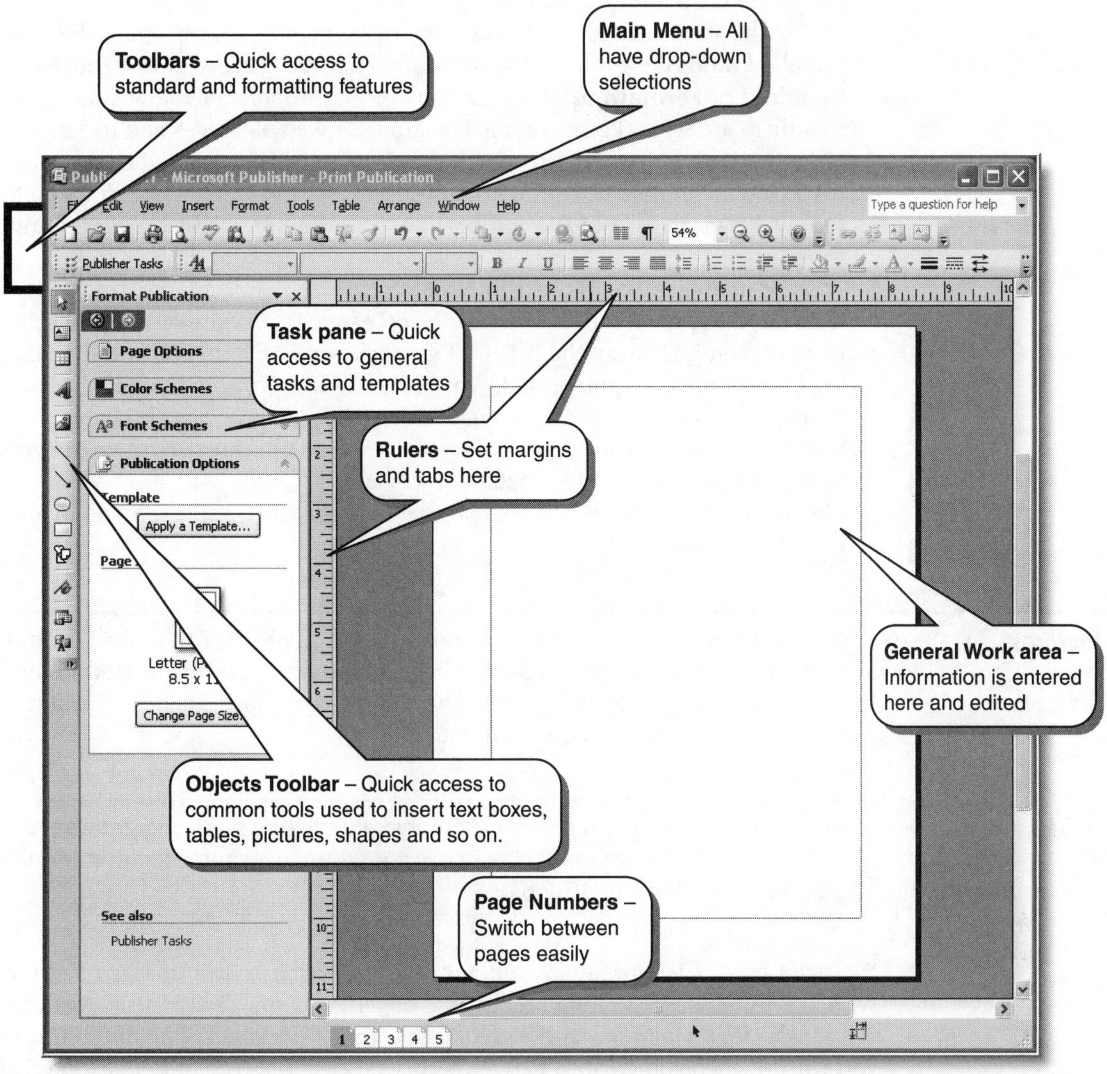

Toolbars – Quick access to standard and formatting features

Main Menu – All have drop-down selections

Task pane – Quick access to general tasks and templates

Rulers – Set margins and tabs here

General Work area – Information is entered here and edited

Objects Toolbar – Quick access to common tools used to insert text boxes, tables, pictures, shapes and so on.

Page Numbers – Switch between pages easily

What tools can be used?

The standard and formatting toolbars have many of the main tools that you will use to create and edit most publications. However, there are many other features that can be used when needed. To find other tools, look for the Toolbar menu (**View >>> Toolbars**) and you will find toolbars that contain specific sets of tools to work with pictures, WordArt, and so on.

Orientation Workout 1: Explore the territory

Turn on the computer and attempt the following:

1. Launch MS Publisher. Select the type of publication that you want to develop. Select a type (e.g., Flyers, Greeting Cards, Letterhead) and then select a specific design. MS Publisher provides a number of optional templates from which to choose. These options are professionally developed and can be used to help with the completion of your project. Try several options and view the different layouts generated by your selection.

2. Examine the main menu (usually found across the top of the screen). Click on each menu title (e.g., File, Edit) and note the various selections available under each. You

won't need all, but it's good to know where to find things. Pay special attention to where the Help menu is located.

3. Under the View menu, drop down to the toolbar selection and make sure the Standard and Formatting toolbars are checked (**View >>> Toolbars >>> Standard** or **Formatting**). These are the common toolbars you will use (also note that there are several others available and later we will access and use them).

4. Note that the tools on the toolbars show icons representing what the tool is for. If you lay the mouse pointer over any specific tool (don't click), the name for the tool will appear. Use of the toolbars is a fast way of accessing commonly used tools.

5. Practice adding elements and information to your project. This can be done, for example, by selecting to insert a text box (**Insert** >>> **Text box** or by selecting the text box icon ⬛ from the side toolbar as shown in Figure 6.1) and then by clicking in the workspace, holding down the mouse button, and dragging the box until it's the size you want. You can adjust this size later. Notice how you can move your text around the workspace by moving the text box. You can also rotate the direction of the text. We go into more detail on this later.

6. Play with it for a few minutes so you get a sense for what can be done and how easy it is to use.

Key features

Several key features have been incorporated within Publisher to assist you and your students as projects are identified, designed, and produced. Here are a few of the items that allow you to quickly and professionally develop projects such as brochures, programs, resumes, signs, cards, and so on.

> **Note:** Each of these key features is demonstrated within a set of mentoring videos on the text's accompanying Web site. Go to the **www.prenhall.com/newby** >>> **Chapter 6** >>> **Mentor Videos.**

Publication Types There are many different types of publications that can be produced with desktop publishing software, such as advertisements, certificates, brochures, flyers, newsletters, programs, and signs. As shown in Figure 6.2, one of the first things you will do when you create a new project is to select the type of publication that you are to design. By first selecting a type, you will then be given access to all kinds of examples and templates for that type of publication.

Predesigned publications and templates Publisher has a number of different premade layouts created by professional designers that are available for your use. One or more of these may match what you need for your publication. Even if the given templates aren't a perfect match for your needs, they provide all types of ideas and possibilities of what can be created. As shown in Figure 6.3, once the type of publication has been selected (e.g., Calendars), then a new window exposing all of the different templates is exposed.

Selecting a template allows you to review the basic design and then add the written information and visual elements needed for your specific publication. Such templates can save you time and effort by giving you a quick, professional start to the project. It's always possible to start from scratch (a blank publication), but the templates allow you to start (and finish) in a much more timely fashion.

In addition, these templates are flexible—that is, you can customize them as needed. Note in Figure 6.4 that you can customize the type of color and font scheme used, as well as paper size, and so on. Once you have created your own or customized one of the given templates, Publisher allows you to save the result as a new template. In this way, when you need it, the template will be available for your use and you won't have to generate it again.

Figure 6.2 Selecting the type of publication to be created within MS Publisher

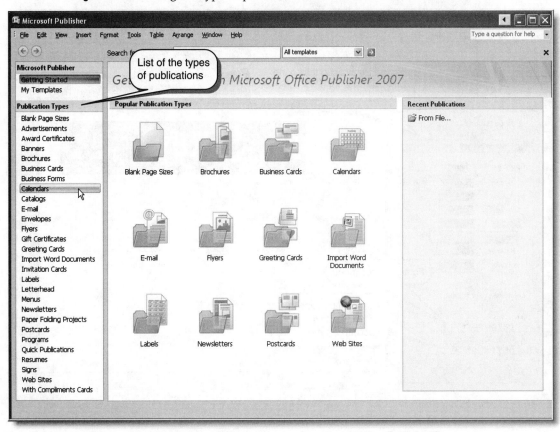

Figure 6.3 Selecting the design/template for the publication

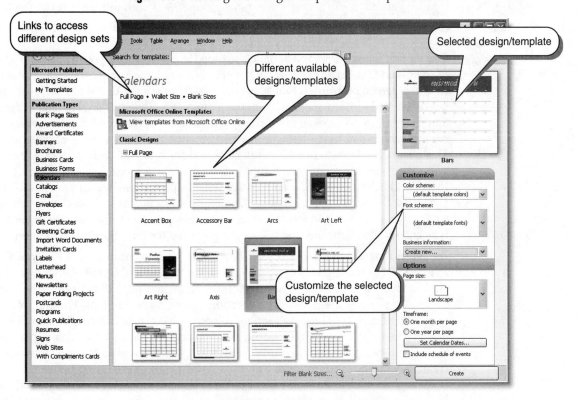

Figure 6.4 Selecting the color and/or font scheme for the publication

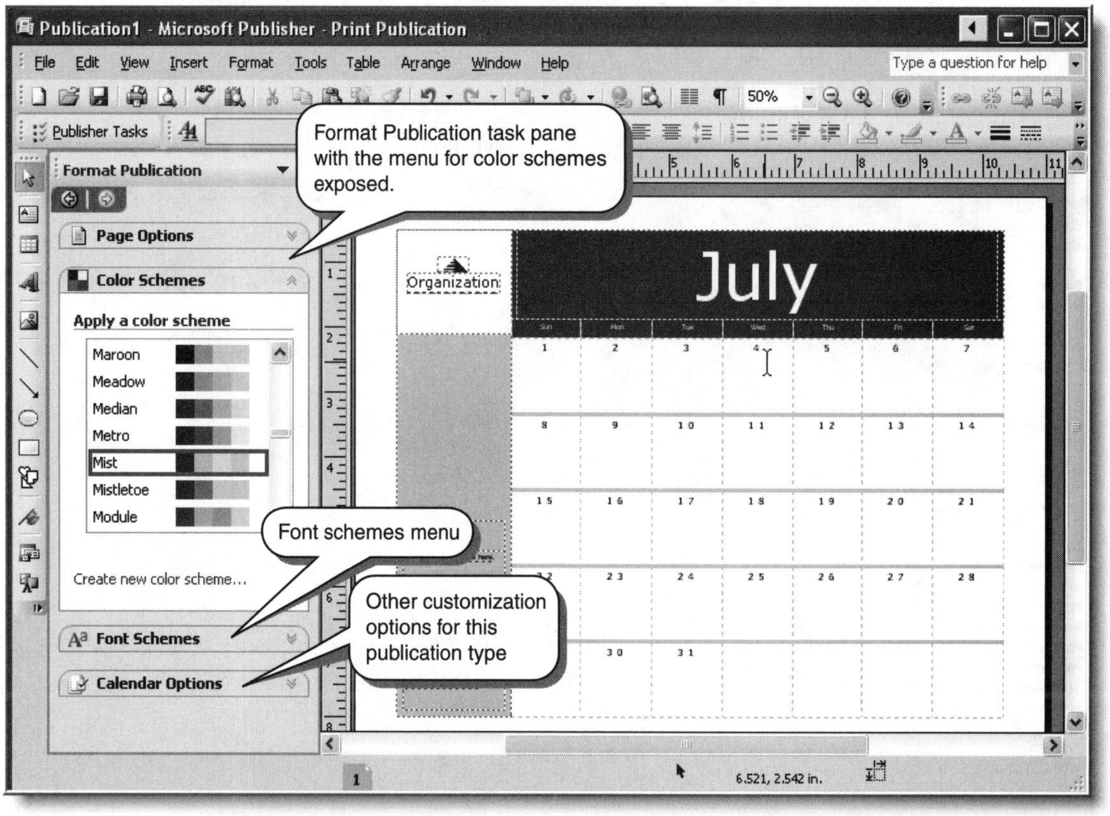

Note: Within this template selection window, the templates have been grouped based on a specified design set (for the calendar templates, these sets include full-page calendars, wallet-size calendars, and some blank sizes that match specific paper sizes). You can access the various grouped sets through the links at the top of the window or by scrolling down with the vertical scroll bar.

Color and Font Schemes With the flexibility provided by this software, you can select all kinds of colors and fonts to be used within your publication. However, for some of us that can lead to potential problems—that is, we may select something that we think looks good but others find problematic. Similar to the templates designed by professional designers and given to you to access and use, designers have also selected schemes or sets of colors and schemes of fonts that work well together within specific types of publications. This allows you to include a variety of color and fonts to add visual appeal, but at the same time you can confidently apply these schemes knowing that they work well together to help your publication be perceived as a professionally creation. As shown in Figure 6.4, the Format Publication task pane gives you access to drop-down menus of various types of color and font schemes. In addition, based on the selected publication type and selected template, you will be given options for the page and publication.

The Master Page Master pages contain the design and layout elements that you want to repeat on multiple pages in a publication. The design and layout elements may include headers and footers, page numbers, pictures, and page dimensions. The use of the master pages helps give your publication a more consistent look. For example, you may want your school logo and school colors to be consistent throughout your publication; therefore, you put the background colors and logo on the master page and they will show up consistently throughout your publication. The Master allows you to create it *once*, and it automatically appears on all pages of the publication.

Within MS Publisher, each type of publication that you select to work with already has one master page associated with it (to provide the page layout). You can access that master and change the layout, add other design elements, and so on. You can also create additional master pages so you can adapt parts of your publication as it is developed (e.g., if you want the interior pages of a brochure to have elements on the master page that vary from those of the front and back page of the brochure).

Here's a list of what you can do with the master pages:

- Create a new Master page (**View** menu >>> **Master Page** >>> on the **Edit Master Pages** toolbar >>> **New Master Page**).
- Access and edit a master page (**View** menu >>> **Master Page** >>> on the **Edit Master Pages** task pane, select the master page to edit).
- Apply a master to a specific publication page (**Format** menu >>> **Apply Master Page** >>> **Apply Master Page** task pane >>> click drop-down menu and select the master page to apply).
- Place design or layout elements on a master page (select element to place on master >>> **Arrange** menu >>> **Send to Master Page**).
- Ignore a master page for a specific part of a publication (**View** menu >>> **Ignore Master Page**).
- Rename a master page (**View** menu >>> **Master Page** >>> click on the arrow next to the master page title that you want to rename >>> **Rename Master Page**).
- Delete a master page (**View** menu >>> **Master Page** >>> click on the arrow next to the master page title that you want to delete >>> **Delete**).

Blank Publications MS Publisher offers a number of blank publications that you can use as a starting point for your own. These allow you to select a specific page size based on the type of publication that you want to create (e.g., booklets, postcards, name tags). The beauty of this selection is that Publisher has included selections that allow you to match your needed size with commercial products (e.g., Avery labels) so that when you create and print, your publication will match exactly the paper that you use from these commercial vendors (see Figure 6.5).

Figure 6.5 Selecting a blank page size

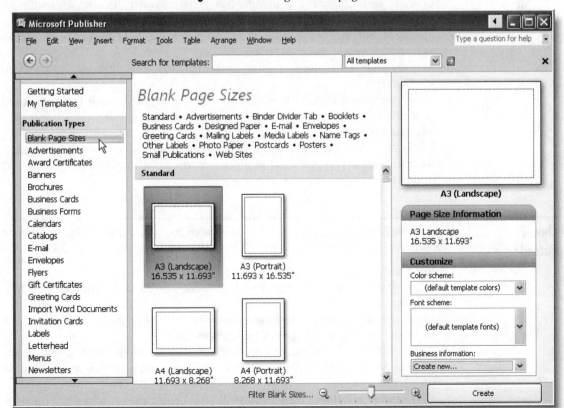

To access the blank publications, simply create a new publication (**File** menu >>> **New**) and select the **Blank Page Sizes** alternative from the **Publication Types** menu. Then click on the link for the type of blank publication you wish to design and use the scroll bar to see all of the alternatives.

Orientation Workout 2: Explore the key features

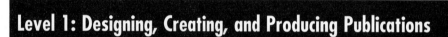

While in Publisher:

1. Create a blank publication with more than one page.
2. Review the Orientation Workout 1 and add some content to your publication (e.g, text boxes with information, a picture).
3. Select and apply a color scheme and/or font scheme.
4. Create a new Master page and add some elements such as a header or footer, or page number.
5. Return to your pages and note the changes made on all of the pages using the Master.

Level 1: Designing, Creating, and Producing Publications

What should you be able to do?

Given specific guidelines and step-by-step procedures, you'll be able to use various tools and techniques of a desktop publisher program (specifically MS Publisher) to design, create, and produce a publication.

What resources are provided?

Basically, Level 1 is divided into a common teaching scenario, selected solutions, and practice exercises (i.e., Workouts). The scenario has been constructed to allow you to examine a problem and how it can be addressed through the use of this software. To do this we have provided the following:

a. Quick reference figures that identify (via visual callouts) all of the key features that have been incorporated within the solution presentation. These allow you to rapidly identify the key features and reference exactly how to include such features within your own work.
b. Step-by-step instructions on how to incorporate all highlighted features within your work.
c. Video mentoring support that support and guide you through the integration of each of the highlighted features (**www.prenhall.com/newby** >>> **Chapter 6** >>> **Mentor Videos**).
d. Workout exercises that allow you to practice identifying and selecting which software features to use, when to use those features, how they should be incorporated, and to what degree they are effective.

How should you proceed?

If you have little or no experience with MS Office 2007 and particularly Publisher, then we suggest you do the following:

1. Read and review Scenario 1.
2. Examine the quick reference figure (Figure 6.7) and all of the numbered highlights or callouts.
3. Using the step-by-step directions given for each highlighted feature, use the software and practice using each of the features.
4. Access the mentoring videos (**www.prenhall.com/newby** >>> **Chapter 6** >>> **Mentor Videos**) that explain each of the features and how they are accomplished within the software.
5. Go to the Workout and work through the problems and exercises as it outlines.

If you have <u>experience</u> with Publisher 2007, you may want to review the scenarios and the quick reference figure first. If any of the features are unfamiliar, then use the step-by-step procedures, as well as the mentoring support videos. Once the review has been completed, then move directly to the Workout exercise and create your own publication by incorporating many of the highlighted features.

Scenario 1: Getting everyone involved

Remember the aluminum can recycling project that Mr. Rena's classes were involved with (see Chapters 3 and 4). After gaining the approval of the school administration for their plans for a schoolwide recycling effort, the SCAR (Students for Can and Aluminum Recycling) committee was formed. In an effort to promote their new schoolwide recycling project, the committee decided to create some signs to distribute around the school. Figure 6.6 is a printout of one of the SCAR signs that was distributed.

Let's take a look at the sign created by this student committee. This sign can be used as a template for other signs that will use a similar format and other features. Several key publishing features were used within the sign.

- Take a close look at Figure 6.7. This figure highlights what has been done to the publication so that it looks like a finished product. Pay attention to the numbered callout bubbles.
- We want you to follow the step-by-step procedures and reproduce the "Save the Cans" sign with all of the key features included. It doesn't have to be exactly the same, but demonstrate that you can carry out the highlighted functions or features.

Figure 6.6 Sample sign created using MS Publisher

Figure 6.7 Highlighted sample sign

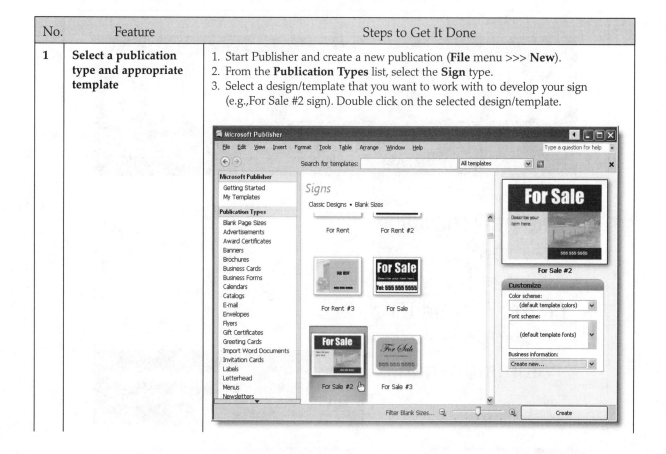

No.	Feature	Steps to Get It Done
1	**Select a publication type and appropriate template**	1. Start Publisher and create a new publication (**File** menu >>> **New**). 2. From the **Publication Types** list, select the **Sign** type. 3. Select a design/template that you want to work with to develop your sign (e.g.,For Sale #2 sign). Double click on the selected design/template.

No.	Feature	Steps to Get It Done
2	**Insert and/or adapt a text box**	A **text box** is one of the best methods used to insert text onto a workspace and then control where it is placed and how it looks. **To insert a text box:** 1. Chose the text box tool or (**Insert** menu >>> **Text Box**). This will make your cursor look like a large plus sign +. Take the cursor and drag a box across your workspace. 2. Type text directly into the text box. Modify your text using font type, size, color, and style changes found on the formatting toolbar. Franklin Gothic Book ▾ 36 ▾ **B** *I* U ≡ ≡ ≡ ≡ ≡ ≡ ≡ ≡ ≡ A A A ▾ A ▾ **To adapt a text box within a template:** 1. Click within the selected text box and select all words that you wish to adapt. 2. Type in the words that you desire. 3. Adapt the text (e.g., color, size, alignment) through the use of the formatting toolbar buttons. 4. Adapt the size of the text box by clicking once in the text box. Handles (i.e., small dots on the corners and sides of the text box) should appear. Textbox with handles 5. Click, hold, and move the handle to adjust the size of the box. Alter the size of the text box until the words fit appropriately.
3	**Adapt the publication's color scheme**	1. Select the colors from the predesigned set of color schemes (**Format** menu >>> **Color Scheme**). This selection can also be made from the **Format Publications** task pane by selecting the drop-down menu under the **Color Scheme** icon and title. 2. If you want to fill a specific area with a chosen color, select the item (e.g., a text box) and then click the arrow next to the fill button on the formatting toolbar. This will reveal the suggested colors that would match the current color scheme and it will also allow other colors to be selected. No Fill More Fill Colors... Fill Effects... Sample Fill Color
4	**Font type, size, style, and color change**	1. Select (highlight) the words you would like to change. 2. On the main menu, select **Format** >>> **Font**. . . . The font window appears.

continued

No.	Feature	Steps to Get It Done

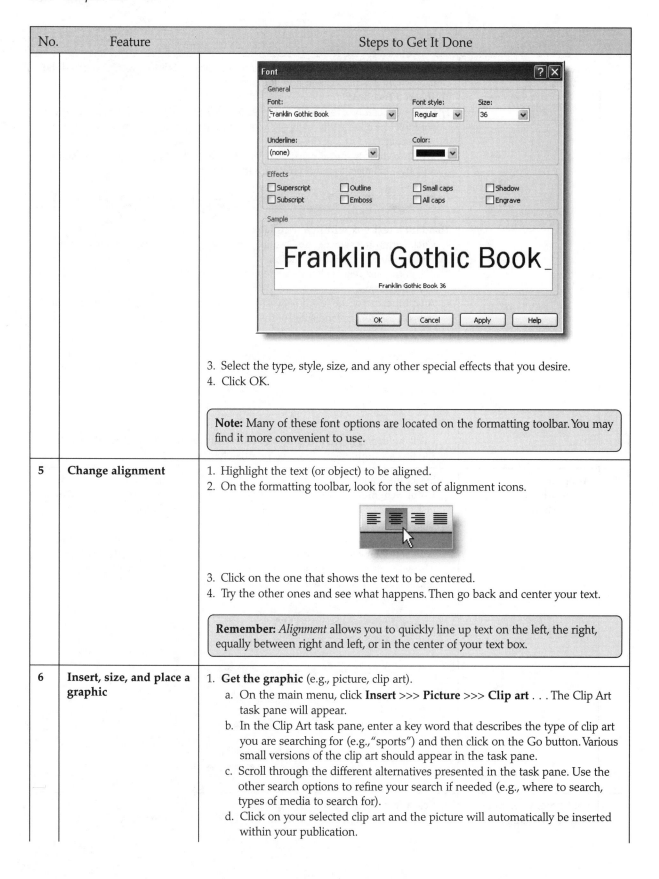

3. Select the type, style, size, and any other special effects that you desire.
4. Click OK.

> **Note:** Many of these font options are located on the formatting toolbar. You may find it more convenient to use.

| 5 | **Change alignment** | 1. Highlight the text (or object) to be aligned.
2. On the formatting toolbar, look for the set of alignment icons. |

3. Click on the one that shows the text to be centered.
4. Try the other ones and see what happens. Then go back and center your text.

> **Remember:** *Alignment* allows you to quickly line up text on the left, the right, equally between right and left, or in the center of your text box.

| 6 | **Insert, size, and place a graphic** | 1. **Get the graphic** (e.g., picture, clip art). |

  a. On the main menu, click **Insert** >>> **Picture** >>> **Clip art** . . . The Clip Art task pane will appear.
  b. In the Clip Art task pane, enter a key word that describes the type of clip art you are searching for (e.g., "sports") and then click on the Go button. Various small versions of the clip art should appear in the task pane.
  c. Scroll through the different alternatives presented in the task pane. Use the other search options to refine your search if needed (e.g., where to search, types of media to search for).
  d. Click on your selected clip art and the picture will automatically be inserted within your publication.

No.	Feature	Steps to Get It Done

Clip Art task pane

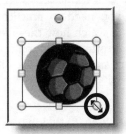

Selected clip art
with handles | **Note:** Some of your selected pictures may not be stored on your hard drive or server. Another option is to go directly to the Microsoft "Clip art on Office Online" site. There should be a direct link located at the bottom of the Clip Art task pane. Once you get to that site, follow the directions for selecting and using their clip art.

2. **Size the graphic.** If your inserted clip art is the perfect size for your publication—great, leave it as it is. However, in many cases, the size will need to be adjusted. Point your mouse at the picture and left click once. Note that a box will be drawn around the picture and handles will be placed at each of the corners and in the middle of each of the sides. You can grab a handle by putting your mouse pointer on the handle (note that your pointer will change into a double-headed arrow), left click, and hold it. Dragging a handle will cause the picture to be altered. Try different handles and see what happens to the shape and size of the picture.

3. **Place the graphic.** Once your picture is inserted and sized appropriately, you can move it to a different location on the page by putting the mouse on top of the **graphic**, clicking, holding, and then dragging it to the new location.

4. **Adapt or adjust the quality of the graphic.** You should also note that once you have selected your picture (the picture has the box around it with the handles) a special **Picture toolbar** appears. This toolbar can be attached directly to the formatting toolbar if you desire. You can access it at any time (**View** menu >>> **Toolbars** >>> **Picture**).

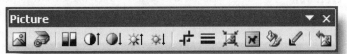

You can use these tools to:
• Adjust the picture (brightness, contrast, color)
• Change the picture style (**border**, shape, special effects)
• Arrange the picture in relation to other items (bring to the front, send to the back)
• Size (crop, alter height and width)

Note: Additional fine-tuning of the picture is also available by accessing the **Format Picture** dialog box (**Format** menu >>> **Picture** . . .). Through a series of tabs, you can select to adjust the color and lines, size, layout, picture quality, and so forth to a much finer degree than using the picture toolbar. This dialog box is also accessible by clicking the ✎ icon on the **Picture toolbar**.

Note: Working with clip art and other graphic files may take a bit of practice. You'll find that some don't look very good when their size is changed to a drastic degree—others work great. You will also find that access to the Internet gives you an endless supply of various clip art, pictures, and so forth that you may want to use and insert within your documents. |
| 7 | **Insert WordArt** | 1. WordArt is a Microsoft object that provides you with various fancy text templates. You can use WordArt instead of a text box to insert text, but all of the text formatting in the WordArt text box will be the same.
2. The simple way to insert WordArt is to select the **WordArt tool** from the **Objects toolbar**. |

continued

No.	Feature	Steps to Get It Done
	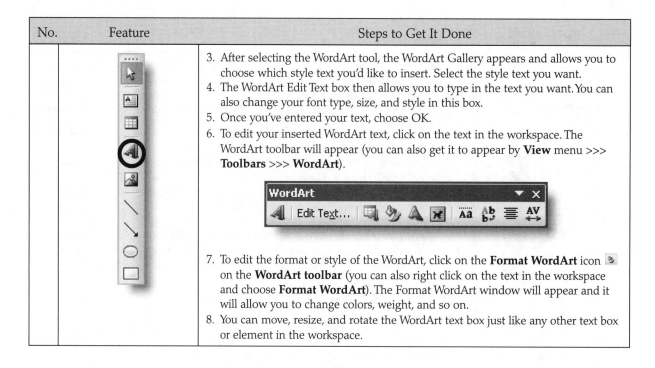	3. After selecting the WordArt tool, the WordArt Gallery appears and allows you to choose which style text you'd like to insert. Select the style text you want. 4. The WordArt Edit Text box then allows you to type in the text you want. You can also change your font type, size, and style in this box. 5. Once you've entered your text, choose OK. 6. To edit your inserted WordArt text, click on the text in the workspace. The WordArt toolbar will appear (you can also get it to appear by **View** menu >>> **Toolbars** >>> **WordArt**). 7. To edit the format or style of the WordArt, click on the **Format WordArt** icon on the **WordArt toolbar** (you can also right click on the text in the workspace and choose **Format WordArt**). The Format WordArt window will appear and it will allow you to change colors, weight, and so on. 8. You can move, resize, and rotate the WordArt text box just like any other text box or element in the workspace.

Level 1a Workout: Practice using basic desktop publishing features

To acquire the needed skills for desktop publishing, you need to practice using Publisher. It generally isn't good enough to just read and watch how these features are developed. One way for you to accomplish this is by creating and formatting your own publications. As these documents are created, select and integrate the different features within your own work.

Here is a basic outline of what you need to do:

1. Review Figure 6.7 and all of the highlighted features that are in that figure.
2. Using Figure 6.7 as a guide, create your own publication for the SCAR committee.
3. Go through the list of features and practice adding them to your publication. Don't worry about matching the example figure exactly. You can adapt and change the features as you add them. Remember, this is a practice workout: *practice integrating as many features as possible.*

> **Note:** Refer to specific feature numbers and the given step-by-step procedures as needed. Additionally, use the mentoring videos to help guide you through any specific procedure that needs additional clarification (see **www.prenhall.com/newby** >>> **Chapter 6** >>> **Mentor Videos**).

Level 1b Workout: Creating your own document

The benefits of desktop publishing software become very apparent as you begin to create and format your own publications. Think about all of the signs, brochures, newsletters, flyers, calendars, cards, Web pages, and so on that you can create for your work, home, school—whatever. Select one or two of those currently in need of being completed and do the following:

1. Select a project that you need or want to complete. If you are having difficulty coming up with a relevant project, open Publisher and review the list of publications that are possible. Think about your school, work, or home and if any of those types would be helpful.
2. Review the features demonstrated within Figure 6.7.

Table 6.1 Level 1 Workout and Practice Checklist Creating and Formatting
a Publication

Publication Content	___ Content is accurate and current.
	___ Content is relevant and cohesive throughout the document.
	___ Content achieves the proper "level" for the intended audience.
	___ Content is free from spelling and grammatical errors.
Publication Format	___ A new publication was created.
	___ Font size, style, and type were varied within the document to add emphasis to headings, and so forth.
	___ All text was placed and aligned in an appealing manner that allowed for clear understanding of the written material.
	___ Attractive, audience-relevant color and font schemes were employed within the publication.
	___ WordArt was employed effectively to gain attention to important text within the publication.
	___ Appropriate graphics (e.g., clip art, pictures, images) were properly selected, sized, and placed within the publication.

3. Format your new document with as many of the features demonstrated in those
   figures as possible. Use Table 6.1 as a checklist to guide your efforts.

> **Note:** Remember and implement the second rule to live by: SAVE, SAVE, SAVE,
> and then SAVE your work again. This was a key principle mentioned at the first of
> this text. Make sure you do that—or it will come back to haunt you sometime down
> the road.
>
> Also think about concepts of Rules 3, 4 and 5: Keep things simple, watch how
> others accomplish what we have described in this chapter, and make sure you
> think about saving the publication as a template that can be adapted and used later
> as needed.

Level 2: Tables, Templates, and Other Good Stuff

**What should you
be able to do?**

You should come to recognize additional desktop publishing features and gain confidence using Help to create, edit, and format several original publications.

The key here is not to memorize all that the software is capable of—it's better to
know some of the basics and when, where, and how to find assistance for all of the
other stuff.

Getting some Help

Similar to Help in Windows, there is also Help in MS Publisher and most other
sophisticated desktop publishing software. To use Help, click the **Help** menu >>>
Microsoft Publisher Help (you can also access Help by clicking on the **Help** icon
on the standard toolbar). A Help window will open, which allows you to examine
topics through a table of contents, browse different sections of the Publisher Help, or
insert a specific question or key word to search the Help for potential answers.

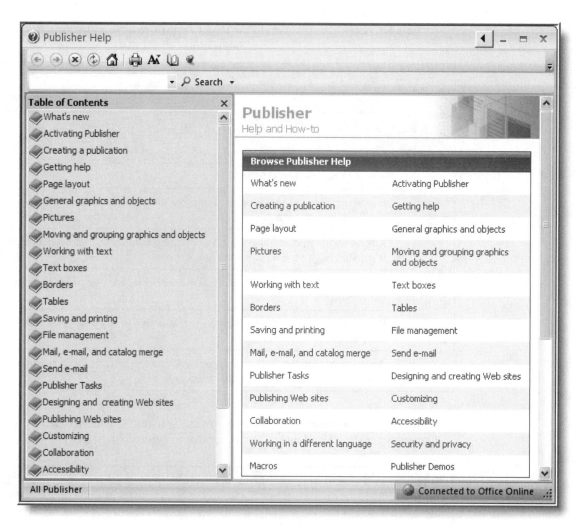

Publisher Help window

Help generally *does not* have all of the answers—but it will have a lot of them. Make sure you become familiar with how it works and how often it can be of assistance.

Scenario 2: The production

Mrs. Perez's fifth-grade class is putting on a play about the American Revolution at the end of the year. Although many have parts in the play, all of the students are involved with various parts of the production. An important part is the planning, designing, and production of the program for the event. Mrs. Perez's students chose the colors, pictures, and full layout of the program, as well as writing the information that the program will contain. The final publication is shown in Figures 6.8 and 6.9. Remember that the program will be folded vertically down the center so the front cover and back page are side-by-side. Thus, it only takes one piece of paper for the four pages. Once this publication is completed, it will be used as a template for future play programs just by cutting and pasting new content as needed.

After reviewing the finished product (Figures 6.8 and 6.9), take a close look at Figure 6.10 and the highlighted sections of the interior two pages of the program. Following the figure there is a description of each of the features that have been added to those pages and how they were accomplished. More importantly, there is also a description of how to find this information within MS Publisher's Help. Take

Figure 6.8 Program back and cover pages

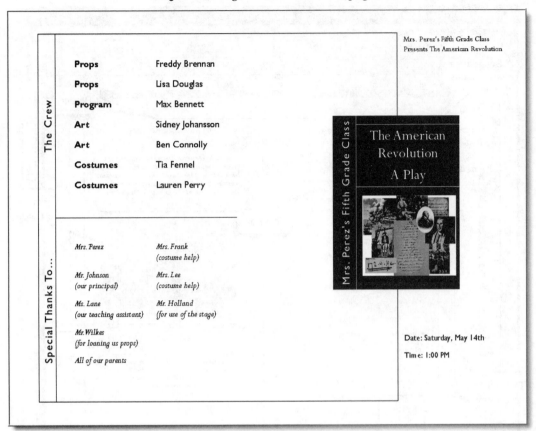

Figure 6.9 Program pages two and three

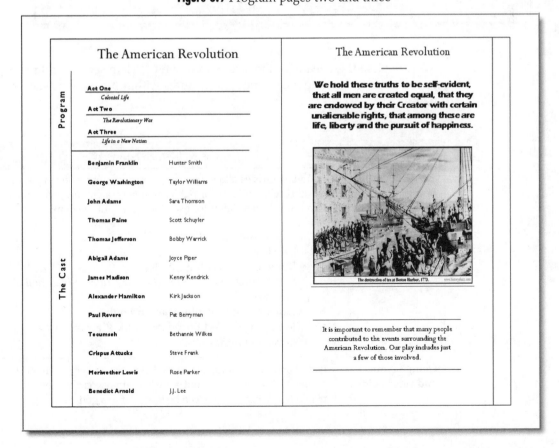

Figure 6.10 Program layout for pages two and three with highlights

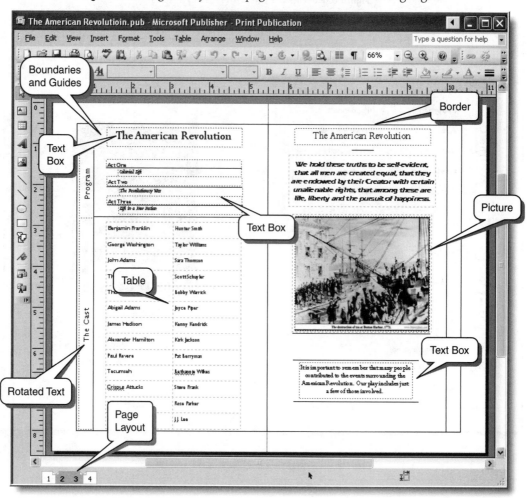

time to explore these features and also to examine the Help section and the explanations given on how to incorporate the features within productions such as this program.

Feature	Steps to Get It Done
Using object boundaries	Boundary **guides** allow you to see the edges of the items you are working with within your publication (e.g., a graphic, a text box). The **boundaries** allows for exact placement of the items on the publication. **Information and procedures:** Publisher Help ● • Key word: **Object boundaries**. • Select: *Hide or show layout guides, ruler guides, and object boundaries*. **Key features to note, explore, and try out:** • To view and use object boundaries, click **View** menu >>> **Borders and Guides**.
Using layout and ruler guides	Layout and ruler guides are used to help position items with exactness on the publication. These guides are lines (that won't be seen when the publication is printed) that can be formed into a grid

Feature	Steps to Get It Done

to ensure that exact placement of the elements on the page is completed.

Information and procedures:

Publisher Help ✹

- Key word: **Layout guides**.
- Select: *Hide or show layout guides, ruler guides, and object boundaries.*

Key features to note, explore, and try out:

- **Make the guides visible** (**View** >>> **Borders and Guides**): You can also go through the same process to make the guides invisible.
- **Baseline guide** (horizontal lines running across the publication): To access and use a baseline guide click **View** >>> **Baseline Guides**.
  - o To change the amount of space between the horizontal lines of the baseline guides, click **Arrange** menu >>> **Layout Guides . . .** The **Layout Guides** window will appear. Click on the **Baseline Guides** tab. The spacing and offset can be set within the Horizontal Baseline section of this window.

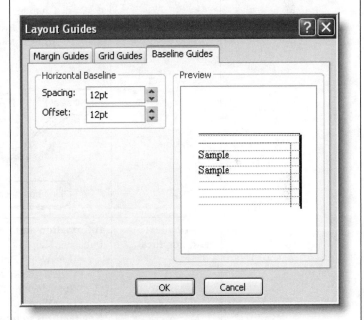

  - o Within the same Layout Guides window (**Arrange** menu >>> **Layout Guides. . . .**), clicking on the **Grid Guides** tab allows you to insert horizontal and vertical guides on the publication layout. The **Margin Guides** tab allows the outer margins of the publication to be adjusted.
- **Ruler guides:** These are additional guides (lines) that can be added to the Publisher workspace. They can be used to help place elements on the publication. An important feature of these guides, however, is that you can move and place them as needed.
  - o To insert a ruler guide: click **Arrange** menu >>> **Ruler guide** >>> **Add Horizontal** (or **Vertical**) **Ruler Guide**. You can add additional ruler guides as they are needed.
  - o To move a ruler guide: Once a ruler guide has been inserted, move your cursor over the top of the placed guide—the cursor will turn into a double-headed arrow. Click, hold, and drag the guide in the direction you desire it to move.

continued

Feature	Steps to Get It Done

Inserting and adapting text boxes	**Information and procedures:**
	Publisher Help ⊙
	• Table of Contents task pane: **Text boxes**
	• Select: any of the topics of interest about text boxes (*e.g.,* ***Create a text box, Align text within a text box***).
	Key features to note, explore, and try out:
	• Text boxes are used to position text on a page within a publication. The box allows you to control where the text is placed and how it looks and is emphasized.
	• To quickly insert and/or adapt a text box, review the explanation given within Scenario 1, Level 1, Feature 2 of this chapter (page 163).
	• There are a number of ways to emphasize the text box and catch the attention of those viewing it. Select your inserted text box and then try the following by only accessing icons on the format toolbar:
	  a. Fill the text box with a color
	  b. Put a border on the text box
	  c. Change the color of the text box border
	  d. Change the font size of text within the textbox
	  e. Change the color of the text within the textbox
	  f. Add shadowing and/or dimensionality to the box

Rotating text (and graphics)	**Information and procedures:** Publisher Help ⊙ • Key word: **Rotate text**. • Select: ***Make text vertical*** and follow the procedures given for "Make text flow vertically within a text box or AutoShape." **Key features to note, explore, and try out:** • To rotate the text box exactly 90°, select the text box and then open the **Format Text Box** window (**Format >>> Text Box**) and then click the **Text Box tab** and click on the **Rotate text within AutoShape by 90°**. • To freely rotate the text box, simply select the text box, then click, hold, and rotate the extended handle. The text will rotate as the mouse is moved in a circular fashion. Selected text box ready to be rotated Text box being rotated

Feature	Steps to Get It Done
	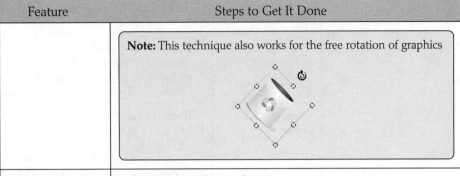 **Note:** This technique also works for the free rotation of graphics
Creating, formatting, and moving tables 	**Information and procedures:** Publisher Help ⊙ • Table of Contents task pane: **Tables**. • Select: any of the topics of interest about text boxes. (*e.g., Create a table, Format a table's size, layout, and cell properties*). **Key features to note, explore, and try out:** • To create a **table**, simply click on the table icon on the **Object toolbar**. The cursor will then turn into a cross hair + on the Publisher workspace. Click, hold, and drag the cursor to the size of the desired table and then release the cursor. A **Create Table** window will appear. In this window: o Select the number of rows and columns for the table. o Select a format from a number of premade table designs (**Table format:**). 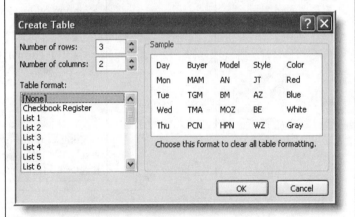 **Note:** You can also create a table and get the **Create Table** window to immediately appear by clicking **Table** menu >>> **Insert** >>> **Table.** • Tables can be altered and changed quite rapidly. Simply select the table and then click **Format** menu >>> **Table** and the **Format Table** window will appear. Within this table, you can alter the colors and lines, size, layout, and cell properties. • To move a table to a new location, select the table and then click, hold, and drag one of the side borders of the table. The table will follow where you move the cursor. Also, once the table is selected, the directional arrows on the keyboard will also move the table in the selected direction.

continued

Feature	Steps to Get It Done
	• To <u>insert a new row or column</u> on a table, click on a cell adjacent to where the new row or column should be inserted, click **Table >>> Insert >>> Row above (or below or Column left or right)**. To <u>delete a row or column</u> use this same procedure (**Table >>> Delete >>> Row or Column**).

Insert graphics or pictures	**Information and procedures:**
	Publisher Help ⊛
	   • Table of Contents task pane: **Pictures**.
	   • Select: *Add pictures and other graphics*.
	Key features to note, explore, and try out:
	To insert a picture or graphic:
	   • Click **Insert** menu >>> **Picture** >>> **From File** . . . and then navigate to your stored picture and select it.
	   • The inserted picture once selected can be sized, rotated, and/or moved similar to a text box. In addition, use of the picture toolbar tools allows the picture to be adapted in several different ways (e.g., color, contrast, crop).

Adding borders to a text box (or picture, object, AutoShape, and so forth)	**Information and procedures:**
	Publisher Help ⊛
	   • Table of Contents task pane: **Borders**.
	   • Select: *Add or remove a border in Publisher*.
	   • Select: *Change the color of fills, lines, and borders*.
	Key features to note, explore, and try out:
	Borders (e.g., a line) are a great way to highlight text and focus the attention of the viewer. To create a border:
	   • Select the text box (or picture, AutoShape, object).
	   • Click **Format** menu >>> **Text box** (or name of item selected).
	   • The **Format Text box** (or your selected item) window will appear.
	   • Select the **Colors and Lines** tab.
	   • Select the line color, border art, placement of lines, and so on.
	
	Note: Within this window (i.e., **Format Text Box**), you can also select a fill color and level of transparency of the fill for the selected text box

Scenario 3: SCAR and the Web

The SCAR (Students for Can and Aluminum Recycling) committee members have an idea for Mr. Rena and how the recycling project could be promoted to a greater degree. They want to develop a Web site that will inform the students, teachers, and parents about the project, its progress, and the difference it is making. With that information, they are hoping others will be more willing to help and contribute to their recycling cause. Although none of the students were skilled with Web editing software (e.g., Expression Web, Dreamweaver) or the use of HTML, they were told that Publisher had Web page templates that could be used to create professionally looking Web sites. Before approaching Mr. Rena and other school teachers and administrators, a small group of students decided to create a draft Web site as a demonstration of what could be done.

They decided that with the use of the Web design templates within Publisher, they could quickly develop the trial site and show it to those they would need. In this case, they just saved their site on a laptop hard drive so they could demonstrate how it would look and work. Later, after completing the final draft and gaining the needed school approvals, they would publish it to the Web.

Figure 6.11 SCAR draft Web site

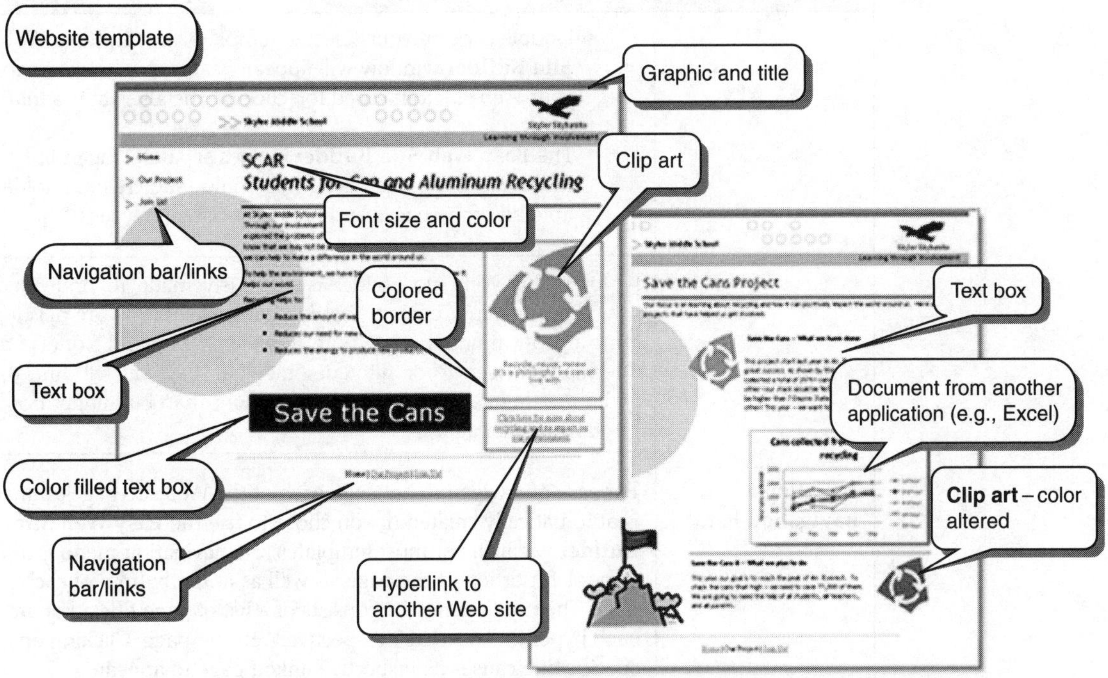

Figure 6.11 reveals the first couple pages of the draft Web site that the committee presented to Mr. Rena. Note that we have also included some highlighted features to indicate those similar to the previous explanations given within Scenarios 1 and 2 and to highlight several new elements (e.g., hyperlinks) that are specific to the development of a Web page publication. Review this Web site here; however, to review the full site, explore it by going to the text Web site (**www.prenhall.com/newby** >>> **Chapter 6** >>> **Example Web site** >>> **SCAR**).

Feature	Steps to Get It Done

Web site prework	Before the actual development of your Web site, there are a number of questions that should be answered (e.g., What is the purpose of the site? Who will use the site?). The answers will direct you on what types of pages should be developed within the site and what the key elements of each of the pages should be and how they should look.
	Information:
	Publisher Help
	    • Table of Contents: **Designing and creating Web sites**.
	    • Select: *Plan your Web site.*

Using Web site templates	**Information and procedures:**
	Publisher Help
	    • Table of Contents task pane: **Publishing Web Sites**.
	    • Select: *Prepare, publish, and maintain your Publisher Web Site* >>> *prepare your Web site* >>> *create your Web Site.*
	Key features to note, explore, and try out:
	    • When you start a new publication (**File** menu >>> **New** . . .), and you select **Web Sites** from the list of publication types, a number of newer and classic design Web site templates will appear.

continued

Feature	Steps to Get It Done
	• Double click on your selected template, and an **Easy Web Site Builder** window will appear. Based on what you want your Web site to be used for, click on the alternatives that apply. • The **Easy Web Site Builder** creates separate pages, links those pages together using hyperlinks, and creates a folder to hold all of the pages and their associated graphics. **Note:** This Web site builder is obviously made for individuals working within a business setting. However, if you are developing an educationally related site, it can still be helpful. Some of the terms will need to be altered somewhat, but you will find that altering them are generally more efficient than building it from a totally blank page.

Inserting a navigation bar	For ease of navigation between each of the Web site pages, a menu is automatically created (if you chose to use the **Easy Web Site Builder** wizard). For most templates, the navigation menu is at the upper left portion of the page, as well as at the bottom of each page. The menu generally consists of a list of page titles that are each hyperlinked to their respective Web site page. Clicking on a specific title causes its respective linked page to appear.
	Information and procedures:
	Publisher Help 🔅
	• Table of Contents task pane: **Designing and creating Web sites**.
	• Select: **Create a hyperlink**.
	Key features to note, explore, and try out:
	• Click on any of the items within the navigation bar and a **Navigation Bar Properties** icon ◁ will appear. Click on that icon and the Navigation bar properties dialog box will appear.
	• Within this window you can add, move, modify, and change the location of the links within the bar.
	
	Navigation Bar Properties [?][X]
	Name:
	`Bottom Navigation Bar`
	Links:
	Home [Add Link...]
	Our Project [Remove Link]
	Join Us! [Modify Link...]
	  [Move Up]
	  [Move Down]
	☑ Update this navigation bar with links to new pages that are added to this publication.
	[OK] [Cancel] [Help]

Feature	Steps to Get It Done

Inserting hyperlinks	Hyperlinks are one of the most powerful features of a Web document. Links allow you to connect Web pages in a site, connect to other Web sites, and connect to separate documents, graphics, audio or video files, and so on.
	Information and procedures:
	Publisher Help 🔘
	   • Table of Contents task pane: **Designing and creating Web sites.**
	   • Select: *Create a hyperlink*.
	Key features to note, explore, and try out:
	   • Select the word(s), graphic, or another item that you want to use as the link.
	   • Click **Insert** menu >>> **Hyperlink**. . . . You can also create a hyperlink using the **Hyperlink** icon 🔘 on either the **Standard** toolbar or the **Web tool** toolbar.
	   • As shown in Figure 6.12, the **Insert Hyperlink** window allows you to create a link to an existing page in your current Web site, explore the Internet to find the site that you desire to link to, find a document or file with which you want to create a link, or enter an exact name of a Web site that should be linked.
	
	Figure 6.12 Insert Hyperlink window
	
	Note: The typical link is a word or list of words that indicate what a click will do (e.g., go to my home page); however, you can also use images and parts of images as links. This would allow you, for example, to click on a picture to go to a site that the picture represents.

Use of text boxes	Just as within print types of publications, text boxes within a Web publication are used to organize information and place it in exact locations on the page.
	Information and procedures:
	Publisher Help 🔘
	   • Table of Contents task pane: **Text boxes**.
	Key features to note, explore, and try out:
	   • Review the information and procedures provided in Scenario 2 (page 172) for *Inserting and adapting text boxes*.

Filling text boxes with color or other stuff	**Information and procedures:**
	Publisher Help 🔘
	   • Table of Contents task pane: **General graphics and objects**.
	   • Select: *Formatting graphics or objects* >>> *Add or delete a shape fill or shape effect*.

continued

Feature	Steps to Get It Done
	Key features to note, explore, and try out: • Click on the text box you want to fill. • On the formatting toolbar, click on the arrow next to the **Fill Color** icon. • Click on the desired color. **Note:** Also review Scenario 1, Feature 3 (***Adapt the publication's color scheme***) from this chapter (page 163), for a description of this process. **Another note:** There may be times when you want the box to "fill" with something more than just a color. When you click the down arrow next to the fill icon on the formatting toolbar, click on the "Fill Effects . . ." alternative. The **Fill Effects** window will allow you to adjust the gradient, texture, pattern, picture, and tint.
Altering fonts size, color, style	**Information and procedures:** Publisher Help • Table of Contents task pane: **Working with text**. • Select: *Fonts >>> Change the font, font size, or font color*. **Key features to note, explore, and try out:** • See Scenario 1, Feature 4 (***Font type, size, style, and color change***) of this chapter (pages 163–164), for a full explanation of this procedure.
Inserting colored borders, lines	Borders and lines can help to organize as well as bring attention to a specific section of your Web site. Borders can be added in a number of ways. **Information and procedures:** Publisher Help • Table of Contents task pane: **Borders**. • Select: *Add or remove a border in Publisher*. • Select: *Change the color of fills, lines, and borders*. **Key features to note, explore, and try out:** • See Scenario 2 (***Adding borders to a text box [or picture, object, AutoShape, and so forth]***) for a full explanation of this procedure (see page 174).
Inserting clip art	**Information and procedures:** Publisher Help • Table of Contents task pane: **Pictures**. • Select: *Clip Art >> Add a clip to your document*. **Key features to note, explore, and try out:** • See Scenario 1, Feature 6 (***Insert, size, and place a graphic***) for a full explanation of this procedure (pages 164–165).
Altering clip art (e.g., color)	**Information and procedures:** Publisher Help • Table of Contents task pane: **Pictures**. • Select: *Clip Art >> Modify clip art*. **Key features to note, explore, and try out:** • Right click on the clip art you want to modify and select **Format Picture . . . .** • The **Format Picture** window will appear. • Click the **Picture** tab selected you can crop the picture, recolor the image, and even compress the size of the image. • Other tabs allow you to alter the fill, lines, border art, size, rotation, layout on the page, and so forth.

Feature	Steps to Get It Done
	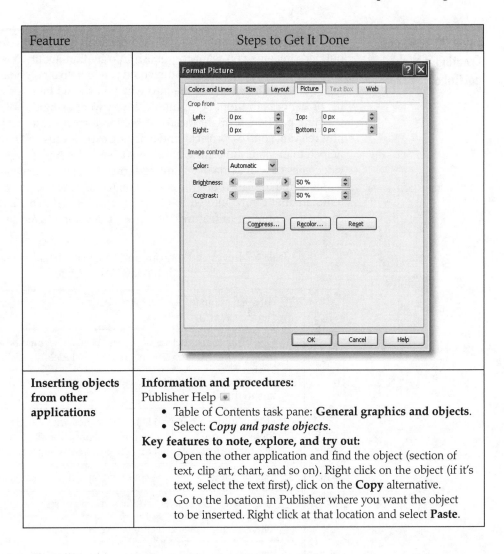

Inserting objects from other applications	**Information and procedures:**
	Publisher Help
	   • Table of Contents task pane: **General graphics and objects**.
	   • Select: *Copy and paste objects*.
	Key features to note, explore, and try out:
	   • Open the other application and find the object (section of text, clip art, chart, and so on). Right click on the object (if it's text, select the text first), click on the **Copy** alternative.
	   • Go to the location in Publisher where you want the object to be inserted. Right click at that location and select **Paste**.

Level 2a Workout: Creating your publication

Now you try it.

1. Think of a program for a play, or perhaps a poster or sign you would usually create by hand to hang up in your room, or use some other way.
2. Select a template for your publication. Try various styles of templates to ensure the selection of that which is most optimal.
3. Create text boxes in the workspace of the desktop publisher and enter the information.
4. Divide it into appropriate sections.
5. Put some of the information into tables.
6. Align, rotate, and format the title and all key headings.
7. Insert an appropriate picture, clip art, or graphic and place it within the workspace.
8. Adjust the picture or clip art in some way (e.g., change color, add a border, fill the picture background with a new color).
9. Redo these steps, except start from a blank publication (without the use of a template design). Note the differences in how the two publications were created.

Note: Each of these key features is demonstrated on the mentoring videos within the text's accompanying Web site. Go to **www.prenhall.com/newby** >>> **Chapter 6** >>> **Mentor Videos.**

Level 2b Workout: Creating a Web portfolio

A major use of the Internet is to allow individuals to publish information. In this workout, let's imagine you want to publish information about yourself. Create a personal "interview" Web portfolio that you would use to help a potential employer review your qualifications and gain insights into why you should be hired and how you can help his or her organization. For example, if you were using the Web portfolio to secure a teaching position, it might include a section for your resume, your teaching philosophy, relevant courses, projects, and teaching experiences you have completed that have helped to prepare you for the position you seek. Examples of your completed projects, video clips of your actual teaching performances, and so on could also be included.

Take time to plan your Web site. Then, using Publisher, select a Web site design or template that can be altered to fit your plans. Use Table 6.2 as a checklist to help incorporate a number of features within your developed Web site.

Table 6.2 Level 2b Workout and Practice Checklist Developing the "Interview" Web Portfolio

Web Site Planning	___ Potential audience for the Web site was considered (e.g., "Who will select to view the site?").
	___ Organizational structure of the site was determined based on the key elements of information that need to be included.
Web Site Content	___ Purpose of the Web site is clearly presented and easily understood by visitors to the site.
	___ Resumé (if incorporated) is well designed with all relevant elements (e.g., contact information, teaching philosophy, work history, goals). It properly targets the correct potential audience (potential employers).
	___ Example projects from previous work and class experiences have been included.
Web Site Format	___ The Web site is attractive and has visual appeal (use of graphics, color, font).
	___ Relevant graphics and pictures have been included.
	___ Relevant links to other sources of information within and outside of the local site have been included as needed.
	___ Ease of navigation through the Web site (effective and useful links, logical navigation points to and from various parts of the site).
	___ Web site is free of typographical and other errors.

Note: Remember to implement the second rule to live by: SAVE, SAVE, SAVE, and then SAVE your work again. This was a key principle mentioned at the first of this text. Make sure you do that—or it will come back to haunt you sometime down the road.

Also think about the concepts in Rules 3, 4, and 5: Keep things simple, watch for how others accomplish what we have described in this chapter, and make sure you think about saving the publication as a template that can be adapted and used later as needed.

Level 3: Integration and Application

What should you be able to do?

Here you need to think of how to use desktop publishing—both in terms of yourself and your students. You should be able to apply the examples given to generate ideas on how to integrate and apply desktop publishing to improve personal productivity, as well as student learning.

Introduction

Within Levels 1 and 2 of this chapter, we focused on desktop publishing from the perspective of you learning to use it. However, to extend its use, you need to begin to think about desktop publishing as a means to enhance the learning experience of students. There are times when integrating desktop publishing within a learning situation may actually improve the learning opportunities and possibilities of the learners. However, there are other times when such integration would be more of a hassle than the potential benefits warrant. Learning to tell the difference can help you be successful in what you develop and use in your classroom.

Desktop publishing integration

Creating the enhanced learning experience: A partial lesson plan

Topic: A study of the people, places, and culture of an African country.

Overview:

Mr. Carpenter, an eighth-grade social studies teacher at Lowell Middle School, is continuing to search for ways for his students to explore Zimbabwe, to find out about the country and its people. With the help of a former student, Jonathon Rogers (who is a university graduate student in Zimbabwe on an internship with an international health and education organization), Mr. Carpenter hopes to guide his students as they explore this fascinating country.

Through the use of e-mail, regular mail, digital photography, and audio recordings, Jonathon should be able to explore Zimbabwe and share his findings with the Lowell social studies classes of Mr. Carpenter.

Specific learning task:

To explore present-day Zimbabwe, the students in Mr. Carpenter's classes are to investigate Zimbabwe and create travel brochures for the country. Each class is divided into smaller cooperative groups who are asked to address the following components in their travel brochure:

1. Country information—maps, climate, size, population, wildlife, currency used, major cities, languages spoken, religions, holidays celebrated.
2. Tourist information—transportation, lodging, dining.
3. Activities—historically significant sites, tours, safaris, entertainment.

Sample learning objectives:

Students will be able to do the following:

1. Identify and describe important elements about life in Zimbabwe.
2. Identify and describe areas of Zimbabwe that would be of interest to outside visitors.

Procedure:

1. Break into the groups and brainstorm the key questions of inquiry to investigate about the selected topic.
2. Research answers for the questions from the view of Zimbabweans.
3. Create a table that lists the questions and potential answers determined through research. Reference the answers to the questions found within the research.
4. Plan a layout of the information to be provided in brochure style.
5. Design and create the brochure incorporating the information gathered.
6. Weigh the importance of information gathered and eliminate information that is not as important, in order for it all to fit.
7. Present the final brochures to be distributed to all members of their class. This could be in the form of individual brochures or a display of some sort.

Questions about desktop publishing integration

Obviously, this lesson can be completed with or without the use of desktop publishing software. Use these reflective questions to explore the value of potentially integrating desktop publishing within such a lesson as outlined by Mr. Carpenter.

- Within this lesson, in what way can desktop publishing be used by Mr. Carpenter, by Jonathon, and by the members of the social studies classes?
- How will the small groups cooperatively brainstorm and plan the publication? Can desktop publishing software be used to facilitate the planning process?
- Will the publication involve the use of visual graphics of some kind? Will the students have easy access to the collection of these graphics?
- In what ways can these brochures be presented to the class? Could other publications, such as bulletin boards, be used to help display the brochures?
- Are there potential problems or pitfalls if desktop publishing is integrated within this lesson and its respective assignments?
- How would the results of this project be altered if the outcome was to be a published Web site instead of the brochure? Would a different potential audience impact the design and/or content of the publication?

Level 3a Workout: Integrating desktop publishing

Now it's your turn. Complete the following steps to this workout as you think about the future use of desktop publishing within an applied setting.

1. Read each of the following situations. Imagine being directly involved in the planning for each of these projects. Select one (or more if you wish) for further consideration.

Advertise a Product

A high school economics class that has been studying business and advertisements has been divided into small groups. Each group has been given a common household product. Their job is to take this product and create print advertising for it, including prices, as though the year is 2050. They must take into consideration what type of advertising to create, such as a catalog, flyer, coupon, and so on.

Service Learning Fund-Raiser

Elementary students at Lavenville School are finding out what service learning is all about. They have decided to work on a schoolwide project to raise funds for playground equipment for a local transitional housing group that is working on a housing project for homeless families. The students will create flyers, signs, and postcards to mail out to area residents that describe the housing project, the benefits it will be for the community, and the important impact the project will have on those in need and on the students helping with the project. Their ultimate goal is to raise awareness to the problem of homelessness and at the same time raise money to help with the playground.

Classroom e-Newsletter

Bramsonner Alternative School is a residential school for students who have had difficulties of one kind or another in the traditional school setting. To provide a constructive activity for the residents and to provide a means for them to work together, showcase their talents, practice their writing skills, and so on, they want to develop an electronic newsletter that could be distributed across the school's intranet. It could include items about school activities and programs, interesting teacher information, current news events, and even exemplary projects that have been developed. If it is completed in a successful manner, perhaps hard copies could be printed and sent to parents and grandparents.

Family Tree

A class that has been studying genealogy is creating individual family trees. They are to diagram the family tree using a software program to produce a professional-looking publication to laminate and keep for future generations.

2. Based on your selected project, consider the following questions found within the Integration Assessment Questionnaire. Mark your response to each question.

Integration assessment questionnaire (IAQ)

Will using **DESKTOP PUBLISHING** software as a part of the project:			
Broaden the learners' perspective on potential solution paths and/or answers?	___Yes	___ No	___ Maybe
Increase the level of involvement and investment of personal effort by the learners?	___Yes	___ No	___ Maybe
Increase the level of learner motivation (e.g., increase the relevance of the to-be-learned task, the confidence of dealing with the task, and/or the overall appeal of the task)?	___Yes	___ No	___Maybe
Decrease the time needed to generate potential solutions?	___Yes	___ No	___ Maybe
Increase the quality and/or quantity of learner practice working on this and similar projects?	___Yes	___ No	___ Maybe
Increase the quality and/or quantity of feedback given to the learner?	___Yes	___ No	___ Maybe
Enhance the ability of the student to solve novel, but similar projects, tasks, and problems in the future?	___Yes	___ No	___ Maybe

3. If you have responded "Yes" to one or more of the IAQ questions, you should consider the use of desktop publishing to enhance the student's potential learning experience.
4. Using the example lesson plan, develop a lesson plan based on your selected project. Within the plan, indicate how and when the learner will use desktop publishing. Additionally, list potential benefits and challenges that may occur when involving this software within the lesson.

Level 3b Workout: Exploring the NETS Standard connection

Developing and executing a lesson plan that integrates the use of desktop publishing directly addresses several of the NETS for both teachers (NETS˚T) and students (NETS˚S). See the Appendix for a full listing of the standards.

Part A:

Generally, the main purpose for learning and using application software is to increase your level of production—that is, to do things faster, better, or both. NETS Standards (NETS*T Standard V and NETS*S Standard 6) help you focus on these productivity objectives for both teachers and students. There are other technology standards, however, that may also be potentially addressed through your knowledge and use of desktop publishing software. Reflect on the following questions and consider the potential impact of spreadsheet integration (refer to the Appendix to review the full sets of standards):

- How can the use of desktop publishing software help develop students' higher order skills and creativity? Is there something about the use of the desktop publisher that may enhance the exploration of alternative ideas, thinking patterns, solutions, or perhaps positively impact overall student creativity? (NETS*T III.C.; NETS*S 2,3, and 4)
- In what ways could desktop publishing be used to facilitate the communication and collaboration between teachers, students, parents, and subject matter experts on specific projects that ultimately impact student learning? (NETS*T V.D.; NET*S 2)

Part B:

Go to the ISTE Web site, **http://cnets.iste.org.** Within that site, select to review either the student or the teacher NETS Standards. Once you have selected the standards to review, select either the student or teacher profiles and look for the corresponding scenarios. Review the scenarios and determine how desktop publishing could be used within several of those situations. While visiting the ISTE Web site and exploring the scenarios, go to the lesson plan search area and select a number of different lesson plans of interest. Review those and determine the role (if any) of desktop publishing within the development, implementation, and assessment of the lesson. Note this from both the perspective of the teacher developing the lesson and from the perspective of the student participating in the implemented lesson.

Further ideas on using desktop publishing as a learning tool

> **Note:** These ideas are to help you generate your own ideas of what could be done. Don't let it bother you if they aren't the right content or grade level—use the idea and adapt it to be helpful within your own situation. These are meant to be a stimulus for additional ideas.

Here are a few ideas that may help you see how the desktop publisher might be beneficial:

1. Teach your high school students how to create a resumé.
2. Have students create a flyer to announce the talent show.
3. Design and create original bookplate or binder labels for classroom books.
4. Create an e-mail newsletter to announce classroom events to parents.
5. Compose and format different types of letters (e.g., business, personal, memo, cover letter, persuasive communication, letter to the editor) and then compare the different styles of writing.
6. Have students develop a brochure about a specific historical topic (e.g., colonial America), their personal work history and skills (e.g., jobs they have worked and what they have done), or places they may someday travel (e.g., Australian Outback).
7. Have learners create original poetry and combine it with an inspirational photo as a background to their written work.

Additional ideas on using the desktop publisher as an assistant

1. **Classroom rules.** A sign that highlights all of the rules of class conduct and consequences when the rule is not followed.
2. **Computer assignment chart.** A chart that allows you to monitor whose turn it is to use the computer.
3. **Certificates.** Creation of certificates for extra effort and merit.
4. **Progress reports.** To keep students (and parents) informed of what has been accomplished and what is still needed.
5. **Work sheets.** Construct various types of work sheets and/or directions for projects.
6. **Calendars.** Develop and use daily, weekly, and/or monthly assignment or work calendars.
7. **Weekly lesson planning.** Develop a table template of all weekly planning for lessons and subjects.
8. **Badges and labels.** Production of name badges for students, class helpers, parents, and others; labels for files, folders, and the like.
9. **Programs.** Develop programs and handouts for school productions.
10. **Newsletters.** Write weekly or monthly classroom newsletters containing relevant information for students and parents. Distribute in hard copies or via the Web.
11. **Permission slips.** Develop permission slips for events such as field trips, bus rides, and authorized school activities.
12. **Volunteer schedules and job responsibilities.** Create a sign that explains job responsibilities and schedules for individuals who volunteer at the school.
13. **Reminders.** Write memos to remind students about projects that they have been assigned or sign up to complete (e.g., bring snacks, give a report).
14. **Banners.** Create banners to hang across the classroom for learning things such as the alphabet, numbers, or a new language.

Chapter 7
WEB EDITING
Expression Web: The Basics of Web Page Development

Introduction

What should you know about Web editors? 	Web editing software allows you to create materials that can be distributed on the World Wide Web (**www**). In this opening section, we want you to know the following: • What a **Web editor** is, what it can do, and how it can help in teaching and learning • How to justify the use of the Web editor as an effective tool—by knowing when and why it should or shouldn't be used

---

Terms to know

HTML	link	WWW
Web page or site	browser	Web editor

What is a Web editor and what does it do?

Web editors are tools used to efficiently and effectively design and develop Web pages. They allow you to insert and manipulate text, graphics, sound, movies, and so on, as well as to create links to other **Web page** elements and other sites on the WWW. For most of us, using a Web editor is very similar to using a word processing program. You can point and click to have items inserted, formatted, highlighted, or sized. In the case of the word processor, the end product generally is something printed in a hard copy, but with the Web editor, the end result is something that can be effectively displayed by a Web **browser** on the Web.

For Web browsers (such as Internet Explorer, Netscape Navigator, or Foxfire) to understand what to display, specific **HTML** (Hypertext Markup Language) codes need to be inserted in the documents you create. You can learn these codes and insert them yourself, or you can have a Web editor do it for you. For most of us, using the editor is faster, does a more sophisticated job, and creates many less mistakes (and headaches).

What are some common Web editors?

• Microsoft's Expression Web[1]
• Macromedia's Dreamweaver
• Adobe's GoLive
• Claris's HomePage
• Microsoft's SharePoint Designer
• Microsoft's FrontPage

[1]Microsoft's Expression Web has replaced Microsoft's FrontPage.

> **Note:** We focus on MS Expression Web in this text. However, all of **what we present can be done in any of the other Web editors listed**. So if you don't have access to MS Expression Web, don't be alarmed—you can still complete the projects and learn the basic skills.

> **Note:** Many of today's word processing programs (and other desktop publishing programs—e.g., Publisher) have an option that allows you to save your documents as HTML. This is simple and easy, however, these programs are not designed specifically for Web page development and they may not be as easy to work with when dealing with advanced features and the editing of Web pages.

Why bother learning how to use a Web editor?

- **It's faster than learning and using HTML.** The editor does the tedious coding for you and thus you can concentrate on the content of your creation.
- **It allows you to use what you already know.** If you know how to use a word processor, many of the same features (e.g., creating a table, inserting a picture, formatting words) will be very familiar to you.
- **It can enhance communication.** Developing Web pages and displaying them on the Web can be a simple way to provide information to your students, parents, colleagues, and administrators.
- **It can lead to greater learning experiences.** Using the editor may allow you to develop learning experiences that can draw on the depth of information found on the Web and thus impact student learning to a greater degree.
- **It allows for creative expression.** Whether working on something for class or developing a personal page for your hobby interest, the tools within the Web editor allow you to be creative in the design and presentation of your information.
- **It's fun.** Learning the basic features of the Web editor is not difficult or time-consuming. You can quickly find projects that are enjoyable to construct and immediately rewarding in their appearance and impact.

How can a Web editor be used at school? A brief list of ideas

By the teacher:

- Ancillary information sites for students to visit and use
- Information boards
- Class or school Web site
- Unit or topical projects
- Virtual field trips

By the student:

- School digital newspaper or magazine
- Publish student projects
- Electronic portfolio
- Develop WebQuest-type projects
- Cooperative group-designed projects

Orientation

What's the workspace look like?

Figure 7.1 is an example of the workspace of a common Web editor (MS Expression Web). Note where you can enter in your information and some of the common toolbars, buttons, and menus located around the workspace.

> **Note:** The toolbars and main menu have several tools specifically designed for Web page development and editing. However, there should be an "air of familiarity" about many of the tools that appear on these toolbars and menus. Yes, many work here as they do in other applications such as word processing and spreadsheets. That should help you start working on this even faster.

Figure 7.1   View of a Microsoft *Expression* Web webpage editing work area

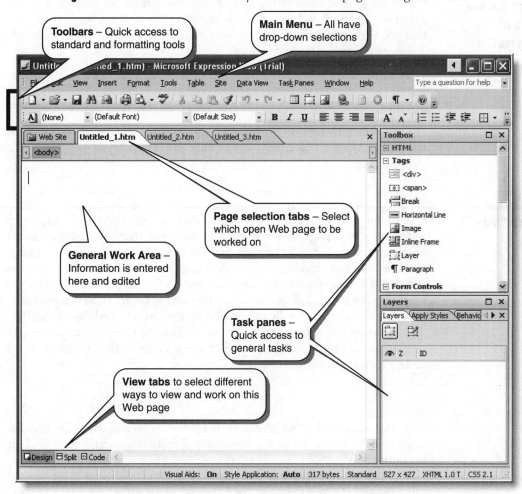

Note: Once you have Expression Web up and running and have entered in a sentence or two, it might be interesting for you to click on the HTML View Tab in the bottom left corner of the work space. This should give you a better appreciation for what the Web editor is doing for you. Without the editor, you would be entering in many of the <b>, <p> type codes to tell the browser how to handle this page when it is encountered on the Web.

What is a "browser"?   A computer application program used to access Web pages on the WWW. The most commonly used browsers are Microsoft's Internet Explorer, Mozilla's Foxfire, and Apple's Safari. These programs allow the user to view and explore pages and sites found on the Web (they do this by accessing and interpreting the HTML code). Web editing software (e.g., Expression Web) is used to design and create Web pages or sites. After the pages have been created and published in some way (e.g., on the Web), browser software is used to access, view, and interact with those published Web pages.

Microsoft Internet Explorer

Mozilla Foxfire

Apple Safari

What are the key elements of a Web page?

When you look at some of the fancy things being done on Web sites, often it is easy to get the feeling that "I will never be able to do that!" Actually, there are three basics that you should learn to do almost everything needed to create an instructional site. You need to know how to create and display

1. Text
2. Images
3. Links

On a difficulty scale of 1–5 (1 being simple, 5 being difficult)—each of these skills falls right around a 1 or 2 (simple, fun, easy to grasp).

What are "links"?

One of the most powerful features about Web pages is their ability to jump from one section of a **Web page or site** to another section of that same page or site or even to another totally independent site on the WWW. Links tell the browser where to go. For example, you can mention on your Web page that some interesting activities can be completed on a different Web site and create a link to that site. Those viewing your page can click on the link and immediately jump to the location that your link has sent them to. Links are generally designated by the linked words being highlighted in a different color (e.g., blue) and underlined. When the browser's mouse pointer passes over an active link, it changes into a "pointed finger" which indicates a click on the mouse button will activate the link.

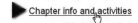
Chapter info and activities

A nice advantage of such links is that if the individual using the browser doesn't want to visit the link, he or she can skip it. If more information is desired, the user is in control of what is seen and experienced.

You can imagine that this may also cause some confusion if too many links are provided and the user gets "lost," or if the user skips some very important information because he or she chose not to explore a specific connection.

Orientation Workout: Explore the territory

Turn on the computer and attempt the following:

1. Launch MS Expression Web.
2. Examine the main menu. Click on each menu title (e.g., File, Edit) and note the various selections that are available under each. You won't need all of these, but it is a good idea to know where to find things. Pay special attention to where the Help Menu is located.
3. Look over the toolbars that are available (**View Menu >>> Toolbars . . .**). Make sure the standard and formatting toolbars are checked or you may wish to check the common toolbar instead.
4. Note that the tools located on the toolbars show icons representing what the tool is for. If you lay the mouse pointer over any specific tool (don't click) the name (tag) for the tool appears. Use of the toolbars is a fast way of accessing commonly used tools.
5. Try entering in a line or two of text on the workspace of the Web editor. Highlight one or two words and then click on various tool icons on the formatting toolbar (e.g., **bold** text icon). Note how your highlighted words change based on the tool that you have selected to use.
6. Also try to save your Web page by using either a drop-down menu (**File >>> Save As . . .**) or the Save icon on the standard toolbar.
7. Try several different functions and see what happens. For example, try making a bulleted or numbered list, within a document, change the font style, size, and color

of one or more words, and then create a table. Try opening the Font format window (**Format >>> Font**) and reviewing what can be done to the fonts that you want to work with in the Web editor.

For more information and a demonstration about Expression Web, please review the Expression Web Orientation video on the text's accompanying Web site (**www.prenhall.com/newby** >>> **Chapter 7** >>> **Mentor Video**).

Level 1: Designing, Creating, and Producing a Course Web Site

What should you be able to do?

Within Level 1, you should be focused on developing skills using the basic tools of simple Web page and site development. At the conclusion of this level, you should be able to create several Web pages, insert text and graphics, and use links effectively by following specific guidelines and step-by-step procedures.

What resources are provided?

Level 1 presents a scenario that might be encountered within your world of teaching. In addition, selected solutions and practice exercises (i.e. Workouts) are presented. The scenario has been constructed to allow you to examine a problem and how it could be addressed through the use of this software. To do this we have provided the following:

a. Quick reference figures that identify (via visual callouts) all of the key features that have been incorporated within the solution presentation. These allow you to rapidly identify the key features and reference exactly how to include such features within your own work.

b. Step-by-step instructions on how to incorporate all highlighted features within your work.

c. Video mentoring support that will guide you through the integration of each of the highlighted features (see the text's accompanying Web site: **www.prenhall.com/ newby**).

d. Workout exercises that allow you to practice identifying and selecting which software features to use, when to use those features, how they should be incorporated, and to what degree they are effective.

How should you proceed?

If you have little or no experience with Microsoft's Expression Web, then we suggest you do the following:

1. Read and review Scenario 1,
2. Examine the quick reference figures (Figures 7.3–7.6) and all of the numbered highlights and callouts,
3. Using the step-by-step directions given for each highlighted feature, use the software, and practice using each of the features,
4. Access the mentoring videos that explain each of the features and how they are accomplished within the software (see the text's accompanying Web site: **www.prenhall.com/newby**).
5. Go to the Workout and work through the problems and exercises as it outlines.

If you have experience with Expression Web (or similar software—e.g., Adobe Dreamweaver), you may want to review the problem scenario and the quick reference figure first. If any of the features are unfamiliar, then use the step-by-step procedures as well as the mentoring support videos. Once the review has been completed, then move directly to the Workout exercise and create your own Web page by incorporating many of the highlighted features.

Scenario 1: Developing a class Web site

Helen Smith's second-grade unit on dinosaurs has always been a fun learning experience for her students. This year, Helen decided to expand it by adding a simple Web site so that students could access it from home and from the school's computer lab. She has started with some simple pages and plans over the next few weeks to add other pages to her site.

Take a close look at Figure 7.2. This is a composite picture of Mrs. Smith's course Web site that includes three individual Web pages. Figures 7.3–7.6 illustrate the individual Web pages of Mrs. Smith's course site. You can also go to this textbook's Web site (**www.prenhall.com/newby**) and review this example site that Mrs. Smith created.

Figure 7.2 Mrs. Smith's Dinosaur Web site

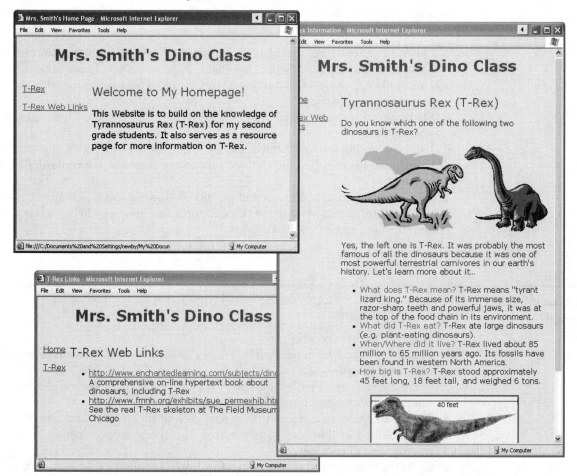

Figure 7.3 View in Expression Web of the basic page layout (template) designed as the starting point for all other Web pages within Mrs. Smith's Web site.

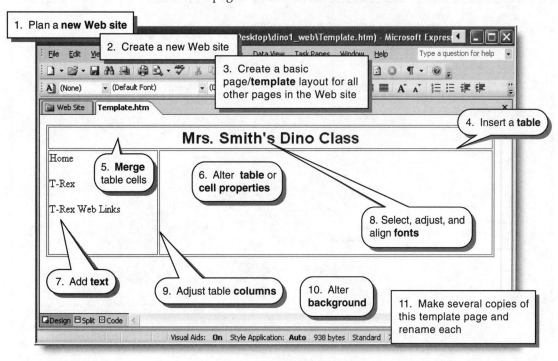

Figure 7.4 Mrs. Smith's home page with page name or title, links, and content added

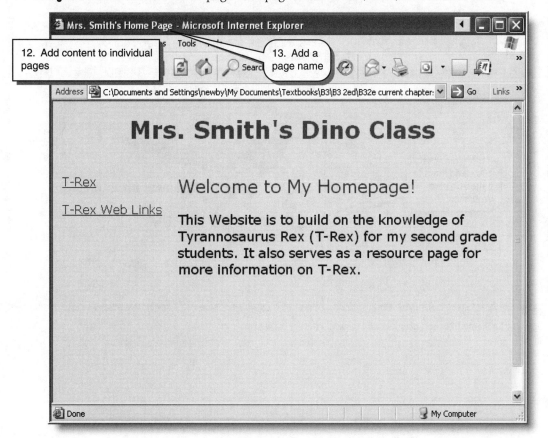

Figure 7.5 T-Rex information page with images and links added.

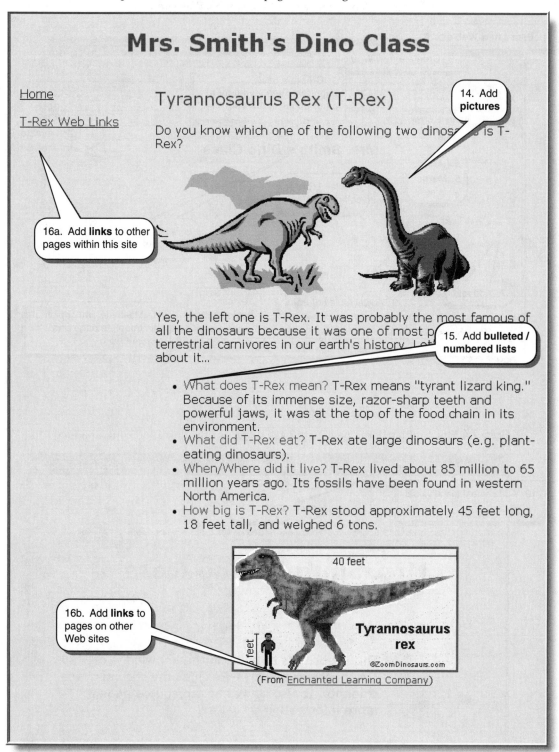

Figure 7.6 T-Rex links page with additional links added

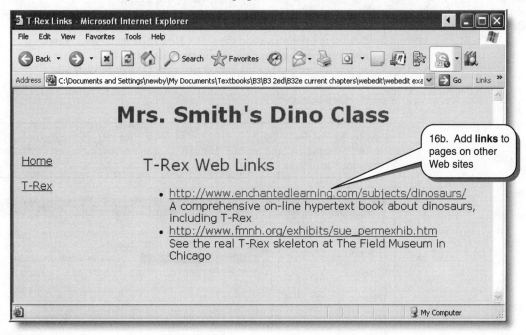

No.	Feature	Steps to Get It Done

1	**Plan your new Web site**	1. Plan what your Web site is going to be all about. Think about the purpose of the Web site, its audience, who may be reviewing it, and your content.
		2. For a Web site to work properly, you need to have the proper folder structure so that everything is ordered and saved correctly. Here is what you should do:
		  a. Create a new folder on the desktop of your computer (or wherever you want the Web site to reside). Name this folder something that you will remember—something like "dino1_Web" will work nicely if you were developing a Web site about dinosaurs.
		  b. Open that new "dino1_Web" folder and create another new folder inside of it. Name this new folder "images." This is the folder that will store all of the pictures you will acquire and use in your Web site. To help you recall how to create a folder inside of a folder, review the Level 1 Workout: (By the numbers) found in Chapter 1.
		
		Note: By keeping everything inside of one "dino1_Web" folder, as you move the folder to different locations (e.g., storage devices, computers, etc.), all of the contents will also be successfully transported. Likewise, by keeping all of the images in one folder ('images') inside of the "dino1_Web" folder, access to the pictures will always be completed correctly.
		
		    📁 dino1_web
		      📁 images
		
		    Also note that it is fine for you to create other folders inside of the "dino1_Web" folder and also inside of the "images" folder. These can be used to help keep everything organized as you build your Web site.
		
		Note: It is generally wise when developing Web pages to limit the names of your folders and Web pages to 8 lowercase characters or less with no spaces or special characters, other than the underscore (_).

continued

No.	Feature	Steps to Get It Done

2	**Create a new Web site**	1. Launch Expression Web (or your Web editing software).
		2. Click on the File menu and then click New (**File** menu >>> **New**).
		3. In the New dialog box, click on the **Web Site** tab.
		    a. If you want a single-page Web site, click **One Page Web Site.**
		    b. If you want to develop a site with more than one page, click the **Empty Web Site** alternative.
		
		Note: In this **New** dialog box (with the **Web Site** tab selected), you can also select "Templates" and review and select from many different professionally designed templates.
		
		4. Click on the **Browse** . . . button and the **New Web Site Location** dialog box will appear. Navigate to the folder that you created in Feature 1 (e.g., "dino1_Web"). Click on your desired folder.
		5. Once selected, click **Open** and the **New** dialog box will reappear with the location and name of your Web site listed in the "Specify the location of the new Web site:" area.
		6. Click OK.
		
		Note: Your selected folder (e.g., "dino1_Web" folder) appearance has been altered to indicate that it is now a Web site folder.
		
		dino1_web dino1_web

3	**Create a simple template page for a consistent page layout**	Templates allow for quick, consistent Web page production. For a basic Web site (3–6 pages), it is often most efficient to create your own template. The template allows you to create needed page elements once and use those same elements across multiple pages. 1. Create a new page (**File** menu >>> **New . . .**). 2. In the **New** dialog box select to create a new Web page (**Page tab** >>> **General** >>> **HTML** >>> **OK**).

No.	Feature	Steps to Get It Done
		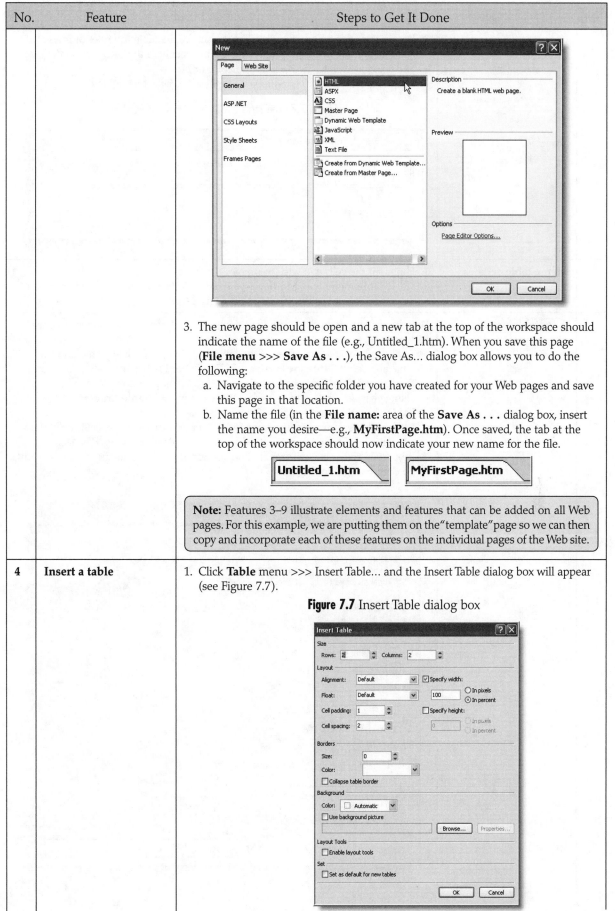

3. The new page should be open and a new tab at the top of the workspace should indicate the name of the file (e.g., Untitled_1.htm). When you save this page (**File menu** >>> **Save As . . .**), the Save As... dialog box allows you to do the following:
   a. Navigate to the specific folder you have created for your Web pages and save this page in that location.
   b. Name the file (in the **File name:** area of the **Save As . . .** dialog box, insert the name you desire—e.g., **MyFirstPage.htm**). Once saved, the tab at the top of the workspace should now indicate your new name for the file.

> **Untitled_1.htm**   **MyFirstPage.htm**

Note: Features 3–9 illustrate elements and features that can be added on all Web pages. For this example, we are putting them on the "template" page so we can then copy and incorporate each of these features on the individual pages of the Web site.

---

4   **Insert a table**

1. Click **Table** menu >>> Insert Table... and the Insert Table dialog box will appear (see Figure 7.7).

Figure 7.7 Insert Table dialog box

continued

No.	Feature	Steps to Get It Done
		2. Within this dialog box you can select the size of the table (number of rows and columns), the table layout, the padding and spacing of the cells, the border size and color, as well as the background color or picture. 3. Figure 7.8 shows an inserted table with all of the cells highlighted. **Figure 7.8** Inserted table in Expression Web 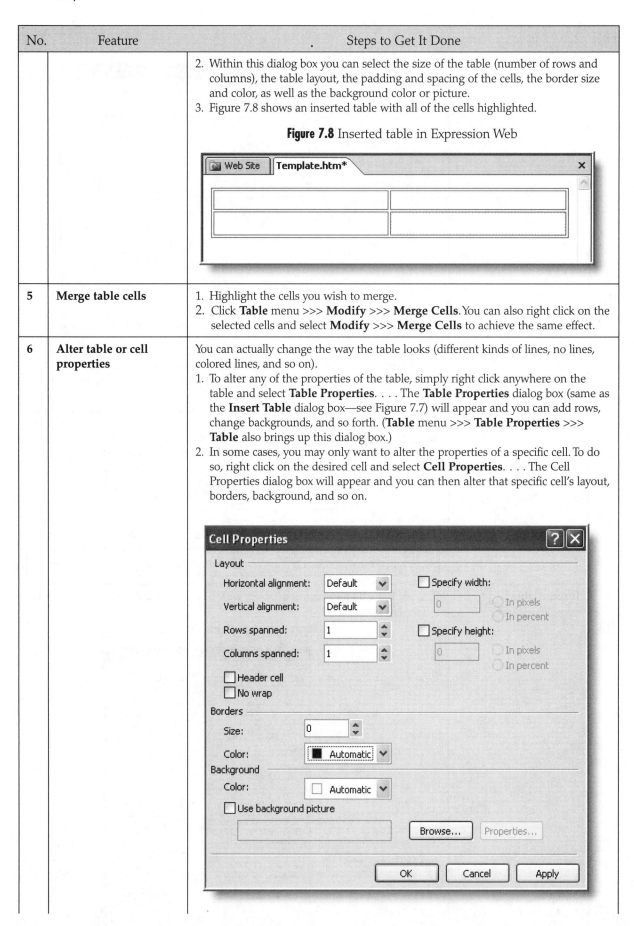
5	**Merge table cells**	1. Highlight the cells you wish to merge. 2. Click **Table** menu >>> **Modify** >>> **Merge Cells**. You can also right click on the selected cells and select **Modify** >>> **Merge Cells** to achieve the same effect.
6	**Alter table or cell properties**	You can actually change the way the table looks (different kinds of lines, no lines, colored lines, and so on). 1. To alter any of the properties of the table, simply right click anywhere on the table and select **Table Properties**. . . . The **Table Properties** dialog box (same as the **Insert Table** dialog box—see Figure 7.7) will appear and you can add rows, change backgrounds, and so forth. (**Table** menu >>> **Table Properties** >>> **Table** also brings up this dialog box.) 2. In some cases, you may only want to alter the properties of a specific cell. To do so, right click on the desired cell and select **Cell Properties**. . . . The Cell Properties dialog box will appear and you can then alter that specific cell's layout, borders, background, and so on.

No.	Feature	Steps to Get It Done
7	**Insert text**	1. Click in the cell where the text is to be inserted. 2. Type in the information that should appear on each of the Web pages within the Web site. For Mrs. Smith's Web site, the title and the main menu of page links are consistent across all of the Web site pages. 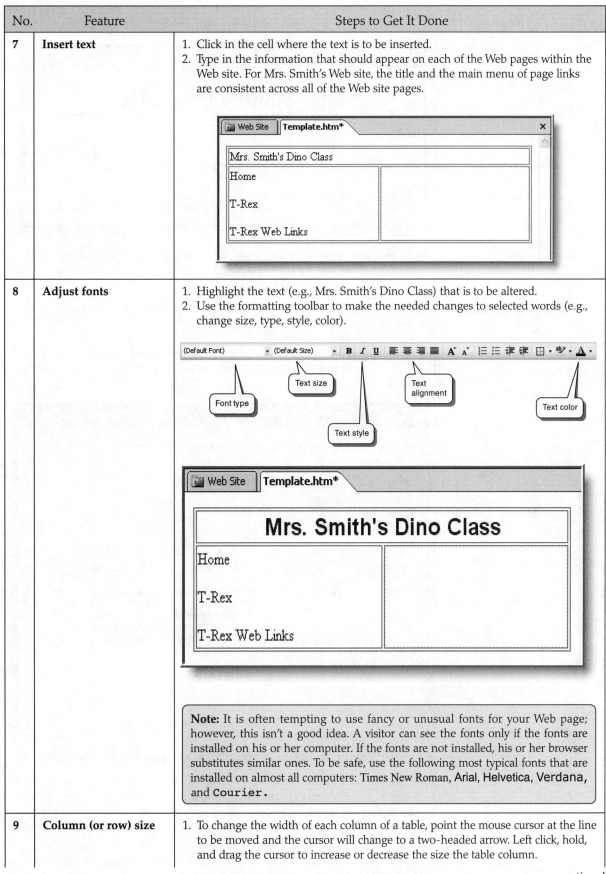
8	**Adjust fonts**	1. Highlight the text (e.g., Mrs. Smith's Dino Class) that is to be altered. 2. Use the formatting toolbar to make the needed changes to selected words (e.g., change size, type, style, color). **Note:** It is often tempting to use fancy or unusual fonts for your Web page; however, this isn't a good idea. A visitor can see the fonts only if the fonts are installed on his or her computer. If the fonts are not installed, his or her browser substitutes similar ones. To be safe, use the following most typical fonts that are installed on almost all computers: Times New Roman, Arial, Helvetica, Verdana, and Courier.
9	**Column (or row) size**	1. To change the width of each column of a table, point the mouse cursor at the line to be moved and the cursor will change to a two-headed arrow. Left click, hold, and drag the cursor to increase or decrease the size the table column.

continued

No.	Feature	Steps to Get It Done
		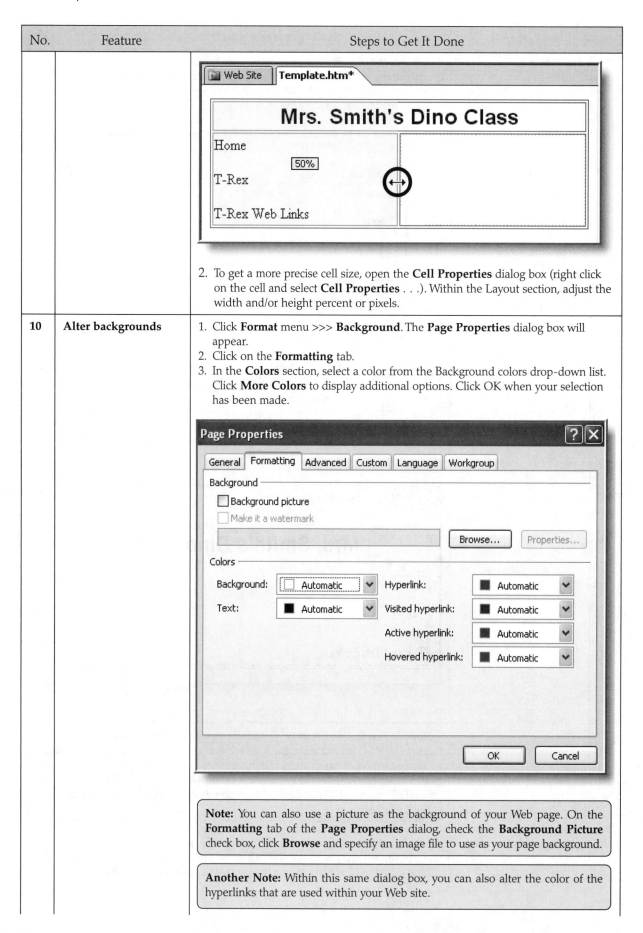 2. To get a more precise cell size, open the **Cell Properties** dialog box (right click on the cell and select **Cell Properties** . . .). Within the Layout section, adjust the width and/or height percent or pixels.
10	**Alter backgrounds**	1. Click **Format** menu >>> **Background**. The **Page Properties** dialog box will appear. 2. Click on the **Formatting** tab. 3. In the **Colors** section, select a color from the Background colors drop-down list. Click **More Colors** to display additional options. Click OK when your selection has been made. **Note:** You can also use a picture as the background of your Web page. On the **Formatting** tab of the **Page Properties** dialog, check the **Background Picture** check box, click **Browse** and specify an image file to use as your page background. **Another Note:** Within this same dialog box, you can also alter the color of the hyperlinks that are used within your Web site.

No.	Feature	Steps to Get It Done

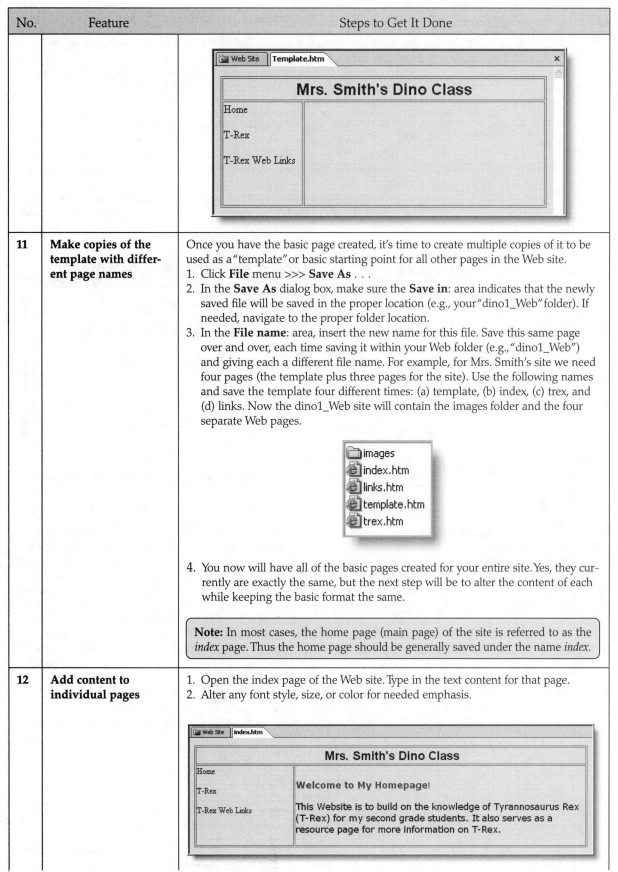

| 11 | Make copies of the template with different page names | Once you have the basic page created, it's time to create multiple copies of it to be used as a "template" or basic starting point for all other pages in the Web site.
1. Click **File** menu >>> **Save As** . . .
2. In the **Save As** dialog box, make sure the **Save in**: area indicates that the newly saved file will be saved in the proper location (e.g., your "dino1_Web" folder). If needed, navigate to the proper folder location.
3. In the **File name**: area, insert the new name for this file. Save this same page over and over, each time saving it within your Web folder (e.g., "dino1_Web") and giving each a different file name. For example, for Mrs. Smith's site we need four pages (the template plus three pages for the site). Use the following names and save the template four different times: (a) template, (b) index, (c) trex, and (d) links. Now the dino1_Web site will contain the images folder and the four separate Web pages. |

4. You now will have all of the basic pages created for your entire site. Yes, they currently are exactly the same, but the next step will be to alter the content of each while keeping the basic format the same.

> **Note:** In most cases, the home page (main page) of the site is referred to as the *index* page. Thus the home page should be generally saved under the name *index*.

| 12 | Add content to individual pages | 1. Open the index page of the Web site. Type in the text content for that page.
2. Alter any font style, size, or color for needed emphasis. |

continued

No.	Feature	Steps to Get It Done
		3. Spell check your work and save your page (**Tools** menu >>> **Spelling** >>> **Spelling** . . .) 4. Add content for each of the other content pages (e.g, *trex* and *links*), and save each of those pages. For content that can be added, see Figure 7.5. 5. After adding the content, save your work.
13	**Web page names**	1. The title of a Web page is the actual name of the page, not the page's file name. When a browser displays the page, it's name shows in the browser's title bar (see Figure 7.4—"Mrs. Smith Home Page" is the title of that Web page). This is helpful for those cruising Web sites and also it helps some Web search engines find materials. 2. To create or change the name of a Web page, *right* click anywhere on the page, and choose **Page Properties** from the pop-up menu. Click the **General** tab and enter the title of the page in the **Title** section. In our example, we titled the index page, "Mrs. Smith's Home Page." Click OK. **Page Properties** [? X] General Formatting Advanced Custom Language Workgroup Location: file:///C:/Documents and Settings/newby/Desktop/dino1_w Title: Mrs. Smith's Home Page Page description: Keywords: Base location: Default target frame: 3. Other information about this page can also be included within this dialog box (e.g., key words, a description of what the page is or its purpose).
14	**Add and adapt pictures (images or graphics)**	**Important info:** Web pages handle pictures different than other software such as word processors. Instead of sticking the picture directly into the document so that it becomes a part of the document, the Web editor inserts a reference that tells the browser where to go to find the picture and then how to display it. When working with images or pictures, then, it is wise to have an "images" folder inside of your "dino1_Web" folder (refer back to Feature 1 for an additional explanation). This is the location that all of your Web site pictures will be stored. If the "dino1_Web" folder is moved to another location on your hard drive or even to another computer or server, the nested "images" folder and all its contents (i.e., the needed pictures or images) will also travel safely with the Web site. 1. Obtain and save the pictures(s) into your site's image folder. a. Pictures from a Web site i. Right click on the picture >>> **Save Picture** As . . . The **Save Picture** dialog box appears. ii. In the **Save Picture** dialog box a. Navigate to your new Web site's image folder b. Name the picture c. Click **Save** b. Pictures from other sources (e.g., computer files) i. Navigate to the folder that contains the file of the picture. ii. Right click on the specific file >>> **Copy**. iii. Navigate to your new Web site's *image* folder. iv. Right click inside of the image folder >>> **Paste**.

No.	Feature	Steps to Get It Done

		2. Insert picture(s) into your Web page.
		  a. On your Web page, place the cursor where you want the image to be inserted.
		  b. Click **Insert** >>> **Picture** >>> **From File** . . . The **Picture** dialog box will appear. Navigate to your images folder where you have saved the to-be-inserted picture. Click on the title of your image and click **Insert**.
		  c. An **Accessibility Properties** dialog box will appear. Enter the alternate text (text you want those viewing your site to read as the picture is being loaded). This text is also helpful for screen reader software to help those listening to your Web page understand what is being displayed.
		  d. Click **Insert** and the picture should now appear at the cursor's position in your Web page.
		3. Adapt your inserted picture
		  a. Once your picture is inserted within your Web page, point your mouse at the picture and left click once. You will note that a box will be drawn around the picture and small squares will be placed at each of the corners and in the middle of each of the sides. These are called **handles**. You can grab a handle by putting your mouse pointer on the handle (note that your pointer will change into a double-headed arrow), left click, and hold. Dragging a handle will cause the picture to be altered. Try different handles and see what happens to the shape and size of the picture.
		
		  b. With your inserted picture selected (the handles should be showing), use the **Picture toolbar** (**View** menu >>> **Toolbars** >>> **Pictures**) to alter the picture in many different ways (e.g., lighten, crop, rotate, order).
		
		  c. Once your picture is inserted and sized appropriately, you can align it by clicking once on it (the handles should appear), and then selecting from the alignment icons on the Formatting toolbar.
		
		Note: Pictures or images come in a variety of formats; however, some Web browsers only support those known as GIF and JPG. GIF format works best for images such as clip art, whereas the JPG format works best for photographic images. If your image is in a different format from GIF or JPG, it will either have to be converted or it will have to be replaced.
		
		Note: It is often helpful to use tables to place images. Think about inserting a table and then placing the images strategically within specific cells of the tables.

15	**Add lists**	1. Enter all of the items to be included in the list. 2. Select all of the items. 3. Click **Format** >>> **Bullets and Numbering** . . . and select from the given options. It is also possible to click on the bullet or number list icon on the formatting toolbar.

continued

No.	Feature	Steps to Get It Done
16a	**Create hyperlinks between pages of your Web site**	A hyperlink (or link) is an electronic connection between text or graphics so that with a simple mouse click, the "linked" information is immediately accessed. As shown in Figure 7.9, links have been created between that Web page and others within Mrs. Smith's Dino Class (e.g., the home page). In this case, clicking on the home page link takes you immediately from the T-Rex page to the Home page. 1. Select (highlight) the words of text that you want to serve as a link to another page within your Web site (e.g., *T-Rex*). 2. Click **Insert** menu >>> **Hyperlink** (You could also click on the hyperlink button on the standard toolbar). 3. The **Insert Hyperlink** dialog box (see Figure 7.9) appears. **Figure 7.9** Insert Hyperlink dialog box used to create links between elements on current page and other elements, pages, sites, or e-mail addresses Type of link desired (e.g., on local computer, e-mail link, other internet site) Navigation buttons to locate other sites to link Other pages in the same folder as the current page you are working on Specifies specific URL address of hyperlink target 4. If you see the desired Web page listed in this window (e.g., T-Rex Information) that you want to link to, click on that title and then click OK. If you don't see it in this list, you can explore your computer files by clicking on the explore button, navigating to the appropriate page, and then clicking OK. 5. Once you click OK, the link will be established and your selected text will change to indicate it now consists of a link (generally, this means that the selected words will be underlined with a changed font color (—generally, it's a blue color.) 6. Link all of the pages in your Web site together using this method. Through the use of such links, individuals can navigate in, out, and through your site.
16b	**Link to other Web sites on the Internet**	As shown in Figures 7.5 and 7.6, other important types of links have to do with connecting your Web page with other sites on the Internet. 1. Use the same first three steps as given in how to "link the pages of your Web site together." 2. Once you have selected your text to be linked and you have the **Insert Hyperlink** window (see Figure 7.9) revealed, type the URL of the Internet resource to which you want to link. Type it into the area designated by the title **Address:**. The **Address** is a URL and generally begins with **"http://www."** If

No.	Feature	Steps to Get It Done
		you simply type in **www,** the http:// will be automatically added for you; however, if you forget the **www,** then the address will be incomplete and it will not make the appropriate link.
		3. If you do not know the Web address that you want the link to lead to, you will need to explore the Web and find that page. You can do that within the **Create Hyperlink** window by using the global explore button and navigating to that desired page.

> **Note:** Once you have created the links, it is a good idea to try them out. Do this by clicking on **File** menu >>> **Preview in Browser**. A browser window will appear and you should be able to check out the link to see if it works appropriately. If there's a problem, delete the link and start the linking process over.

> **Note:** Text isn't the only thing that can be "linked." You can also highlight a graphic and click **Insert** >>> **Hyperlink**. Using the same linking process, a click on the graphic will then send the browser to the desired location.

Level 1a Workout: Practice using basic Web page development features

1. First, examine Mrs. Smith's actual Web site. Launch your browser (e.g., Internet Explorer) and navigate to the text's Web site (**www.prenhall.com/newby** >>> **Chapter 7** >>> **Example Web Sites** >>> **Dino1** >>> **index**). Double click on the "index" page and the browser should begin to display Mrs. Smith's Web site.
2. Go through the site and note all of the text, formatting, pictures, and links.
3. Launch your Web page editor application program (e.g., Microsoft Expression Web).
4. Using Mrs. Smith's Web site as an example, create a sample Web page that includes several of the features highlighted in Figures 7.3–7.6.

> **Note:** Refer to specific feature numbers and the given step-by-step procedures as needed. Additionally, use the mentoring videos to help guide you through any specific procedure that needs additional clarification (**www.prenhall.com/newby** >>> **Chapter 7** >>> **Mentor Videos**).

Level 1b Workout: Creating your own Web site

Developing Web sites benefit both teachers and students as they learn to store and organize all types of digital materials, explore related items, and discover relationships and how things can be linked together. Think about all of the exciting places that can be visited, the unique ways in which information can be structured and disseminated, and so on. For this Workout, select a topic that you wish to explore (e.g., a favorite hobby, author, critical turning point in history, profession, medical procedure). Do the following:

1. Review the features demonstrated within Figure 7.3–7.6.
2. Create a new Web site based upon your selected topic. Develop three or four pages within the Web site. On one page introduce your topic and then develop pages that provide information, insight, guidance, and so on to anyone visiting the site.
3. Format your Web site with as many of the features demonstrated in those figures as possible. Use Table 7.1 as a checklist to guide your efforts.

Table 7.1 Level 1 Workout and Practice Checklist Creating and Formatting a Web Site

Web Site Content	____ Content is accurate and current.
	____ Content is relevant, cohesive, and interesting throughout the document.
	____ Content achieves the proper "level" for the intended audience.
	____ Content is free from spelling and grammatical errors.
Web Site format	____ Ease of navigation throughout the site (e.g., ease of finding and using page navigational links).
	____ All pages had elements (e.g., backgrounds, common fonts) that helped the site be one cohesive unit.
	____ All images display appropriately.
	____ Appropriate graphics (e.g., clip art, pictures, images) were properly selected, sized, and placed within the Web pages.
	____ Font size, style, and type were varied within the Web site to add emphasis to headings, and so forth.
	____ All internal and external links work correctly.
	____ All references and credits are appropriately cited.

Level 2: Web Site Templates, Bookmarks, and Other Good Stuff

What should you be able to do?

The use of a Web editor to develop Web pages can be a very helpful tool. The goal in this level is for you to expand your skills with several additional features of the Web editor; however, the most important goal is for you to develop a skill of working with the Help feature to gain the guidance you need to find solutions to future questions and problems.

Getting some Help

Similar to Help in Windows and other Office 2007 applications, there is also Help in MS Expression Web and most other sophisticated Web editing software. To use Help, click the **Help** menu >>> **Microsoft Expression Web Help** (you can also access Help by clicking on the Help icon ⊛ on the standard toolbar). A Help window will open that allows you to examine topics through a table of contents, browse different sections of the Expression Web Help, or insert a specific question or key word to search the Help for potential answers.

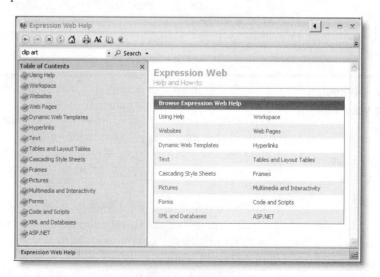

Expression Web Help window

Help generally *does not* have all of the answers—but it will have a lot of them. Make sure you get a good sense for how it works and how often it can be of assistance.

Scenario 2:
The Catacombs

Over Christmas break Brayden James and his family were traveling to Paris for a winter vacation. To leave school prior to the completion of the semester, Brayden had to promise Mr. Chesterton, his English teacher, that he would report back about the most interesting thing he "discovered" during his travels. Although Brayden knew Mr. Chesterton was probably expecting a written page or two about the Eifel Tower, he actually discovered something that was quite a bit different from the normal Paris tourist sight. Brayden decided to report about the Catacombs of Paris.

To compile the report in a way that could quickly be accessed by his teacher—and all of his friends and relatives—Brayden decided to create a small Web site.

Let's take a look at a printout of a couple pages (see Figures 7.10–7.14) from his finished work. You can explore the full site for yourself by launching your Internet browser, and navigating to **www.prenhall.com/newby** >>> **Chapter 7** >>> **catacombs** >>> **default.htm**.

Figure 7.10 Home page for Brayden's Catacomb Web site

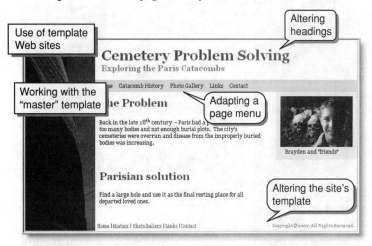

Figure 7.11 Content page for Catacomb Web site

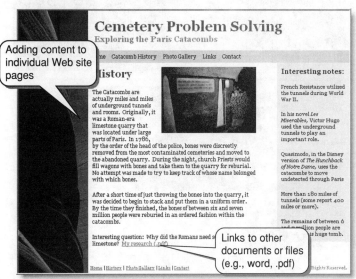

Figure 7.12 Picture gallery from Catacomb Web site

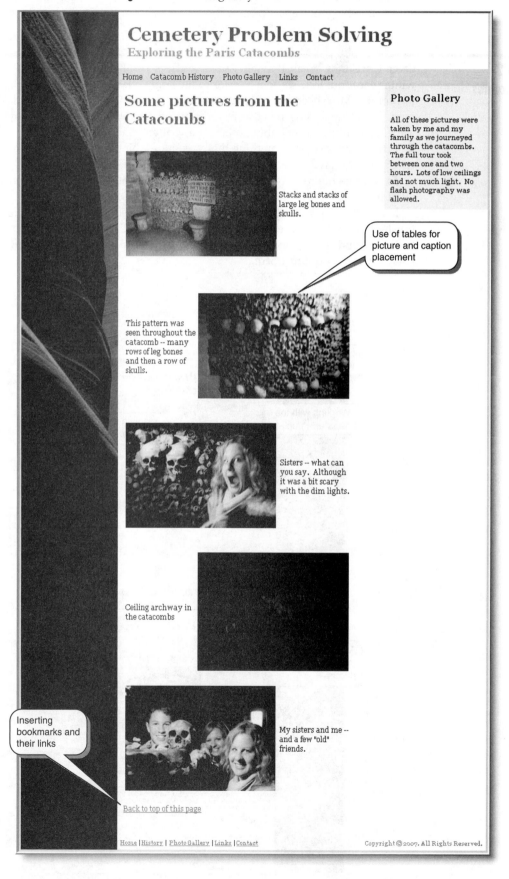

Figure 7.13 Related Web sites

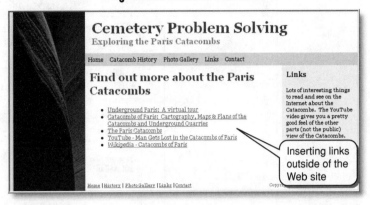

Figure 7.14 Contact page

Feature	Steps to Get It Done
Using Web site templates	There are a number of predesigned and developed Web sites created within Expression Web. Accessing one of these allows you to already have much of the design work completed (by a professional web designer). Then you just insert your content, alter the links, pictures, and so forth, publish, and your work is done. **Information and procedures:** • Create a new Web site (**File** menu >>> **New** >>> **Web Site** . . .) • The **New** dialog box will appear. Click the **Web Site** tab, then click **Templates**. • Click on the various predesigned Web sites (e.g., Organization 1) and examine it in the Preview window. Examine other example sites in the Preview window. Note the three types of templates (Organizations, Personal, and Small Business).

continued

Feature	Steps to Get It Done
	• Use the **Specify the location of the new Web site:** section to indicate where you want your Web site to be located (use **Browse**) to go to the location and create a folder for the site. • Click OK after selecting the template and location. **Key features to note, explore, and try out:** • In the Preview window, you can only see a small view of the home page of the template and the basic design. Once the site is selected and created, you can review all of its pre-designed pages. You may have to set up several template sites before you find the one that has the predesigned pages that you desire. • Don't worry if the template you select isn't perfect—you can change and adapt the pages as needed to get the perfection you seek. The idea behind the predesigned templates is that you can focus on your content and not worry about the little details (e.g., sidebar colors, location of the headings, matching colors of headings and sidebars, and so on).
Working with the master template	Once you have created a Web site by selecting one of the available templates, your Web site folder will be created and contain several pages (these were all designed by the individual who created the template site).

Feature	Steps to Get It Done
	One of those pages is the master.dwt (master dynamic Web template). This page contains all of the elements that will be seen on all pages of the Web site (note Figures 7.10–7.14) and all of the elements that are constant across all of the pages (e.g., large left sidebar image, main heading and subheading, navigation bar, copyright notice). This is the page you change to alter any of these. The beauty of this is that when you make one change on this page (**master.dwt**), the change will occur on all pages of the site. **Information and procedures:** Expression Web Help 🔘 • Key word: Template (**or .dwt**). • Select: *How to Create a Dynamic Web Template.* • Select: *Dynamic Web Templates* (general info on what these template are and why they are useful).
Altering headings, page menus, and so forth on the master template	**Information and procedures:** • Within Expression Web, open the master.dwt (site template). • Select the heading (or whichever element you want to change) that needs to be altered and enter the desired changes. • Save the changes (**File** menu >>> **Save**). • A **Microsoft Expression Web** dialog box will appear and tell you how many pages are attached to this master template and it will ask if you want to update those pages. Selecting **Yes** immediately changes all attached pages of the entire site. **Note:** You can also add or delete elements on the master template. When that is done those items will change on all attached pages. This includes adding links, pictures, and so on.
Adding content to individual Web site pages	**Information and procedures:** • In Expression Web, open the page where you want to insert your content • The Web site template you selected will already have nonsense content inserted. Select that content and replace it with your desired content. • The page adapts (gets shorter or longer) as you enter your information. **Note:** Each page in the template Web site has been set up for specific elements on that page. This is known as a "style sheet" and it helps to make sure the page remains consistent and elements are published reliably in the same location. If you find that you don't want an element that is already on your selected page, highlight the material, delete it. It will not appear when the site is published. For more information on cascading style sheets (CSS), see Expression Web Help 🔘. • Table of Contents task pane: *Cascading Style Sheets*
Linking to other documents (e.g., word, .pdf)	**Information and procedures.** Expression Web Help 🔘 • Table of Contents task pane: **Hyperlinks.** • Select: *Hyperlinks* (general information). • Select: *How to Create or Modify a Hyperlink.*

continued

Feature	Steps to Get It Done
	Key features to note, explore, and try out: • Place a copy of the document or file that you want to link to within your Web site folder (in this way, if the folder is moved to another computer or server, the document will also go with the site and the link will continue to work). • Review the steps explained in Feature 16a for Scenario 1 (page 202) of this chapter. Follow those procedures for creating a link—but link to the document or file instead of another Web page.
Using tables for placing pictures and captions	**Information and procedures:** Expression Web Help • Table of Contents task pane: **Tables and Layout Tables** >>> **Layout Tables.** • Select: *Layout Tables* (general information). • Select: *How to Format a Layout Table*. **Key features to note, explore, and try out:** • Refer to Features 4, 5, and 6 in Scenario 1 (pages 195–196) of this chapter for a full description of how to insert and work with tables. • Even though you are working within the style requirements of the template, you can still insert tables (and other things such as images) within those style sheet elements. **Note:** Pictures and other items within a Web page have a tendency to move around without notice when they are displayed (different browsers perform functions a bit differently). The use of tables helps to secure where the item on the page will be published once they are up on the Web.
Inserting bookmarks	Bookmarks (also known as "anchors") are a set of one or more characters on a page that serves as the target of a link. Bookmarks are very handy, especially when a Web page is long, because they provide a means for jumping from one location to another within the same page (or even in another page). In our example (see Figure 7.12), a bookmark has been placed at the top of a page (you can't see it from the view of the browser) and when you click on the associated link (in our example, the link has been placed at the bottom of the longer page), the browser immediately takes you to the bookmark (in this case, the top of the page). This is a simple and efficient way of getting to specific locations on a Web page. **Information and procedures:** Expression Web Help • Table of Contents task pane: **Hyperlinks.** • Select: *How to Add or Remove a Bookmark.* **Key features to note, explore, and try out:** • Place your cursor at the bookmark (target) location. Then click **Insert** menu >>> **Bookmark**. The **Bookmark** dialog box will open. It will ask you to enter a name for your bookmark. Insert something descriptive (e.g., top). • Go to the location on the page where the link needs to be inserted and enter the link. Highlight your link name, click **Insert** menu >>> **Hyperlink**. The **Insert Hyperlink** dialog box will appear. Click on the **Link to: Place in this Document** button and all bookmarks that you have inserted and named in this document will appear. Select the appropriate target bookmark and click OK.

Feature	Steps to Get It Done
	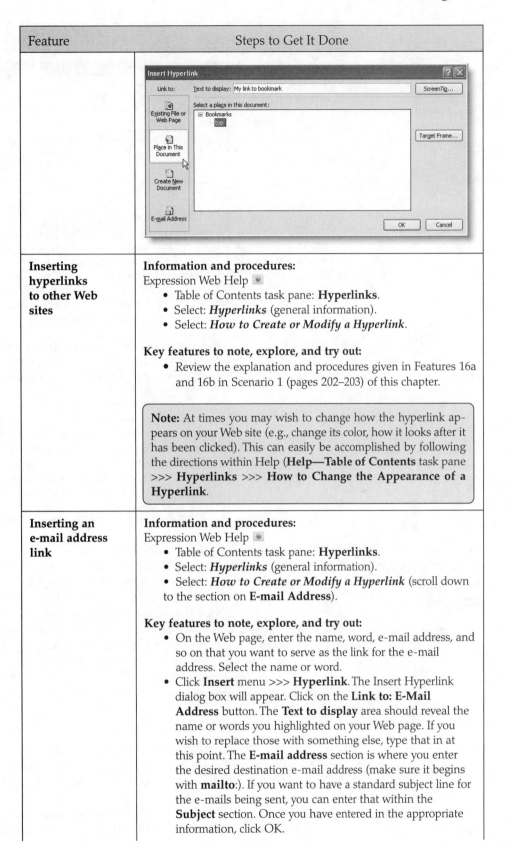

Inserting hyperlinks to other Web sites	**Information and procedures:**
	Expression Web Help
	   • Table of Contents task pane: **Hyperlinks**.
	   • Select: *Hyperlinks* (general information).
	   • Select: *How to Create or Modify a Hyperlink*.
	
	Key features to note, explore, and try out:
	   • Review the explanation and procedures given in Features 16a and 16b in Scenario 1 (pages 202–203) of this chapter.
	
	Note: At times you may wish to change how the hyperlink appears on your Web site (e.g., change its color, how it looks after it has been clicked). This can easily be accomplished by following the directions within Help (**Help—Table of Contents** task pane >>> **Hyperlinks** >>> **How to Change the Appearance of a Hyperlink**.

Inserting an e-mail address link	**Information and procedures:**
	Expression Web Help
	   • Table of Contents task pane: **Hyperlinks**.
	   • Select: *Hyperlinks* (general information).
	   • Select: *How to Create or Modify a Hyperlink* (scroll down to the section on **E-mail Address**).
	
	Key features to note, explore, and try out:
	   • On the Web page, enter the name, word, e-mail address, and so on that you want to serve as the link for the e-mail address. Select the name or word.
	   • Click **Insert** menu >>> **Hyperlink**. The Insert Hyperlink dialog box will appear. Click on the **Link to: E-Mail Address** button. The **Text to display** area should reveal the name or words you highlighted on your Web page. If you wish to replace those with something else, type that in at this point. The **E-mail address** section is where you enter the desired destination e-mail address (make sure it begins with **mailto:**). If you want to have a standard subject line for the e-mails being sent, you can enter that within the **Subject** section. Once you have entered in the appropriate information, click OK.

continued

Feature	Steps to Get It Done
	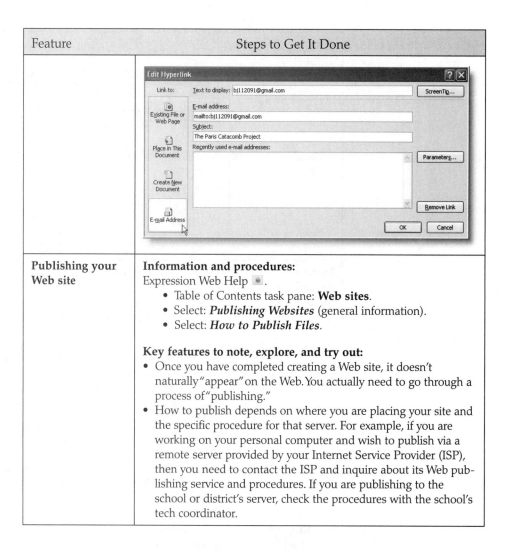
Publishing your Web site	**Information and procedures:** Expression Web Help ⊙. • Table of Contents task pane: **Web sites**. • Select: *Publishing Websites* (general information). • Select: *How to Publish Files*. **Key features to note, explore, and try out:** • Once you have completed creating a Web site, it doesn't naturally "appear" on the Web. You actually need to go through a process of "publishing." • How to publish depends on where you are placing your site and the specific procedure for that server. For example, if you are working on your personal computer and wish to publish via a remote server provided by your Internet Service Provider (ISP), then you need to contact the ISP and inquire about its Web publishing service and procedures. If you are publishing to the school or district's server, check the procedures with the school's tech coordinator.

Level 2a Workout: Producing class Web sites

Return to Scenario 1 of this chapter and review the simple Web page developed for Mrs. Smith's class about dinosaurs. Suppose Mrs. Smith has challenged the students in her class to "extend" and add relevant pages to her site (e.g., a page about the different types of dinosaurs, a page about the places where the dinosaurs roamed, what it would have been like to live during the time of the dinosaurs, what have we now that reminds us that there was once a time when dinosaurs roamed, and perhaps links to other similar sites that would help students and their families learn about this topic). Imagine that you have been asked to help assist a group of her students to complete several new dino site pages using Expression Web or a similar type of Web editing software.

Do the following:

1. Outline the Web site planning that you would have to do and that you would need to help the students accomplish before actual use of the software.
2. Review the key features discussed in both Scenario 1 and Scenario 2 and include those relevant to your pages.
3. Review the chapter's mentoring videos (**www.prenhall.com/newby** >>> **Chapter 7** >>> **Mentor Videos**) and select those that you think would be best for all of your students to review prior to attempting to create these Web pages.
4. Create several relevant, draft Web pages with active links that you could use as examples for the students you'll be guiding through this process. Note the potential "trouble spots" within the Web development process that you may need to spend some extra time on to be sure the students understand how it works appropriately.

**Level 2b Workout:
Service learning and
Web development
skills**

Acquiring skills to publish on the Web is something that can be personally fun, exciting, fulfilling, and helpful. Soon, as you develop your Web skills, you will begin to notice that others need and ask for your Web development skills.

With that in mind, let's think about what you can learn by offering your services to others. For example, what could you learn about the local humane society if you volunteered to create a Web site for that organization? What about a Web site for a new show that will open at a local art gallery or museum? What about the learning that would occur if you created a site about a specific part of algebra that has always given you problems—perhaps one that involved various ways to develop solutions, links to how individuals around the world have attempted to teach this process, and so on. What about a Web site that teaches individuals how to evaluate and purchase their first car, a good horse, or even how to be a better babysitter?

For this workout, take some time to find someone or some organization that needs the Web development help you can provide. Explore the needs of that individual and/or organization and then create a five-or six-page Web site based on that need. As you develop that site, keep a simple journal. Within, it include the following:

- What are the basic needs of the organization or individual?
- What did you have to explore to get the needed information?
- What are some of the ideas that you considered that could be included in the site?
- What were the key technical aspects that you had to figure out about the software to complete this project? What offered the most challenge? What was easy to accomplish?
- What were some of the key things that you learned about the organization that you didn't know before you began this project?

Develop a Web site that could be used by your selected organization. Use Table 7.2 as a checklist to remind yourself of the different features that could be included and addressed within your project.

Table 7.2 Level 2b Workout and Practice Checklist Providing Service Through Web Site Development

Web Site Planning	___ A journal was created that addressed several key questions about the needs for the site, the gathering of information, possible solutions, and technical information.
	___ Potential audience for the Web site was considered (e.g.,"Who will select to view the site?").
	___ Organizational structure of the site was determined based on the key elements of information that needed to be included.
Web Site Content	___ The purpose of the Web site is clearly presented and easily understood.
	___ Content is well organized and structured, easy to read, and offers complete coverage of the topic.
	___ Examples, demonstrations, explanations are given as needed within the content.
Web Site Format	___ The Web site is attractive and has visual appeal (use of graphics, color, font).
	___ Relevant graphics and pictures have been included.
	___ Relevant links to other sources of information within and outside of the local site have been included as needed.
	___ Ease of navigation through the Web site (effective and useful links, logical navigation points to and from various parts of the site).
	___ Web site is free of typographical and other grammatical errors.

> **Note:** Remember to implement the second rule to live by: SAVE, SAVE, SAVE, and then SAVE your work again. This was a key principle mentioned at the first of this text. Make sure you do that—or it will come back to haunt you sometime down the road.
>
>   Also think about the concepts in Rules 3, 4, and 5: Keep things simple, watch for how others accomplish what we have described in this chapter, and make sure you think about saving the publication as a template that can be adapted and used later as needed.

Level 3: Integration and Application

What should you be able to do?

Here's where you get to use this software to help yourself and your students. In this section you begin to see all possibilities once you understand the basics of building Web pages. You can use these examples as a springboard to launch ideas on ways to improve levels of student learning and your personal productivity.

Introduction

Accessing information and activities on the Internet has proven very beneficial for both students and teachers. Early within the school experience search strategies are learned to effectively utilize the benefits of the information on the Web. The ability to create and publish materials on the Internet adds a whole new set of benefits for both teachers and students. Examine the following lesson plan. We think you'll find this example can help you envision how effective Web development experiences might enhance student learning, as well as the capabilities of teachers and the effectiveness of their lessons.

Web site development integration

Creating the enhanced learning experience: A partial lesson plan

Topic: A study of the people, places, and culture of an African country.

Overview:

One of the goals for Mr. Carpenter, the eighth-grade social studies teacher at Lowell-Middle School, was to have his students come to view the world from a more global perspective. He wanted his students to examine and compare other cultures, lifestyles, and people to grasp the benefits and challenges of a very complex, diverse world. By exploring the differences, as well as the similarities, the Lowell students might be more open to attempting new experiences, be more willing to broaden their perception of people and potential friends, be more able to see areas where their service now or in the future may have a dramatic impact on other individuals, and perhaps be more able to solve some common problems.

   Jonathon Rogers, a past student of Mr. Carpenter, is now working on a college internship with an international health and education organization in the country of Zimbabwe. Through his help and other reference materials, the students in Mr. Carpenter's classes are able to explore this different culture, make some comparisons, and gain insights.

Specific learning task:

To further their study of Zimbabwe, Mr. Carpenter's students are to examine specific aspects of life within this country. Individually, they are to select from one of the questions below and then attempt to answer it by referencing materials on the Web and other sources. Students are encouraged to find or obtain firsthand accounts (with Jonathon's possible help) to confirm their research.

Questions:

- On any given day, what is it like to live in Harare (or any other major city), Zimbabwe?
- On any given day, what is it like to live in rural Zimbabwe away from the big cities?
- What do people do in Zimbabwe for entertainment (e.g., music, movies, sports)?
- What special occasions do people celebrate and how are those occasions celebrated?
- Are people religious? What do they believe and how do they show their beliefs?

Once completed, the class as a whole will develop a Web site to assemble and link all of the pieces. Students will work as designers, developers, and evaluators of the Web site to be sure it works and the information is correct.

Sample Learning Objectives:

Students will be able to do the following:

1. Explain and describe lifestyles of the common people within Zimbabwe.
2. Identify and describe the different forms of entertainment that Zimbabweans enjoy, as well as the special occasions that they celebrate.
3. Describe the religions of Zimbabwe and how individuals of that country worship.
4. Describe the process of gathering research information on the Web and the process needed to develop and evaluate a Web site.

Procedure:

1. Have the students select a question they wish to investigate.
2. Research answers for the questions by using the Web and other library resources. Contact Jonathon to see if he has contact with individuals who could give additional insights into some of these answers.
3. Divide the class into Web designers–developers and Web evaluators. Have them work interactively to develop the plans for the Web site and to evaluate and give feedback on those ideas. Depending on the ideas, it may be best to divide the class and create more than one Web site.
4. Create and confirm the initial Web plan. Have Jonathon review and note places where additional information could be added by him and his contacts.
5. Develop and evaluate the remaining portions of the Web site. Add the needed graphics, audio, and video as available.
6. Post the site live on the Web and, if possible, have Jonathon get feedback from several classes of students in Zimbabwe. Get some suggestions from them and rework the site based upon those suggestions.
7. Make the final changes to the site.

Questions About Web Development Integration

Most of the lesson objectives identified for this lesson plan could be accomplished without the development of a specific Web site. However, reflect on the following questions and think about the potential value that the integration of the Web site development may add to what is learned.

- In what ways can the Web environment facilitate the access and use of additional sources of information to support knowledge and understanding of the Zimbabwean people and culture?
- How can the planning, development, and evaluation processes involved in the Web site production impact the students creating the site? If access were possible, can students in Zimbabwe be used to help develop and/or evaluate the site in some way? What advantage would this add to the overall production process for Mr. Carpenter's students?

- Can the site be used to expand the understanding of students in other middle schools?
- How can the Web site be used to focus the efforts of all students working on the collaborative project? What additional interpersonal and communication skills can they learn from the collaborative Web development effort?
- Can the use of graphics, and/or audio and video clips within the hyperlinked environment of the Web increase what students gain from developing and using the site?
- How can this Web site and its development be used to bring together students from different areas of the globe to work together and communicate to a greater degree? What value is there in students from diverse areas and cultures cooperatively working on projects?
- What potential problems or pitfalls should one be wary of when attempting to create such a class Web site?

Level 3a Workout: Integrating Web development

Once you have had a chance to review the lesson plan—and examine and ponder the questions concerning integration—it's time for you to develop your own plan. Complete the following steps to this Workout.

1. Read each of the following situations. Imagine being directly involved in the planning for each of these projects. Select one (or more if you wish) for further consideration.

Creating a Sister Site

Students in Mt. Pleasant Junior High School have had an ongoing pen pal relationship with students in their sister city of Hof, Germany. In fact, some students from each city have occasionally traveled to the sister city for a short visit. Students have been challenged at both schools to think of ways to expand on these cultural exchanges in order for others to experience the similarities and differences between the schools, towns, and individuals from the different countries.

Living in Another Time

If you were allowed to be a commoner (i.e., a normal person) from the past, discuss your life and what you have discovered as you have ventured through it. Explain what life is like, show pictures of your surroundings, indicate what your goals would be, and tell about interesting people you have met or have heard about who lived during your time. For example, be a newspaper delivery boy during the days of Jesse James and explain what life was like then. Be a young girl who travels by wagon train with your family from Ohio to a gold rush town in California in the late 1840s. Explain what it was like to be recruited to march and fight for England during the Crusades. What would it have been like to be a young black man in South Africa during the heated days of Apartheid? What would it have been like to be a young white person in the same place and time? Is there a way to compare those experiences with what we experience today?

Professional Insights

Wouldn't it be nice to sit down and discuss various occupations with individuals who are currently involved in that line of work? What would it be like to be a scientist, or a judge, or a traffic patrolman, or an oceanographer, or even a dance instructor? Is it possible to create a job site that helps individuals investigate different professions and what those who are currently in those jobs have to say about them?

National Debt WebQuest

In a high school current issues class, a group of students converge together for a special project investigating issues concerning the national debt. Although a huge amount of information can be accessed via the Internet, organizing that information into a coherent unit is a challenging problem. One student suggests they attempt to select materials to help teach other students in their class about the key issues involved in their topic and another member mentions that a WebQuest may be a possible way of accomplishing this task.

2. Based on your selected project, consider the following questions that concern the integration of Web Development. Mark your response to each question.

Integration assessment questionnaire (IAQ)

Will using **WEB DEVELOPMENT** software as a part of the project:			
Broaden the learners' perspective on potential solution paths and/or answers?	___Yes	___No	___Maybe
Increase the level of involvement and investment of personal effort by the learners?	___Yes	___No	___Maybe
Increase the level of learner motivation (e.g., increase the relevance of the to-be-learned task, the confidence of dealing with the task, and/or the overall appeal of the task)?	___Yes	___No	___Maybe
Decrease the time needed to generate potential solutions?	___Yes	___No	___Maybe
Increase the quality and/or quantity of learner practice working on this and similar projects?	___Yes	___No	___Maybe
Increase the quality and/or quantity of feedback given to the learner?	___Yes	___No	___Maybe
Enhance the ability of the student to solve novel but similar projects, tasks, and problems in the future?	___Yes	___No	___Maybe

3. If you have responded "Yes" to one or more of the IAQ questions, you should consider the use of Web editing software to enhance the student's potential learning experience.
4. Using the example lesson plan, develop a lesson plan based on this project. Within the plan, indicate how and when the learner will develop web-based materials. Additionally, list potential benefits and challenges that may occur when involving this software within the lesson.

Level 3b Workout: Exploring the NETS Standard connection

Developing and executing a lesson plan that integrates the use of Web editors and Web site development directly addresses several of the Standards for both teachers (NETS*T) and students (NETS*S). See the Appendix for a full listing of the standards.

Part A:

Generally, the main purpose for learning and using application software is to increase your level of production—that is, to do things faster, better, or both. NETS Standards (NETS*T Standard V and NETS*S Standard 6) help us focus on these productivity objectives for both teachers and students. There are other technology standards, however, that may also be potentially addressed through your knowledge and use of Web editing software. Reflect on the following questions and consider the potential impact of Web editor integration (refer to the Appendix to review the full sets of standards):

- How can the use of Web editing software help to develop students' higher order skills and creativity? Is there something about the development of a Web site that promotes organization, writing, analysis, research, as well as message design skills? In what ways can the development of a collaborative Web site be used to increase communication, leadership, and decision making skills of both students and teachers? (NETS*T III.C. and NETS*S 1,2,3, and 4)
- In what ways can Web editing software and the development of a Web page or site be used to facilitate the communication and collaboration between teachers, students, parents, and subject matter experts on specific projects that ultimately impact student learning? Are there alternative means of communicating information that would allow for diverse audiences to better grasp the meaning of the information? (NETS*T V.D. and VI.B.; NET*S 2)
- How could the development of WebQuests, Web scavenger hunts, and so on be used to successfully manage learning activities designed for a specific student audience? (NET*T II.D.)
- In what positive ways could the knowledge that student work would be published on the Web impact the quality of work produced? (NET*S 1 and 5)

Part B:

Go to the ISTE Web site **http://cnets.iste.org**. Within that site, select to review either the student or the teacher NETS Standards. Once you have selected the standards to review, select either the student or teacher profiles and look for the corresponding scenarios. Review the scenarios and determine how Web editors could be used within several of those situations.

While visiting the ISTE Web site and exploring the scenarios, go to the lesson plan search area and select a number of different lesson plans of interest. Review those and determine the role (if any) of Web editors within the development, implementation, and assessment of the lesson. Note this from both the perspective of the teacher developing the lesson and the perspective of the student participating in the implemented lesson.

Further ideas on using a Web editor as a learning tool

- Research content and develop Web sites about specific topics or subject matter.
- Research and locate various information Web sites and then construct a Web site that links and references these information sites
- Develop WebQuests, scavenger hunts, and ThinkQuests.
- Develop a site that incorporates and demonstrates proper visual design.
- Create a cooperative group project that involves the research, design, and development of a comprehensive Web site about a selected topic of interest.
- Develop a site that compares viewpoints and/or materials. For example, have them compare the educational philosophies of various secondary level schools across the country or across several different countries. Likewise, have them compare the governments of different countries and link important sites that explain the pros and cons of each type.
- Develop sites that incorporate the use of various activities from applications programs such as presentation programs (e.g., PPT) and or word processing (e.g., Word).
- Develop data collection instruments (e.g., surveys) that can be sent out via a published Web site and collect data for various Web projects.
- Design Web sites about specific areas of interest (e.g., favorite pet, favorite class in school, special place to visit with one's family, and so forth).

Additional ideas on using a Web editor as an assistant

- Create a Web site for basic administrative information and information exchange. This can be a Web site that students, parents, and administrators can go to to receive specific information (e.g., class information).
- Use the Web editor to develop a specific course or class Web site. This site can include the syllabus, activities, explanations, linked information and sites, and important information and announcements that students need constant access to.
- In terms of support material for classroom activities, ancillary Web sites can be created to hold things such as class notes (overheads) and even additional media (audio and visual) presentations.
- Help to show additional viewpoints of a specific concept, idea, or philosophy. Develop a Web site that links different viewpoints to give the students wider perspectives on what is being learned.
- Develop a portion of a course Web site that contains a question and answer section. This can be similar to a searchable database that stores key questions and responses to important class questions. Students (or parents, administrators, and so on) can submit questions that are then posted with a response. Other students can then review the different questions and responses that have been posted.

Appendix
NATIONAL EDUCATIONAL TECHNOLOGY STANDARDS FOR TEACHERS*

All classroom teachers should be prepared to meet the following standards and performance indicators.

I. Technology Operations and Concepts	*Teachers demonstrate a sound understanding of technology operations and concepts. Teachers:* A. demonstrate introductory knowledge, skills, and understanding of concepts related to technology (as described in the ISTE National Educational Technology Standards for Students). B. demonstrate continual growth in technology knowledge and skills to stay abreast of current and emerging technologies.
II. Planning and Designing Learning Environments and Experiences	*Teachers plan and design effective learning environments and experiences supported by technology. Teachers:* A. design developmentally appropriate learning opportunities that apply technology-enhanced instructional strategies to support the diverse needs of learners. B. apply current research on teaching and learning with technology when planning learning environments and experiences. C. identify and locate technology resources and evaluate them for accuracy and suitability. D. plan for the management of technology resources within the context of learning activities. E. plan strategies to manage student learning in a technology-enhanced environment.
III. Teaching, Learning, and the Curriculum	*Teachers implement curriculum plans that include methods and strategies for applying technology to maximize student learning. Teachers:* A. facilitate technology-enhanced experiences that address content standards and student technology standards. B. use technology to support learner-centered strategies that address the diverse needs of students. C. apply technology to develop students' higher-order skills and creativity. D. manage student learning activities in a technology-enhanced environment.

*Reprinted with permission from *National Educational Technology Standards for Teachers: Preparing Teachers to Use Technology,* © 2002, ISTE ® (International Society for Technology in Education), www.iste.org. All rights reserved.

| **IV. Assessment and Evaluation** | *Teachers apply technology to facilitate a variety of effective assessment and evaluation strategies. Teachers:* |

A. apply technology in assessing student learning of subject matter using a variety of assessment techniques.
B. use technology resources to collect and analyze data, interpret results, and communicate findings to improve instructional practice and maximize student learning.
C. apply multiple methods of evaluation to determine students' appropriate use of technology resources for learning, communication, and productivity.

| **V. Productivity and Professional Practice** | *Teachers use technology to enhance their productivity and professional practice. Teachers:* |

A. use technology resources to engage in ongoing professional development and lifelong learning.
B. continually evaluate and reflect on professional practice to make informed decisions regarding the use of technology in support of student learning.
C. apply technology to increase productivity.
D. use technology to communicate and collaborate with peers, parents, and the larger community in order to nurture student learning.

| **VI. Social, Ethical, Legal, and Human Issues** | *Teachers understand the social, ethical, legal, and human issues surrounding the use of technology in PK–12 schools and apply that understanding in practice. Teachers:* |

A. model and teach legal and ethical practice related to technology use.
B. apply technology resources to enable and empower learners with diverse backgrounds, characteristics, and abilities.
C. identify and use technology resources that affirm diversity.
D. promote safe and healthy use of technology resources.
E. facilitate equitable access to technology resources for all students.

NATIONAL EDUCATIONAL TECHNOLOGY STANDARDS FOR STUDENTS: THE NEXT GENERATION*

"What students should know and be able to do to learn effectively and live productively in an increasingly digital world . . ."

1. Creativity and Innovation	*Students demonstrate creative thinking, construct knowledge, and develop innovative products and processes using technology. Students:* a. apply existing knowledge to generate new ideas, products, or processes. b. create original works as a means of personal or group expression. c. use models and simulations to explore complex systems and issues. d. identify trends and forecast possibilities.
2. Communication and Collaboration	*Students use digital media and environments to communicate and work collaboratively, including at a distance, to support individual learning and contribute to the learning of others. Students:* a. interact, collaborate, and publish with peers, experts or others employing a variety of digital environments and media. b. communicate information and ideas effectively to multiple audiences using a variety of media and formats. c. develop cultural understanding and global awareness by engaging with learners of other cultures. d. contribute to project teams to produce original works or solve problems.
3. Research and Information Fluency	*Students apply digital tools to gather, evaluate, and use information. Students:* a. plan strategies to guide inquiry. b. locate, organize, analyze, evaluate, synthesize, and ethically use information from a variety of sources and media. c. evaluate and select information sources and digital tools based on the appropriateness to specific tasks. d. process data and report results.
4. Critical Thinking, Problem-Solving & Decision-Making	*Students use critical thinking skills to plan and conduct research, manage projects, solve problems and make informed decisions using appropriate digital tools and resources. Students:*

---

*Reprinted with permission from *National Educational Technology Standards for Students, Second Edition*, © 2007, ISTE ® (International Society for Technology in Education), www.iste.org. All rights reserved.

a. identify and define authentic problems and significant questions for investigation.
b. plan and manage activities to develop a solution or complete a project.
c. collect and analyze data to identify solutions and/or make informed decisions.
d. use multiple processes and diverse perspectives to explore alternative solutions.

5. Digital Citizenship

Students understand human, cultural, and societal issues related to technology and practice legal and ethical behavior. Students:

a. advocate and practice safe, legal, and responsible use of information and technology.
b. exhibit a positive attitude toward using technology that supports collaboration, learning, and productivity.
c. demonstrate personal responsibility for lifelong learning.
d. exhibit leadership for digital citizenship.

6. Technology Operations and Concepts

Students demonstrate a sound understanding of technology concepts, systems and operations. Students:

a. understand and use technology systems.
b. select and use applications effectively and productively.
c. troubleshoot systems and applications.
d. transfer current knowledge to learning of new technologies.

GLOSSARY

action button In MS PowerPoint, a ready-made button which can be created, inserted, and hyperlinked within a presentation. By clicking on the button, the hyperlinked activity is carried out. See also *button.*

active window Describes the window that is currently selected or being used.

alignment How text is positioned on a screen, page, or specific portion of a page or screen. Left alignment lines all text flush on the left margin. Right alignment creates flush text on the right margin. Center alignment creates text that is centered in the middle of the page and full alignment creates flush margins on both right and left margins.

animations Special visual or sound effects added to an object or text. For example, in PowerPoint, having bulleted lists of items enter and leave a presentation at specific times or based on specific actions.

applications software Programs used by the computer to assist in specific tasks (e.g., word processing, desktop publishing, presentation development). See also *computer applications.*

audio clips Sound and music files that can be hyperlinked, accessed, and played within Web pages and other electronic files.

background Pictures or text that are placed on a screen, slide, or within a text document to appear behind other elements. Backgrounds are generally used to add color and interest to the screen, slide, and so forth.

bookmark Identifies a specific reference location in a Web document that can be referred or linked to. For example, the top of a long Web document can be bookmarked and later accessed when a link to the top of the document bookmark is clicked or activated.

border Lines around cells, tables, or pages that add emphasis, interest, and/or organizational clarity.

border art: Selected graphics that can be inserted continuously around the edges of a page, picture, or paragraph border within a document.

boundary guides see *Layout guides*

browser Computer applications, such as Internet Explorer, Mozilla Foxfire, or Apple Safari used for accessing the World Wide Web.

bullet list Dots or other symbols placed immediately before each item within a list. This design feature adds emphasis and facilitates organization of materials. See *number list.*

button A specific location on a computer screen that triggers an action when clicked.

cell A single block in a spreadsheet grid, formed by the intersection of a row and a column.

cell reference Identifies a cell or a range of cells in a spreadsheet program (e.g., cell reference "D5" identifies the cell where column D and row 5 intersect).

chart A graphic representation of a data set of numbers. Charts can add visual appeal and facilitate comparisons, patterns, and trends in data. Charts are also referred to as graphs.

click To press and release a button on a computer mouse.

click and hold To depress the computer mouse button and keep it depressed until a specific action has occurred or been completed.

click, hold, and drag Use to move an item (e.g., icon) from one location to another on the computer screen. Completed by pointing the mouse pointer at the item to be moved, depressing the mouse button, holding the mouse button down, and then moving the mouse to the new location and releasing the button.

clip art Previously prepared graphics that can be accessed, selected, and inserted within files such as word processed documents, presentation programs, or Web pages.

clipboard Temporary storage in the computer's memory.

columns A vertical arrangement of cells in a table or spreadsheet. In most common spreadsheets the columns are initially designated by letters (e.g., column D, column F).

commands Tools used within application programs (e.g., font color command within MS Word is the tool that allows for the selection of the font color to be used within the document).

command groups Logical collection of tools or commands organized together under a specific tab on the ribbon (e.g., in MS Word on the Home tab there is a "Font" command group that includes commands to control font type, size, highlighting, color, and so on).

computer applications Computer programs designed to perform tasks such as word processing, desktop publishing, mathematical or statistical calculations, and so forth. See also *applications software*.

contextual commands Tools or commands that only appear on the ribbon when a specific object is selected (e.g., if an image is selected, the contextual command tab for the Picture Tools appears on the ribbon within MS Office).

custom animation A sound or visual effect that has been added to an object or text within a PowerPoint presentation. See also *animation*.

database An organized collection of information, often stored on a computer.

design templates A prepared layout designed to ease the process of creating a product in certain computer applications, e.g. a slide design and color scheme for presentation software or a standard Web page layout.

desktop A description of the screen that appears after the computer has been turned on. The computer screen is commonly compared to the top of a desk that contains folders, files, and various tools for working

dialog box expander A small button generally located next to the command group name on the ribbon. Clicking on this button opens a dialog box that is related to the associated command group. For example, clicking on the Font command group dialog box expander opens the font command dialog box, where additional selections can be made.

drag To move a selected item, icon, and text on a computer screen, point the mouse pointer at the target item, click and hold the mouse button, and move the mouse. The selected item will follow the mouse movement until the mouse button is released.

field Each individual category of information recorded in a database (e.g., a student's first name).

file Any data saved onto a hard disk or other storage device (e.g., a word document file, a spreadsheet file). Also, within a database, this refers to a group of related database records.

fill A spreadsheet feature that allows one to automatically continue a series of numbers, number and text combinations, dates, or time periods based on an established pattern. Commonly used in a spreadsheet program to automatically allow a specific equation or function to be applied to additional rows or columns of data.

fill color A feature that allows for a color, shading, or pattern to be added to an enclosed figure, text box, and so on.

fill handle A small box in the lower right corner of an active spreadsheet cell. It can be used to complete a fill. See *fill*.

filter A means to select a subset of records or data in a table or worksheet based upon certain selected criteria.

folder An icon that represents where applications, documents, and other folders are located. It is considered an organizational device that serves a similar purpose to a file folder found inside an office filing cabinet.

font The appearance (typeface and size) of text on the computer screen and/or in printed form. Typefaces include Times New Roman, Arial, Courier, and so on.

footers Information that appears in an area at the bottom of a document page (e.g., page number, title of document, date, logo). Footers can be set to appear at the bottom of all or selected pages of multiple page document. See also *headers*.

format A process to design how a document will look (e.g., type of font, selection of borders, use of color). Also used to describe the preparation or initialization of a disk or other electronic storage device to receive digital information.

formula A mathematical expression (equation) that directs an electronic spreadsheet to perform various kinds of calculations on the numbers entered in it.

function Predefined formulas used in spreadsheets or databases that perform calculations. See *formulas*.

gadgets Miniprograms that are displayed within the sidebar of the Windows Vista screen. These miniprograms might include a display of the time, weather, stock updates, news headings, and the like.

gallery A collection of related, displayed items (e.g., a group of) from which a selection can be made. For example, when WordArt or SmartArt is selected, a collection of alternatives (i.e., a gallery) is displayed within a pop-up window from which an alternative can be selected.

grammar check Ancillary feature of word processors that identifies a range of grammatical and format errors such as improper capitalization, lack of subject–verb agreement, split infinitives, and so on. Suggestions on corrections to the errors may also be provided by the check.

graphic Any pictorial representation of information such as charts, graphs, animated figures, or photographic reproductions. Frequently referred to (especially within Web page development) as *images*.

handles Small squares that appear around a selected object that can be dragged to alter the size and shape of the object.

handout page A version of a PowerPoint presentation that can be printed. The handout page can be constructed to include various numbers of slides per page and space for notes to be written.

headers Information that appears in an area at the top of a document page (e.g., page number, title of document, date, logo). Headers can be set to appear at the top of all or selected pages of multiple-page documents. See also *footers*.

Help Built-in resource within most applications programs that supplies practical advice, tutorials, and/or demonstrations on the use of the software and its various features.

hold Depressing a mouse button and not releasing it until some task is completed (e.g., depressing until a specific menu appears on the screen or until the dragging of an icon has been completed). See also *click and hold; click, hold, and drag*.

HTML See *Hypertext Markup Language*

hyperlinks Connections between items or elements (e.g., text, objects) within a hyper environment. For example, an action such as the playing of a sound clip is executed when a connected (i.e., hyperlinked) icon is clicked. Hyperlink is frequently referred to simply as *link*.

Hypertext Markup Language The authoring "language" used to define Web pages. Commonly referred to as HTML.

icon A small pictorial or graphical representation of a computer hardware function or component.

images See *graphics*.

integration Within a classroom setting, the use of the computer in ways that facilitate the learning of subject matter or content (e.g., accessing additional information, incorporation of graphics, calculation and charting of data).

Internet A network of computer networks that links computers worldwide

keyboard The most common computer peripheral device used for inputting information. Keyboards can vary in size, shape, type, and arrangement of keys to input data.

layout guides Margin, column, row, and baseline lines used to create a grid of boundaries so that text, graphics, and objects can be properly aligned within a document or publication.

links See *hyperlinks*.

mail merge Inserting data from applications programs such as databases or spreadsheets into a form letter or document.

margins Blank space outside the boundaries of the text and/or images on a document page. Margins can also pertain to specific blank areas within table or spreadsheet cells.

Master slide A template that stores information concerning font styles, placeholder sizes and positions, background design, and color schemes for a presentation program such as PowerPoint.

menu On-screen list of available options (e.g., File menu consists of options to open a new document, save the current document, close the current document, and so forth.)

Microsoft Excel Spreadsheet software created by Microsoft Corporation to organize, analyze, calculate, and present data such as budgets and grades.

Microsoft Expression Web Software created by Microsoft Corporation for the purpose of developing and editing Web pages.

Microsoft Office A set of application software developed by Microsoft Corporation that typically includes programs such as MS Word (word processing), MS PowerPoint (presentation software), MS Access (database management), MS Excel (spreadsheet), and MS Outlook (planning and calendaring).

Microsoft PowerPoint Presentation software created by Microsoft Corporation to plan, organize, design, and deliver professional presentations.

Microsoft Publisher Desktop publishing software created by Microsoft Corporation to create professional-looking handouts, awards, brochures, calendars, newsletters, and Web sites.

Microsoft Word Word processing software created by Microsoft Corporation to plan, organize, and produce professionally looking text documents (e.g., letters, papers, reports).

mouse A pointing device used to select and move information on the computer display screen. As the mouse is physically moved, a pointer on the computer screen moves in a similar fashion. The mouse typically has one to three buttons that may be used for selecting or entering information.

normal view In MS PowerPoint, normal view is the main editing view used to write and design presentations.

notes page In MS PowerPoint, each notes page shows a small version of the slide and the notes that go with the slide. This can be used as an easy way to create speaker's notes to accompany the presentation.

number list Sequential numbers or letters placed immediately before each item within a list. This design feature adds emphasis and facilitates organization of materials. See *bullet list*.

Office button Located in the upper-right corner of the Microsoft Office applications, this button allows access to the basic open, save, and print commands. It replaces the old *file* menu of pre-2007 versions of MS Office.

page border Various types of line styles, graphics, and colors that can be added to the edge of a document page to increase interest and emphasis.

page orientation The direction (e.g., vertical or portrait; horizontal or landscape) of a page layout.

page setup Option that allows for the selection of page margins, orientation, layout, and paper size.

peripherals Devices (e.g., printers, external hard drives, keyboards) that connect to the computer.

point Manipulation of a mouse (or trackball, touchpad, and so on) to select a specific word, graphic, or location on a computer screen.

presentation software Computer software designed for the production and display of computer text and images, intended to replace the functions typically associated with the slide and overhead projectors.

Quick access toolbar Generally located in the upper-left corner (next to the Office button), this toolbar contains commands that are frequently used and that are independent of the tab currently being displayed. This toolbar is customizable and often includes such things as undo, redo, and save.

Quick styles Allow one to select different colors, fonts, and effects that can be combined within a specific theme. Quick styles always match the theme and have been created by professional visual designers.

record A collection of related fields within a database of information. See also *field* and *database*.

recycle bin The location where deleted files are stored. Deleted files can be recovered from this storage location or can be permanently deleted by emptying the recycle bin.

ribbon The area within MS Office 2007 applications that contains the command tabs, command groups, and individual commands. The ribbon is designed to hold logically grouped commands to facilitate the completion of specific activities.

row A horizontal arrangement of cells in a table or spreadsheet. In most common spreadsheets the rows are initially designated by numbers (e.g., row 2, row 232).

ruler A bar displayed across the top of the document window that is marked in units of measurement (e.g., inches.). Margins, tabs, and column widths for example, can be set through the use of the ruler.

search A common feature within application programs to find words, numbers, and/or characters within a file. Additionally, operating systems can use searches to locate specific files, folders, programs, and so forth.

section break A mark used to show the end of a section.

sections The layout of a document can be altered by dividing it into sections. Each section can be formatted in a different manner (e.g., one section with two-column format and another section with single column format) and divided by the section break.

select   To indicate that a text or object will be used or worked with by the program. To select, point the mouse pointer and click and/or by drag across the text or object. Once "selected," the text or object will be highlighted in some fashion (e.g., color change). To remove the selection, a mouse click on anything other than the selected item will remove the selected status.

shading   A darkening or coloring of the background behind text or graphics. It is used to add emphasis and interest to a table, paragraph, cell, page, and the like.

sidebar   A long, vertical area that is displayed on the side of the Windows Vista desktop. It contains gadgets that provide information (e.g., the weather, stock prices, time).

slide   The fundamental unit within a presentation (e.g., PowerPoint). It can contain graphics, text, sounds, movies, and action buttons.

slide layout   The manner in which elements (headings, text, lists, graphics) on a slide are arranged. In MS PowerPoint, for example, templates can be selected from the slide layout menu and used to automatically arrange slide elements.

slide show view   In MS PowerPoint, slide show view shows how the presentation will look when given to an audience. The full screen is used and all animations, graphics, links are activated.

slide sorter view   In MS PowerPoint, this view is of the full set of presentation slides in thumbnail form. Slide sorter view allows for easy reorganization, addition, and deletion of slides, as well as the review of transition and animation effects, and so on.

SmartArt   A gallery of predesigned visual layouts that can be adapted to communicate information, ideas, and messages.

sort   Arranging data in a spreadsheet or database in ascending or descending order.

spell check   A feature in applications programs that searches through a file and reports any instances of text that do not match a built-in dictionary. In most cases, it offers suggestions on possible alternative spellings.

spreadsheet   A general purpose computer calculating tool. It is generally arranged in rows and columns. It can also hold various types of data (e.g., images, texts, numbers) which can be sorted and filtered similar to a database.

Start menu   Options displayed when the Start button on the taskbar is clicked. Options generally include access to programs, help, search, and shut down procedures.

style   Text style refers to the appearance of a character without changing size or typeface (e.g., using bold or italics).

system software   The basic operating software that tells the computer how to perform its fundamental functions.

table   Data set up in a row–column format. Cells within the table can contain text and graphics. Tables are often used to organize and present information.

task bar   A bar usually displayed at the bottom of the screen that contains the Start button, open document icons, and buttons to activate programs.

task panes   Small windows within an application program that provide easy access to commonly used commands.

template   A type of stored document that contains previously generated formats and/or content (e.g., text, page layouts, columns). Use of the template as a starting point allows for the efficient creation of new, but similar, documents. For example, a template office memo allows for the previously created header, footer, school logo, and the like of the template to be included so that only new information needs to be added.

text box   An object that can be added to a document, worksheet, Web page, etc. that sets off or emphasizes a section of text. It can be readily positioned, colored, and borders added for extra emphasis within a document.

text wrapping   The automatic arrangement of text from the end of one line to the beginning of the next line. Text may be wrapped within cells of a table or spreadsheet, within paragraphs on pages, and in reference to inserted graphics and objects. See *word wrap.*

themes   Previously completed design settings (e.g., coordinated colors, fonts, styles that have been created by professional visual designers) can be applied within a document, file, or presentation.

toolbar   Bars generally displayed at the top or bottom of a screen of application software that contain shortcuts to useful features and tools (e.g., shortcut to save a file, shortcut to open a document or create a new document). Use of the toolbars eliminates the need to go to the menu options.

touchpad   Input device generally found on a laptop computer that serves a similar function as a mouse. The pad allows for a finger or stylus to be used to control the position of the pointer or cursor on the screen.

trackball　Input device that serves a similar function as the mouse input device. The device is similar to an inverted mouse where the user rotates the ball with a thumb or forefinger to guide the pointer or cursor on the screen.

URL　Uniform Resource Locator. The unique address for every Internet or World Wide Web page, containing the protocol type, the domain, the directory, and the name of the site or page.

video clips　Digital video files that can be hyperlinked, accessed, and viewed within Web pages and other electronic files.

view buttons　buttons within the applications program (e.g., MS Word) that allow the document or file to be displayed in different formats (e.g., as a Web page, two pages side by side).

view menu　A specific area where a selection can be made about how the workspace of an application should be set up (e.g., for editing, notes, outlining).

view tab　A tab option on the main ribbon of most applications programs that allows one to select various ways to view a document or file of data, as well as how the document should be displayed.

watermark　Text or pictures that appear behind text in a document. For example, a picture of a mountain that is printed behind text about a trip to the mountains. Often a watermark is washed out, or lightened, so that it doesn't hinder how the main text is viewed. Watermarks are generally intended to add interest or information to printed documents.

Web　See WWW.

Web-based documents　Documents that are accessed via the Internet and World Wide Web.

Web browser　See *browser*.

Web editor　Software that allows for the creation and editing of materials that can be distributed on the World Wide Web

Web page development　The design and creation of a hypertext document appropriate for publishing on the World Wide Web. Generally, this is accomplished using Web editing software or HTML.

Web site　A set of interrelated Web pages usually operated by a single entity (e.g., company, school, organization, or individual).

WebQuest　An inquiry-oriented activity in which most of the information used by learners is drawn from the World Wide Web.

"What if..."　When using a spreadsheet program, statements beginning with this phrase are used to signify how the spreadsheet may be used to make predictions and/or estimations.

Windows　A specific type of computer operating system produced and marketed by Microsoft Corporation. Versions include Windows XP and Windows Vista.

Windows Explorer　A software program within the Windows operating system that allows one to navigate to and access various folders and files.

window　A portion of the computer screen that displays information or a program. Multiple windows can be revealed at the same time (e.g., a window revealing an office memo in a word processing document, another revealing a spreadsheet chart, and another accessing information on the Internet). Size, number, and location of windows revealed on the computer screen can be altered by the user.

WordArt　A gallery of predesigned text styles such as shadowed or mirrored text that can be included within a document.

word processing　The act of creating a document through the use of word processor software.

word processor　A computer program for writing that supports the entry, editing, revising, formatting, storage, retrieval, and printing of text.

word wrap　A feature of a word processor that automatically shifts the next whole word to the next line of the document when a line of text in a computer document is filled. See *text wrapping*.

workspace　The main screen space within an application program (e.g., word processor) where the main amount of work is completed (i.e., text, data, and graphics are inserted and edited).

workbook　A set or collection of worksheets from a spreadsheet program saved under a single file name.

worksheet　An area of rows and columns in a spreadsheet program in which text, numeric values, and formulas are entered.

WWW　World Wide Web (or the Web). An information retrieval system on the Internet that relies on a point-and-click hypertext navigation system.

INDEX